The Anti-Interfaith Abrahamic Faith

By Gregory Heary

The example of Abraham's faith is the example of the faith of his forefathers Noah and Adam. Both Adam and Noah had one and the same doctrinal religion which Abraham practiced as well. None of these prophets practiced multiple religions nor instructed their offspring it was allowed to differ regarding religion. Today many different religions lay claim to Abraham as one of their founding preachers and there is a popular interfaith cooperative movement to focus on similarities between the sectarian groups ignoring and overlooking major theological differences and disputes in the name of tolerance or mutual understanding. This is not what Abraham would want. More importantly it is not what the God of Abraham wants, whose opinion outweighs all the multitudes of human opinions on the matter of religious dialogue. Why focus the spotlight on Abraham instead of his God? Because the differing definitions of that God exist with wildly different ways of worshipping make evident the incompatibility and idiocy of having a multitude of religions having valid claims to Abraham as one of their own members or founders. So this book is written to disprove the claim that there is a concept such as "Abrahamic faiths", which we have done utilizing the very same religious texts those claiming to follow Abraham hold as spiritually authoritative. It is hoped the reader will learn the faith of Abraham and intelligently abandon the heretical notion that there are multiple ways to adhere to Abraham's singular religion.

At the time of this writing three major religions allege to be Abrahamic in origin and are popularly believed by the masses to be justified in this claim. However there are more than three faiths professing to be descended from Abraham. Some of the less popular religions that make the same Abrahamic claim as Judaism, Christianity and Islam include:

- Mandaeism
- Bahaism
- Druzim
- Rastafarianism
- Azalism

Why then are not these religions lumped in together with the top three claimants in the name of interfaith tolerance and understanding as well? Mandaeism even goes a step closer than Judaism as they believe in Prophet John but stop short of belief in Jesus and Muhammad, so Mandaists (also known as Sabians) have more in common with Christians and Muslims than Jews do but the media doesn't even mention them as existing let alone validify their claims to Abraham. While Bahaism has over 8.5 million followers at the time of this writing. So how can "civilized religious society" just throw them into the trash when they claim to descend from Abraham too? Is it not unequal and unfair? Or are the claims to Abraham merely based on statistics where if you have a certain number of adherents to your faith then your claim is acceptable to join the club but if your numbers are below the necessary minimum then your claim is rejected as foolish? What is that number of validity? Do numbers even matter? If numbers of claimants don't matter then what does?

The "Children of Abraham Institute" was founded in 2001 and claims the goal of the movement was primarily peace and the avoidance of military conflict namely in Israel/Palestine, the middle east and elsewhere amongst the three religious groups of Jews, Christians and Muslims. This Children of Abraham institute was co-founded by the older "Society for Scriptural Reasoning" whose motto is, "three scriptures on the table, no agendas under the table". They purport to study all the scriptures of the three major religions together in the name of friendship and appreciation of overlapping similarities. However anyone who actually studies any one of those scriptures will realize that such overlap while interesting doesn't negate the intolerance monotheism inherently breeds among its adherents. For if there is one God naturally there is one right way and many wrong ways to worship. Hence heresy comes about through people picking the wrong ways that are not based on legitimate prophetic textual instructions. All heretics within monotheistic denominations claim to worship God so why then are heretics not embraced as much as these Abrahamic claimants collude together? Afterall the point is worshipping God right? The goal is not Abraham but the God of Abraham. So technically based on the interfaith ideals all heresy should be tolerated to a greater extent than the claims to Abrahamic faiths are because similarities in worshipping God should take precedent over similar claims to following a human prophet. Yet the absurdity of allowing all heresies is well known to be blasphemously intolerable to all people with religious inclination. So why make this exception for Abrahamic heresies? Primarily because some Scriptures from some religions say God promised things to Abraham among which were certain portions of land. Therefore a claim to follow Prophet Abraham is much more than a claim to a religious inheritance but it is also a claim of political authority over highly prized real estate in the middle east. Therefore know that the Abrahamic faiths movement is partially political propaganda to diffuse the rival political and territorial claims of religious groups in the middle east. Since the minor 5 religions that lay claim to Abraham have no political authority it is for this reason their claims to follow Abraham at the interfaith feasts are rejected. It is only people who have military capabilities that get a table at the interfaith conferences because it is a form of diplomacy disguised as religious dialogue. This is because everybody knows religious wars are typically bloodier and thereby more expensive or costly than non-religious wars. So in the interest of economics it was decided that secularization of the middle eastern conflicts were necessary in the hopes of preventing worldwide interreligious disunity and conflict. Simply put, on a global level Jews, Christians and Muslims are living too close together and intermingled to afford to be at war religiously in never-ending conversion based mortal combat. Thereby to justify religious living together peacefully without any warfare nor attempts at converting each other this doctrine of Abrahamic faiths came about because if we all belong to Abraham's blessed inheritance then there is no longer any reason to worry about territorial disputes nor religious conversion from one group to the others. This way people can maintain God gave certain land to Abraham and everyone wins it because we all are entitled rather than just one group. So in a nutshell, emphasis on the nuttiness of the doctrine, all Abrahamic faiths no longer have to fight each other over land nor doctrine because compromise is key to comfortable living in the world free from conflicts. Basically since in the past people felt religious groups didn't fight fairly now in the name of religion they've decided we shouldn't fight at all or even argue or disagree about doctrines peacefully in confrontational conversion motivated ways.

However there are alternative ways to attain peace without dragging Abraham's name into the mud of heretical interfaith dialogues. Also even if peace is not attained sometimes it is better for war to occur than for there to be peace wherein principles and ethics and religion itself is sacrificed. Is religion more important than peace? Or is peace more important than your religion? Truly we must determine whether Abraham would desire people to fight for the sake of his religion or to be at peace no matter the price such a peace would cost to your faith. It is evident to anyone with any knowledge of Abrahamic texts that Abraham was a lifelong fighter for justice and monotheism against polytheism and evil injustice. So peace is attainable under religiously acceptable conditions but peace is also attainable under religiously unacceptable conditions. The interfaith Abrahamic faiths doctrines are unacceptable conditions for peace. War is simply not inevitable nor is it the worst thing that can happen in the world. If the faith of Abraham is abandoned in the name of Abraham for the sake of peace and tolerance this would waste all the sacrifices of those adherents to the faith of Abraham for there would be no more religion that was linked to Abraham in such a case, instead all we would have would be people with a meaningless label. I dislike violence and war as do most people but I dislike the destruction of religion more than the destruction of the world. Whereas the dismantling of the creed of Abrahamic intolerance for falsehood is too high a cost to pay for world peace. So I hope the negotiations of religious compromise in the name of Abrahamic faiths cease because it is without foundation nor precedent among the alleged Abrahamic faiths. Such a interfaith movement in the name of Abraham will only serve to fuel heresy and extremism despite what such movements claim to intend or act for. They will fail to attain peace and their followers will fail to attain paradise because of forsaking the faith of Abraham by hijacking his name for the sake of a faith other than what he taught humanity.

We propose as a step towards a peaceful solution that the claims to following Abraham be examined and compared with the attributed Abrahamic texts the claimants propose to show the faith of Abraham. Then all can better determine who is following Abraham as their texts depict him and who is not so the faith of Abraham can be identified. The Abrahamic claims can be tested. The problem with this method would only be if the texts are illegitimate or have been corrupted or tampered with. Whereas ironically nobody amongst the Abrahamic faiths claims to have any Scripture penned by Abraham's own hand. Nor do we even with any certainty know the language of Abraham. The language of Abraham is labeled as proto-Canaanite but nobody today knows that language or what its alphabet even looked like. Thus all the evidence or testimony regarding the popular person of Abraham is considered as hearsay evidence in languages different than what he is scholastically decreed to have spoken. Now if the text is revelation from God then such hearsay evidence is true and reliable but it is still hearsay nonetheless because it is not from the subject of the study themselves directly. So due to the fact that there is no handwritten Scripture of Abraham available for us to analyze today to best determine the faith of Abraham then we must use non-direct testimony from other sources. Despite there being to date 8 various alleged Abrahamic faiths, since only the three major religions of Judaism, Christianity and Islam are bunched together at the political interfaith roundtable I have chosen these three claims to focus on. This is because they have more textual attributions to Abraham than the rest and we don't want to be the person responsible for adding to the interfaith mix of nonsense. The goal of this book is to reduce the claims of Abrahamic faiths from 3+ to 1 not increase the number at the diplomatic dialogues. We all agree Abraham didn't teach 8 religions. Yet currently there is a popular heretical movement amongst religious crowds that are claiming he is responsible for three. So let us examine the three claimants' textual attributions to Abraham from the Jewish Hebrew Tanakh, the Christian Greek New Testament and the Muslim Arabic Quran and Hadith.

Abrahamic data from the Jewish Hebrew Tanakh

Book of Bereshit(Genesis) 12:1-20

אוַיֹּ֤אמֶר יְהוָה֙ אֶל־אַבְרָ֔ם לֶךְ־לְךָ֛ מֵאַרְצְךָ֥ וּמִמּֽוֹלַדְתְּךָ֖ וּמִבֵּ֣ית אָבִ֑יךָ אֶל־הָאָ֖רֶץ אֲשֶׁ֥ר אַרְאֶֽךָּ׃

בוְאֶֽעֶשְׂךָ֙ לְג֣וֹי גָּד֔וֹל וַאֲבָ֣רֶכְךָ֔ וַאֲגַדְּלָ֖ה שְׁמֶ֑ךָ וֶֽהְיֵ֖ה בְּרָכָֽה׃

גוַאֲבָֽרֲכָה֙ מְבָ֣רֲכֶ֔יךָ וּמְקַלֶּלְךָ֖ אָאֹ֑ר וְנִבְרְכ֣וּ בְךָ֔ כֹּ֖ל מִשְׁפְּחֹ֥ת הָאֲדָמָֽה׃

דוַיֵּ֣לֶךְ אַבְרָ֗ם כַּאֲשֶׁ֨ר דִּבֶּ֤ר אֵלָיו֙ יְהוָ֔ה וַיֵּ֥לֶךְ אִתּ֖וֹ ל֑וֹט וְאַבְרָ֗ם בֶּן־חָמֵ֤שׁ שָׁנִים֙ וְשִׁבְעִ֣ים שָׁנָ֔ה בְּצֵאת֖וֹ מֵחָרָֽן׃

הוַיִּקַּ֣ח אַבְרָם֩ אֶת־שָׂרַ֨י אִשְׁתּ֜וֹ וְאֶת־ל֣וֹט בֶּן־אָחִ֗יו וְאֶת־כָּל־רְכוּשָׁם֙ אֲשֶׁ֣ר רָכָ֔שׁוּ וְאֶת־הַנֶּ֖פֶשׁ אֲשֶׁר־עָשׂ֣וּ בְחָרָ֑ן וַיֵּצְא֗וּ לָלֶ֙כֶת֙ אַ֣רְצָה כְּנַ֔עַן וַיָּבֹ֖אוּ אַ֥רְצָה כְּנָֽעַן׃

ווַיַּעֲבֹ֤ר אַבְרָם֙ בָּאָ֔רֶץ עַ֚ד מְק֣וֹם שְׁכֶ֔ם עַ֖ד אֵל֣וֹן מוֹרֶ֑ה וְהַֽכְּנַעֲנִ֖י אָ֥ז בָּאָֽרֶץ׃

זוַיֵּרָ֤א יְהוָה֙ אֶל־אַבְרָ֔ם וַיֹּ֕אמֶר לְזַ֨רְעֲךָ֔ אֶתֵּ֖ן אֶת־הָאָ֣רֶץ הַזֹּ֑את וַיִּ֤בֶן שָׁם֙ מִזְבֵּ֔חַ לַיהוָ֖ה הַנִּרְאֶ֥ה אֵלָֽיו׃

חוַיַּעְתֵּ֨ק מִשָּׁ֜ם הָהָ֗רָה מִקֶּ֛דֶם לְבֵֽית־אֵ֖ל וַיֵּ֣ט אָהֳלֹ֑ה בֵּֽית־אֵ֤ל מִיָּם֙ וְהָעַ֣י מִקֶּ֔דֶם וַיִּֽבֶן־שָׁ֤ם מִזְבֵּ֙חַ֙ לַֽיהוָ֔ה וַיִּקְרָ֖א בְּשֵׁ֥ם יְהוָֽה׃

טוַיִּסַּ֣ע אַבְרָ֔ם הָל֥וֹךְ וְנָס֖וֹעַ הַנֶּֽגְבָּה׃

יוַיְהִ֥י רָעָ֖ב בָּאָ֑רֶץ וַיֵּ֨רֶד אַבְרָ֤ם מִצְרַ֙יְמָה֙ לָג֣וּר שָׁ֔ם כִּֽי־כָבֵ֥ד הָרָעָ֖ב בָּאָֽרֶץ׃

יאוַיְהִ֕י כַּאֲשֶׁ֥ר הִקְרִ֖יב לָב֣וֹא מִצְרָ֑יְמָה וַיֹּ֙אמֶר֙ אֶל־שָׂרַ֣י אִשְׁתּ֔וֹ הִנֵּה־
נָ֣א יָדַ֔עְתִּי כִּ֛י אִשָּׁ֥ה יְפַת־מַרְאֶ֖ה אָֽתְּ׃

יבוְהָיָ֗ה כִּֽי־יִרְא֤וּ אֹתָךְ֙ הַמִּצְרִ֔ים וְאָמְר֖וּ אִשְׁתּ֣וֹ זֹ֑את וְהָרְג֥וּ אֹתִ֖י
וְאֹתָ֥ךְ יְחַיּֽוּ׃

יגאִמְרִי־נָ֖א אֲחֹ֣תִי אָ֑תְּ לְמַ֙עַן֙ יִֽיטַב־לִ֣י בַעֲבוּרֵ֔ךְ וְחָיְתָ֥ה נַפְשִׁ֖י
בִּגְלָלֵֽךְ׃

ידוַיְהִ֕י כְּב֥וֹא אַבְרָ֖ם מִצְרָ֑יְמָה וַיִּרְא֤וּ הַמִּצְרִים֙ אֶת־הָ֣אִשָּׁ֔ה כִּֽי־יָפָ֥ה
הִ֖וא מְאֹֽד׃

טווַיִּרְא֤וּ אֹתָהּ֙ שָׂרֵ֣י פַרְעֹ֔ה וַֽיְהַֽלְל֥וּ אֹתָ֖הּ אֶל־פַּרְעֹ֑ה וַתֻּקַּ֥ח הָאִשָּׁ֖ה
בֵּ֥ית פַּרְעֹֽה׃

טזוּלְאַבְרָ֥ם הֵיטִ֖יב בַּעֲבוּרָ֑הּ וַֽיְהִי־ל֤וֹ צֹאן־וּבָקָר֙ וַחֲמֹרִ֔ים וַעֲבָדִים֙
וּשְׁפָחֹ֔ת וַאֲתֹנֹ֖ת וּגְמַלִּֽים׃

יזוַיְנַגַּ֙ע יְהֹוָ֧ה ׀ אֶת־פַּרְעֹ֛ה נְגָעִ֥ים גְּדֹלִ֖ים וְאֶת־בֵּית֑וֹ עַל־דְּבַ֥ר שָׂרַ֖י
אֵ֥שֶׁת אַבְרָֽם׃

יחוַיִּקְרָ֤א פַרְעֹה֙ לְאַבְרָ֔ם וַיֹּ֕אמֶר מַה־זֹּ֖את עָשִׂ֣יתָ לִּ֑י לָ֚מָּה לֹא־
הִגַּ֣דְתָּ לִּ֔י כִּ֥י אִשְׁתְּךָ֖ הִֽוא׃

יטלָמָ֤ה אָמַ֙רְתָּ֙ אֲחֹ֣תִי הִ֔וא וָאֶקַּ֥ח אֹתָ֛הּ לִ֖י לְאִשָּׁ֑ה וְעַתָּ֕ה הִנֵּ֥ה
אִשְׁתְּךָ֖ קַ֥ח וָלֵֽךְ׃

כוַיְצַ֥ו עָלָ֛יו פַּרְעֹ֖ה אֲנָשִׁ֑ים וַֽיְשַׁלְּח֥וּ אֹת֛וֹ וְאֶת־אִשְׁתּ֖וֹ וְאֶת־כָּל־אֲשֶׁר־
לֽוֹ׃

1 And the Lord said to Abram, "Go forth from your land
and from your birthplace and from your father's house,
to the land that I will show you. 2 And I will make you

into a great nation, and I will bless you, and I will aggrandize your name, and [you shall] be a blessing. 3 And I will bless those who bless you, and the one who curses you I will curse, and all the families of the earth shall be blessed in you." 4 And Abram went, as the Lord had spoken to him, and Lot went with him, and Abram was seventy five years old when he left Haran. 5 And Abram took Sarai his wife and Lot his brother's son, and all their possessions that they had acquired, and the souls they had acquired in Haran, and they went to go to the land of Canaan, and they came to the land of Canaan. 6 And Abram passed through the land, until the place of Shechem, until the plain of Moreh, and the Canaanites were then in the land. 7 And the Lord appeared to Abram, and He said, "To your seed I will give this land," and there he built an altar to the Lord, Who had appeared to him.8 And he moved from there to the mountain, east of Beth el, and he pitched his tent; Beth el was to the west and Ai was to the east, and there he built an altar to the Lord, and he called in the name of the Lord. 9 And Abram traveled, continually traveling southward. 10 And there was a famine in the land, and Abram descended to Egypt to sojourn there because the famine was severe in the land. 11 Now it came to pass when he drew near to come to Egypt, that he said to Sarai his wife, "Behold now I know that you are a woman of fair appearance. 12 And it will come to pass when the

Egyptians see you, that they will say, 'This is his wife,' and they will slay me and let you live. 13 Please say [that] you are my sister, in order that it go well with me because of you, and that my soul may live because of you." 14 And it came to pass when Abram came to Egypt, that the Egyptians saw the woman, that she was very pretty. 15 And Pharaoh's princes saw her, and they praised her to Pharaoh, and the woman was taken to the house of Pharaoh. 16 And he benefited Abram for her sake, and he had flocks and cattle and he donkeys and men servants and maid servants, and she donkeys and camels. 17 And the Lord plagued Pharaoh [with] great plagues as well as his household, on account of Sarai, Abram's wife. 18 And Pharaoh summoned Abram, and he said, "What is this that you have done to me? Why did you not tell me that she was your wife? 19 Why did you say, 'She is my sister,' so that I took her to myself for a wife? And now, here is your wife; take [her] and go." 20 And Pharaoh commanded men on his behalf, and they escorted him and his wife and all that was his.

Book of Bereshit(Genesis) 13:1-18

אוַיַּעַל אַבְרָם מִמִּצְרַיִם הוּא וְאִשְׁתּוֹ וְכָל־אֲשֶׁר־לוֹ וְלוֹט עִמּוֹ
הַנֶּגְבָּה:

בוְאַבְרָם כָּבֵד מְאֹד בַּמִּקְנֶה בַּכֶּסֶף וּבַזָּהָב:

גוֹהֵלֵךְ לְמַסָּעָיו מִנֶּגֶב וְעַד־בֵּית־אֵל עַד־הַמָּקוֹם אֲשֶׁר־הָיָה שָׁם אָהֳלֹה בַּתְּחִלָּה בֵּין בֵּית־אֵל וּבֵין הָעָי:

דאֶל־מְקוֹם הַמִּזְבֵּחַ אֲשֶׁר־עָשָׂה שָׁם בָּרִאשֹׁנָה וַיִּקְרָא שָׁם אַבְרָם בְּשֵׁם יְהֹוָה:

הוְגַם־לְלוֹט הַהֹלֵךְ אֶת־אַבְרָם הָיָה צֹאן־וּבָקָר וְאֹהָלִים:

ווְלֹא־נָשָׂא אֹתָם הָאָרֶץ לָשֶׁבֶת יַחְדָּו כִּי־הָיָה רְכוּשָׁם רָב וְלֹא יָכְלוּ לָשֶׁבֶת יַחְדָּו:

זוַיְהִי־רִיב בֵּין רֹעֵי מִקְנֵה־אַבְרָם וּבֵין רֹעֵי מִקְנֵה־לוֹט וְהַכְּנַעֲנִי וְהַפְּרִזִּי אָז יֹשֵׁב בָּאָרֶץ:

חוַיֹּאמֶר אַבְרָם אֶל־לוֹט אַל־נָא תְהִי מְרִיבָה בֵּינִי וּבֵינֶךָ וּבֵין רֹעַי וּבֵין רֹעֶיךָ כִּי־אֲנָשִׁים אַחִים אֲנָחְנוּ:

טהֲלֹא כָל־הָאָרֶץ לְפָנֶיךָ הִפָּרֶד נָא מֵעָלָי אִם־הַשְּׂמֹאל וְאֵימִנָה וְאִם־הַיָּמִין וְאַשְׂמְאִילָה:

יוַיִּשָּׂא־לוֹט אֶת־עֵינָיו וַיַּרְא אֶת־כָּל־כִּכַּר הַיַּרְדֵּן כִּי כֻלָּהּ מַשְׁקֶה לִפְנֵי | שַׁחֵת יְהֹוָה אֶת־סְדֹם וְאֶת־עֲמֹרָה כְּגַן־יְהֹוָה כְּאֶרֶץ מִצְרַיִם בֹּאֲכָה צֹעַר:

יאוַיִּבְחַר־לוֹ לוֹט אֵת כָּל־כִּכַּר הַיַּרְדֵּן וַיִּסַּע לוֹט מִקֶּדֶם וַיִּפָּרְדוּ אִישׁ מֵעַל אָחִיו:

יבאַבְרָם יָשַׁב בְּאֶרֶץ־כְּנָעַן וְלוֹט יָשַׁב בְּעָרֵי הַכִּכָּר וַיֶּאֱהַל עַד־סְדֹם:

יגוְאַנְשֵׁי סְדֹם רָעִים וְחַטָּאִים לַיהֹוָה מְאֹד:

ידוַיהֹוָה אָמַר אֶל־אַבְרָם אַחֲרֵי הִפָּרֶד־לוֹט מֵעִמּוֹ שָׂא נָא עֵינֶיךָ וּרְאֵה מִן־הַמָּקוֹם אֲשֶׁר־אַתָּה שָׁם צָפֹנָה וָנֶגְבָּה וָקֵדְמָה וָיָמָּה

טוכִּי אֶת־כָּל־הָאָרֶץ אֲשֶׁר־אַתָּה רֹאֶה לְךָ אֶתְּנֶנָּה וּלְזַרְעֲךָ עַד־
עוֹלָם׃

טזוְשַׂמְתִּי אֶת־זַרְעֲךָ כַּעֲפַר הָאָרֶץ אֲשֶׁר | אִם־יוּכַל אִישׁ לִמְנוֹת
אֶת־עֲפַר הָאָרֶץ גַּם־זַרְעֲךָ יִמָּנֶה׃

יזקוּם הִתְהַלֵּךְ בָּאָרֶץ לְאָרְכָּהּ וּלְרָחְבָּהּ כִּי לְךָ אֶתְּנֶנָּה׃

יחוַיֶּאֱהַל אַבְרָם וַיָּבֹא וַיֵּשֶׁב בְּאֵלֹנֵי מַמְרֵא אֲשֶׁר בְּחֶבְרוֹן וַיִּבֶן־שָׁם
מִזְבֵּחַ לַיהוָה׃

1 And Abram came up from Egypt, he and his wife and all that was his, and Lot with him, to the south. 2 And Abram was very heavy with cattle, with silver, and with gold. 3 And he went on his journeys, from the south and until Beth el, until the place where his tent had been previously, between Beth el and between Ai. 4 To the place of the altar that he had made at first, and Abram called there in the name of the Lord. 5And also Lot, who went with Abram, had flocks and cattle and tents. 6 And the land did not bear them to dwell together, for their possessions were many, and they could not dwell together. 7 And there was a quarrel between the herdsmen of Abram's cattle and between the herdsmen of Lot's cattle, and the Canaanites and the Perizzites were then dwelling in the land. 8 And Abram said to Lot, "Please let there be no quarrel between me and between you and between my herdsmen and between your herdsmen, for we are kinsmen. 9 Is not all the land before you? Please part from me; if [you go] left, I will go right, and if [you go] right, I will go left." 10 And Lot raised his eyes, and he saw the entire plain of the Jordan, that it was entirely watered; before the Lord destroyed Sodom and Gomorrah, like the garden of the Lord, like the land of Egypt, as you come to Zoar. 11 And Lot chose for himself the entire plain of the Jordan, and Lot traveled from the east, and they parted from one another. 12 Abram dwelt in the land of Canaan, and Lot dwelt in the cities of the plain, and he pitched his tents until Sodom. 13 And the people of Sodom were very evil and sinful against the Lord. 14 And the Lord said to Abram after Lot had parted from him, "Please raise your eyes and see, from the place where you are, northward and southward and eastward and westward. 15 For all the land that you see I will give to you and to your seed to eternity. 16 And I will make your seed like the dust of the earth, so that if a man will be able to count the dust of the earth, so will your seed be counted. 17 Rise, walk in the land, to its length and to its breadth, for I will give it to you." 18 And Abram pitched his tents, and he came, and he dwelt in the plain of Mamre, which is in Hebron, and there he built an altar to the Lord.

Book of Bereshit 14:9-24

טאֵת כְּדָרְלָעֹמֶר מֶלֶךְ עֵילָם וְתִדְעָל מֶלֶךְ גּוֹיִם וְאַמְרָפֶל מֶלֶךְ
שִׁנְעָר וְאַרְיוֹךְ מֶלֶךְ אֶלָּסָר אַרְבָּעָה מְלָכִים אֶת־הַחֲמִשָּׁה:

יוְעֵמֶק הַשִּׂדִּים בֶּאֱרֹת בֶּאֱרֹת חֵמָר וַיָּנֻסוּ מֶלֶךְ־סְדֹם וַעֲמֹרָה
וַיִּפְּלוּ־שָׁמָּה וְהַנִּשְׁאָרִים הֶרָה נָּסוּ:

יאוַיִּקְחוּ אֶת־כָּל־רְכֻשׁ סְדֹם וַעֲמֹרָה וְאֶת־כָּל־אָכְלָם וַיֵּלֵכוּ:

יבוַיִּקְחוּ אֶת־לוֹט וְאֶת־רְכֻשׁוֹ בֶּן־אֲחִי אַבְרָם וַיֵּלֵכוּ וְהוּא יֹשֵׁב
בִּסְדֹם:

יגוַיָּבֹא הַפָּלִיט וַיַּגֵּד לְאַבְרָם הָעִבְרִי וְהוּא שֹׁכֵן בְּאֵלֹנֵי מַמְרֵא
הָאֱמֹרִי אֲחִי אֶשְׁכֹּל וַאֲחִי עָנֵר וְהֵם בַּעֲלֵי בְרִית־אַבְרָם:

ידוַיִּשְׁמַע אַבְרָם כִּי נִשְׁבָּה אָחִיו וַיָּרֶק אֶת־חֲנִיכָיו יְלִידֵי בֵיתוֹ
שְׁמֹנָה עָשָׂר וּשְׁלֹשׁ מֵאוֹת וַיִּרְדֹּף עַד־דָּן:

טווַיֵּחָלֵק עֲלֵיהֶם | לַיְלָה הוּא וַעֲבָדָיו וַיַּכֵּם וַיִּרְדְּפֵם עַד־חוֹבָה
אֲשֶׁר מִשְּׂמֹאל לְדַמָּשֶׂק:

טזוַיָּשֶׁב אֵת כָּל־הָרְכֻשׁ וְגַם אֶת־לוֹט אָחִיו וּרְכֻשׁוֹ הֵשִׁיב וְגַם אֶת־
הַנָּשִׁים וְאֶת־הָעָם:

יזוַיֵּצֵא מֶלֶךְ־סְדֹם לִקְרָאתוֹ אַחֲרֵי שׁוּבוֹ מֵהַכּוֹת אֶת־כְּדָרְלָעֹמֶר
וְאֶת־הַמְּלָכִים אֲשֶׁר אִתּוֹ אֶל־עֵמֶק שָׁוֵה הוּא עֵמֶק הַמֶּלֶךְ:

יחוּמַלְכִּי־צֶדֶק מֶלֶךְ שָׁלֵם הוֹצִיא לֶחֶם וָיָיִן וְהוּא כֹהֵן לְאֵל עֶלְיוֹן:

יטוַיְבָרֲכֵהוּ וַיֹּאמַר בָּרוּךְ אַבְרָם לְאֵל עֶלְיוֹן קֹנֵה שָׁמַיִם וָאָרֶץ:

כוּבָרוּךְ אֵל עֶלְיוֹן אֲשֶׁר־מִגֵּן צָרֶיךָ בְּיָדֶךָ וַיִּתֶּן־לוֹ מַעֲשֵׂר מִכֹּל:

כאוַיֹּאמֶר מֶלֶךְ־סְדֹם אֶל־אַבְרָם תֶּן־לִי הַנֶּפֶשׁ וְהָרְכֻשׁ קַח־לָךְ:

כבוַיֹּאמֶר אַבְרָם אֶל־מֶלֶךְ סְדֹם הֲרִמֹתִי יָדִי אֶל־יְהוָה אֵל עֶלְיוֹן
קֹנֵה שָׁמַיִם וָאָרֶץ:

כגאם־מָחוּט וְעַד שְׂרוֹךְ־נַעַל וְאִם־אֶקַּח מִכָּל־אֲשֶׁר־לָךְ וְלֹא
תֹאמַר אֲנִי הֶעֱשַׁרְתִּי אֶת־אַבְרָם:

כדבִּלְעָדַי רַק אֲשֶׁר אָכְלוּ הַנְּעָרִים וְחֵלֶק הָאֲנָשִׁים אֲשֶׁר הָלְכוּ
אִתִּי עָנֵר אֶשְׁכֹּל וּמַמְרֵא הֵם יִקְחוּ חֶלְקָם:

9 With Chedorlaomer the king of Elam and Tidal the king
of Goyim and Amraphel the king of Shinar and Arioch
the king of Ellasar, four kings against the five. 10 Now
the valley of Siddim was [composed of] many clay pits,
and the kings of Sodom and Gomorrah fled and they fell
there, and the survivors fled to a mountain. 11 And they
took all the possessions of Sodom and Gomorrah and all
their food, and they departed. 12 And they took Lot and
his possessions, the son of Abram's brother, and they
departed, and he was living in Sodom. 13 And the
fugitive came and he told Abram the Hebrew, and he was
living in the plain of Mamre the Amorite, the brother of
Eshkol and the brother of Aner, who were Abram's
confederates. 14 And Abram heard that his kinsman had
been taken captive, and he armed his trained men, those
born in his house, three hundred and eighteen, and he
pursued [them] until Dan. 15 And he divided himself
against them at night, he and his servants, and smote
them, and pursued them until Hobah, which is to the left
of Damascus. 16 And he restored all the possessions, and
also Lot his brother and his possessions he restored, and
also the women and the people. 17 And the king of Sodom

came out toward him, after his return from smiting Chedorlaomer and the kings who were with him, to the valley of Shaveh, which is the valley of the king. 18 And Malchizedek the king of Salem brought out bread and wine, and he was a priest to the Most High God. 19 And he blessed him, and he said, "Blessed be Abram to the Most High God, Who possesses heaven and earth. 20 And blessed be the Most High God, Who has delivered your adversaries into your hand," and he gave him a tithe from all. 21 And the king of Sodom said to Abram, "Give me the souls, and the possessions take for yourself." 22 And Abram said to the king of Sodom, "I raise my hand to the Lord, the Most High God, Who possesses heaven and earth. 23 Neither from a thread to a shoe strap, nor will I take from whatever is yours, that you should not say, 'I have made Abram wealthy.' 24 Exclusive of what the lads ate, and the share of the men who went with me; Aner, Eshkol, and Mamre they shall take their share."

As a sidenote within this chapter "Hebrew" is mentioned which might seem obvious since it is a Hebrew book. However historically the language of Hebrew did not exist in the time of Abram/Abraham and didn't even exist in the time of Moses, David or Solomon. So these Hebrew texts should not be confused with the divine revelation of the Torah because they are translations by default.

Only God can translate God accurately. Just as a fish cannot translate a human neither can a human translate God. By saying a translation is divine revelation then you are saying the translator was divine. To say a translation is *"the word of God"* it means you consider the translator to be God since it is their words you are referencing and not God's words even if they were translating God's words, which typically isn't the case anyways. Truly if you have revelation of God get translated the only way it can be considered revelation is if God translated it himself. Simply claiming a translator was "inspired" doesn't count, just as nobody could say God inspired them to translate my book because accurate translations are not possible unless they are done by the original author themself. So the common claim that the translated biblical passages are the "inspired word of God" is false for so many reasons. That a translation is done by a human is enough proof that translations are not divine revelations or 100% accurate because humans don't know every word in a language. God knows every word and knows the best word to use to convey the correct meaning, humans don't and thus can never ever translate another human 100% correctly, let alone God the Creator of the Universe. Regarding the Hebrew Jewish Bible it is not traceable back to Moses and Moses, David and Solomon didn't even speak or write Hebrew. So the bible is not only scholastically inauthentically transcribed but it's not even in the same language the prophets to whom such writings are alleged to have come from spoke. Just on that fundamental point alone, that the Tanakh or Old Testament is written in a language Abraham, Ishmail, Isaac, Jacob, Joseph, Noah, Job, Jonah, Adam, Moses, David, Solomon, Lot, Seth, Enoch and most biblical characters never spoke disqualifies them as authentic religiously useable texts. Forget translations, copies, forgeries, lack of chains of transmission. The books are in different languages than the prophets they purport to teach us about, hence they could never be from those prophets and could never be the divine revelation given to those prophets. There is absolutely zero connection between the biblical prophets and the biblical texts. Research from paleolinguists indicates that the Hebrew language didn't even exist at the time Moses received his commandments but came into being approximately 1,000 years after Moses, and the oldest fragment of paleo-Hebrew writing that exists is over 250 years after the earliest possible date Moses is believed to have died. So nobody really knows what language Moses spoke or what language his revelation was in either, and we don't have the Ark of the covenant or any original handwritten documents from Moses to read in order to find out. Although it is reported the original Torah was written by God in Gold lettering on Emerald or Pearl tablets. However everyone knows we don't have the original Mosaic Torah tablets, there are no Torah relics alleged to have been touched by Moses available today. The Jewish Kabbalists even thought 2 whole books were missing from the modern Torah and that the Hebrew alphabet lacked one of the letters that the original Torah was in. Thus the Hebrew language dislocated the Torah and the Hebrew version was missing a good chunk of information due to Hebrew missing letters of the alphabet of the language of the Torah. So Abraham didn't speak Hebrew but is believed to have spoken "proto-Canaanite", which is a dead language and is the reason why we don't have access to the Scripture called the Suhuf which was given to Abraham. I mention this so you take these Hebrew Jewish Scriptures within context for what they are and don't confuse them as being written by Abraham or Moses when they are not.

Book of Bereshit(Genesis) 15:1-18

אאחַ֣ר | הַדְּבָרִ֣ים הָאֵ֗לֶּה הָיָ֤ה דְבַר־יְהֹוָה֙ אֶל־אַבְרָ֔ם בַּֽמַּחֲזֶ֖ה
לֵאמֹ֑ר אַל־תִּירָ֣א אַבְרָ֗ם אָֽנֹכִי֙ מָגֵ֣ן לָ֔ךְ שְׂכָֽרְךָ֖ הַרְבֵּ֥ה מְאֹֽד:

בוַיֹּ֣אמֶר אַבְרָ֗ם אֲדֹנָ֤י יֱהֹוִה֙ מַה־תִּתֶּן־לִ֔י וְאָֽנֹכִ֖י הוֹלֵ֣ךְ עֲרִירִ֑י וּבֶן־
מֶ֣שֶׁק בֵּיתִ֔י ה֖וּא דַּמֶּ֥שֶׂק אֱלִיעֶֽזֶר:

גוַיֹּ֣אמֶר אַבְרָ֔ם הֵ֣ן לִ֔י לֹ֥א נָתַ֖תָּה זָ֑רַע וְהִנֵּ֥ה בֶן־בֵּיתִ֖י יוֹרֵ֥שׁ אֹתִֽי:

דוְהִנֵּ֨ה דְבַר־יְהֹוָ֤ה אֵלָיו֙ לֵאמֹ֔ר לֹ֥א יִירָֽשְׁךָ֖ זֶ֑ה כִּי־אִם֙ אֲשֶׁ֣ר יֵצֵ֣א
מִמֵּעֶ֔יךָ ה֖וּא יִירָשֶֽׁךָ:

הוַיּוֹצֵ֨א אֹת֜וֹ הַח֗וּצָה וַיֹּ֙אמֶר֙ הַבֶּט־נָ֣א הַשָּׁמַ֔יְמָה וּסְפֹר֙ הַכּ֣וֹכָבִ֔ים
אִם־תּוּכַ֖ל לִסְפֹּ֣ר אֹתָ֑ם וַיֹּ֣אמֶר ל֔וֹ כֹּ֥ה יִהְיֶ֖ה זַרְעֶֽךָ:

ווְהֶֽאֱמִ֖ן בַּֽיהֹוָ֑ה וַיַּחְשְׁבֶ֥הָ לּ֖וֹ צְדָקָֽה:

זוַיֹּ֖אמֶר אֵלָ֑יו אֲנִ֣י יְהֹוָ֗ה אֲשֶׁ֤ר הֽוֹצֵאתִ֙יךָ֙ מֵא֣וּר כַּשְׂדִּ֔ים לָ֧תֶת לְךָ֛
אֶת־הָאָ֥רֶץ הַזֹּ֖את לְרִשְׁתָּֽהּ:

חוַיֹּאמַ֑ר אֲדֹנָ֣י יֱהֹוִ֔ה בַּמָּ֥ה אֵדַ֖ע כִּ֥י אִֽירָשֶֽׁנָּה:

טוַיֹּ֣אמֶר אֵלָ֗יו קְחָ֥ה לִי֙ עֶגְלָ֣ה מְשֻׁלֶּ֔שֶׁת וְעֵ֥ז מְשֻׁלֶּ֖שֶׁת וְאַ֣יִל מְשֻׁלָּ֑שׁ
וְתֹ֖ר וְגוֹזָֽל:

יוַיִּֽקַּֽח־ל֣וֹ אֶת־כָּל־אֵ֗לֶּה וַיְבַתֵּ֤ר אֹתָם֙ בַּתָּ֔וֶךְ וַיִּתֵּ֥ן אִֽישׁ־בִּתְר֖וֹ
לִקְרַ֣את רֵעֵ֑הוּ וְאֶת־הַצִּפֹּ֖ר לֹ֥א בָתָֽר:

יאוַיֵּ֥רֶד הָעַ֖יִט עַל־הַפְּגָרִ֑ים וַיַּשֵּׁ֥ב אֹתָ֖ם אַבְרָֽם:

יבוַיְהִ֤י הַשֶּׁ֙מֶשׁ֙ לָב֔וֹא וְתַרְדֵּמָ֖ה נָֽפְלָ֣ה עַל־אַבְרָ֑ם וְהִנֵּ֥ה אֵימָ֛ה
חֲשֵׁכָ֥ה גְדֹלָ֖ה נֹפֶ֥לֶת עָלָֽיו:

יגוַיֹּאמֶר לְאַבְרָם יָדֹעַ תֵּדַע כִּי־גֵר | יִהְיֶה זַרְעֲךָ בְּאֶרֶץ לֹא לָהֶם וַעֲבָדוּם וְעִנּוּ אֹתָם אַרְבַּע מֵאוֹת שָׁנָה:

ידוְגַם אֶת־הַגּוֹי אֲשֶׁר יַעֲבֹדוּ דָּן אָנֹכִי וְאַחֲרֵי־כֵן יֵצְאוּ בִּרְכֻשׁ גָּדוֹל:

טווְאַתָּה תָּבוֹא אֶל־אֲבֹתֶיךָ בְּשָׁלוֹם תִּקָּבֵר בְּשֵׂיבָה טוֹבָה:

טזוְדוֹר רְבִיעִי יָשׁוּבוּ הֵנָּה כִּי לֹא־שָׁלֵם עֲוֹן הָאֱמֹרִי עַד־הֵנָּה:

יזוַיְהִי הַשֶּׁמֶשׁ בָּאָה וַעֲלָטָה הָיָה וְהִנֵּה תַנּוּר עָשָׁן וְלַפִּיד אֵשׁ אֲשֶׁר עָבַר בֵּין הַגְּזָרִים הָאֵלֶּה:

יחבַּיּוֹם הַהוּא כָּרַת יְהוָה אֶת־אַבְרָם בְּרִית לֵאמֹר לְזַרְעֲךָ נָתַתִּי אֶת־הָאָרֶץ הַזֹּאת מִנְּהַר מִצְרַיִם עַד־הַנָּהָר הַגָּדֹל נְהַר־פְּרָת:

1 After these incidents, the word of the Lord came to Abram in a vision, saying, "Fear not, Abram; I am your Shield; your reward is exceedingly great." 2 And Abram said, "O Lord God, what will You give me, since I am going childless, and the steward of my household is Eliezer of Damascus?" 3 And Abram said, "Behold, You have given me no seed, and behold, one of my household will inherit me." 4 And behold, the word of the Lord came to him, saying, "This one will not inherit you, but the one who will spring from your innards-he will inherit you." 5 And He took him outside, and He said, "Please look heavenward and count the stars, if you are able to count them." And He said to him, "So will be your seed." 6 And he believed in the Lord, and He accounted it to him as righteousness. 7 And He said to him, "I am the Lord, Who brought you forth from Ur of the Chaldees, to

give you this land to inherit it." 8 And he said, "O Lord God, how will I know that I will inherit it?" 9 And He said to him, "Take for Me three heifers and three goats and three rams, and a turtle dove and a young bird." 10 And he took for Him all these, and he divided them in the middle, and he placed each part opposite its mate, but he did not divide the birds. 11 And the birds of prey descended upon the carcasses, and Abram drove them away. 12 Now the sun was ready to set, and a deep sleep fell upon Abram, and behold, a fright, a great darkness was falling upon him. 13 And He said to Abram, "You shall surely know that your seed will be strangers in a land that is not theirs, and they will enslave them and oppress them, for four hundred years. 14 And also the nation that they will serve will I judge, and afterwards they will go forth with great possessions. 15 But you will come to your forefathers in peace; you will be buried in a good old age. 16 And the fourth generation will return here, for the iniquity of the Amorites will not be complete until then." 17 Now it came to pass that the sun had set, and it was dark, and behold, a smoking furnace and a fire brand, which passed between these parts. 18 On that day, the Lord formed a covenant with Abram, saying, "To your seed I have given this land, from the river of Egypt until the great river, the Euphrates river.

Book of Bereshit(Genesis) 16:1-6

אוְשָׂרַי֙ אֵ֣שֶׁת אַבְרָ֔ם לֹ֥א יָלְדָ֖ה ל֑וֹ וְלָ֛הּ שִׁפְחָ֥ה מִצְרִ֖ית וּשְׁמָ֥הּ הָגָֽר:

בוַתֹּ֨אמֶר שָׂרַ֜י אֶל־אַבְרָ֗ם הִנֵּה־נָ֞א עֲצָרַ֤נִי יְהוָֹה֙ מִלֶּ֔דֶת בֹּא־נָא֙ אֶל־שִׁפְחָתִ֔י אוּלַ֥י אִבָּנֶ֖ה מִמֶּ֑נָּה וַיִּשְׁמַ֥ע אַבְרָ֖ם לְק֥וֹל שָׂרָֽי:

גוַתִּקַּ֞ח שָׂרַ֣י אֵֽשֶׁת־אַבְרָ֗ם אֶת־הָגָ֤ר הַמִּצְרִית֙ שִׁפְחָתָ֔הּ מִקֵּץ֙ עֶ֣שֶׂר שָׁנִ֔ים לְשֶׁ֥בֶת אַבְרָ֖ם בְּאֶ֣רֶץ כְּנָ֑עַן וַתִּתֵּ֥ן אֹתָ֛הּ לְאַבְרָ֥ם אִישָׁ֖הּ ל֥וֹ לְאִשָּֽׁה:

דוַיָּבֹ֥א אֶל־הָגָ֖ר וַתַּ֑הַר וַתֵּ֨רֶא֙ כִּ֣י הָרָ֔תָה וַתֵּקַ֥ל גְּבִרְתָּ֖הּ בְּעֵינֶֽיהָ:

הוַתֹּ֨אמֶר שָׂרַ֣י אֶל־אַבְרָם֘ חֲמָסִ֣י עָלֶיךָ֒ אָֽנֹכִ֗י נָתַ֤תִּי שִׁפְחָתִי֙ בְּחֵיקֶ֔ךָ וַתֵּ֨רֶא֙ כִּ֣י הָרָ֔תָה וָאֵקַ֖ל בְּעֵינֶ֑יהָ יִשְׁפֹּ֥ט יְהוָֹ֖ה בֵּינִ֥י וּבֵינֶֽיךָ:

ווַיֹּ֨אמֶר אַבְרָ֜ם אֶל־שָׂרַ֗י הִנֵּ֤ה שִׁפְחָתֵךְ֙ בְּיָדֵ֔ךְ עֲשִׂי־לָ֖הּ הַטּ֣וֹב בְּעֵינָ֑יִךְ וַתְּעַנֶּ֣הָ שָׂרַ֔י וַתִּבְרַ֖ח מִפָּנֶֽיהָ:

1 Now Sarai, Abram's wife, had not borne to him, and she had an Egyptian handmaid named Hagar. 2 And Sarai said to Abram, "Behold now, the Lord has restrained me from bearing; please come to my handmaid; perhaps I will be built up from her." And Abram hearkened to Sarai's voice. 3 So Sarai, Abram's wife, took Hagar the Egyptian, her handmaid, at the end of ten years of Abram's dwelling in the land of Canaan, and she gave her to Abram her husband for a wife. 4 And he came to Hagar, and she conceived, and she saw that she was pregnant, and her mistress became unimportant in her eyes. 5 And Sarai said to Abram, "May my injustice be upon you! I gave my handmaid into your bosom, and she saw that she had become pregnant, and I became unimportant in her eyes. May the Lord judge between me and you!" 6 And Abram said to Sarai, "Here is your handmaid in your hand; do to her that which is proper in your eyes." And Sarai afflicted her, and she fled from before her.

Book of Bereshit(Genesis) 16:15-16

טווַתֵּ֧לֶד הָגָ֛ר לְאַבְרָ֖ם בֵּ֑ן וַיִּקְרָ֨א אַבְרָ֧ם שֶׁם־בְּנ֛וֹ אֲשֶׁר־יָלְדָ֥ה הָגָ֖ר יִשְׁמָעֵֽאל׃

טזוְאַבְרָ֕ם בֶּן־שְׁמֹנִ֥ים שָׁנָ֖ה וְשֵׁ֣שׁ שָׁנִ֑ים בְּלֶֽדֶת־הָגָ֥ר אֶת־יִשְׁמָעֵ֖אל לְאַבְרָֽם׃

15 And Hagar bore a son to Abram, and Abram named his son, whom Hagar had borne, Ishmael. 16 And Abram was eighty-six years old, when Hagar bore Ishmael to Abram.

Book of Bereshit(Genesis) 17:1-27

אוַיְהִ֣י אַבְרָ֔ם בֶּן־תִּשְׁעִ֥ים שָׁנָ֖ה וְתֵ֣שַׁע שָׁנִ֑ים וַיֵּרָ֨א יְהֹוָ֜ה אֶל־אַבְרָ֗ם וַיֹּ֤אמֶר אֵלָיו֙ אֲנִי־אֵ֣ל שַׁדַּ֔י הִתְהַלֵּ֥ךְ לְפָנַ֖י וֶהְיֵ֥ה תָמִֽים׃

בוְאֶתְּנָ֥ה בְרִיתִ֖י בֵּינִ֣י וּבֵינֶ֑ךָ וְאַרְבֶּ֥ה אוֹתְךָ֖ בִּמְאֹ֥ד מְאֹֽד׃

גוַיִּפֹּ֥ל אַבְרָ֖ם עַל־פָּנָ֑יו וַיְדַבֵּ֥ר אִתּ֛וֹ אֱלֹהִ֖ים לֵאמֹֽר׃

דאֲנִ֕י הִנֵּ֥ה בְרִיתִ֖י אִתָּ֑ךְ וְהָיִ֕יתָ לְאַ֖ב הֲמ֥וֹן גּוֹיִֽם׃

הוְלֹא־יִקָּרֵ֥א ע֛וֹד אֶת־שִׁמְךָ֖ אַבְרָ֑ם וְהָיָ֤ה שִׁמְךָ֙ אַבְרָהָ֔ם כִּ֛י אַב־הֲמ֥וֹן גּוֹיִ֖ם נְתַתִּֽיךָ׃

וְהִפְרֵתִ֤י אֹֽתְךָ֙ בִּמְאֹ֣ד מְאֹ֔ד וּנְתַתִּ֖יךָ לְגוֹיִ֑ם וּמְלָכִ֖ים מִמְּךָ֥ יֵצֵֽאוּ:

וַהֲקִמֹתִ֨י אֶת־בְּרִיתִ֜י בֵּינִ֣י וּבֵינֶ֗ךָ וּבֵ֨ין זַרְעֲךָ֧ אַחֲרֶ֛יךָ לְדֹרֹתָ֖ם לִבְרִ֣ית עוֹלָ֑ם לִהְי֤וֹת לְךָ֙ לֵֽאלֹהִ֔ים וּֽלְזַרְעֲךָ֖ אַחֲרֶֽיךָ:

וְנָתַתִּ֣י לְ֠ךָ וּלְזַרְעֲךָ֨ אַחֲרֶ֜יךָ אֵ֣ת | אֶ֣רֶץ מְגֻרֶ֗יךָ אֵ֚ת כָּל־אֶ֣רֶץ כְּנַ֔עַן לַאֲחֻזַּ֖ת עוֹלָ֑ם וְהָיִ֥יתִי לָהֶ֖ם לֵאלֹהִֽים:

וַיֹּ֤אמֶר אֱלֹהִים֙ אֶל־אַבְרָהָ֔ם וְאַתָּ֖ה אֶת־בְּרִיתִ֣י תִשְׁמֹ֑ר אַתָּ֛ה וְזַרְעֲךָ֥ אַֽחֲרֶ֖יךָ לְדֹרֹתָֽם:

זֹ֣את בְּרִיתִ֞י אֲשֶׁ֣ר תִּשְׁמְר֗וּ בֵּינִי֙ וּבֵ֣ינֵיכֶ֔ם וּבֵ֥ין זַרְעֲךָ֖ אַחֲרֶ֑יךָ הִמּ֥וֹל לָכֶ֖ם כָּל־זָכָֽר:

וּנְמַלְתֶּ֕ם אֵ֖ת בְּשַׂ֣ר עָרְלַתְכֶ֑ם וְהָיָה֙ לְא֣וֹת בְּרִ֔ית בֵּינִ֖י וּבֵינֵיכֶֽם:

וּבֶן־שְׁמֹנַ֣ת יָמִ֗ים יִמּ֥וֹל לָכֶ֛ם כָּל־זָכָ֖ר לְדֹרֹֽתֵיכֶ֑ם יְלִ֣יד בָּ֔יִת וּמִקְנַת־כֶּ֙סֶף֙ מִכֹּ֣ל בֶּן־נֵכָ֔ר אֲשֶׁ֛ר לֹ֥א מִזַּרְעֲךָ֖ הֽוּא:

הִמּ֧וֹל | יִמּ֛וֹל יְלִ֥יד בֵּֽיתְךָ֖ וּמִקְנַ֣ת כַּסְפֶּ֑ךָ וְהָיְתָ֧ה בְרִיתִ֛י בִּבְשַׂרְכֶ֖ם לִבְרִ֥ית עוֹלָֽם:

וְעָרֵ֣ל | זָכָ֗ר אֲשֶׁ֤ר לֹֽא־יִמּוֹל֙ אֶת־בְּשַׂ֣ר עָרְלָת֔וֹ וְנִכְרְתָ֛ה הַנֶּ֥פֶשׁ הַהִ֖וא מֵעַמֶּ֑יהָ אֶת־בְּרִיתִ֖י הֵפַֽר:

וַיֹּ֤אמֶר אֱלֹהִים֙ אֶל־אַבְרָהָ֔ם שָׂרַ֣י אִשְׁתְּךָ֔ לֹא־תִקְרָ֥א אֶת־שְׁמָ֖הּ שָׂרָ֑י כִּ֥י שָׂרָ֖ה שְׁמָֽהּ:

וּבֵרַכְתִּ֣י אֹתָ֔הּ וְגַ֨ם נָתַ֧תִּי מִמֶּ֛נָּה לְךָ֖ בֵּ֑ן וּבֵֽרַכְתִּ֙יהָ֙ וְהָֽיְתָ֣ה לְגוֹיִ֔ם מַלְכֵ֥י עַמִּ֖ים מִמֶּ֥נָּה יִהְיֽוּ:

וַיִּפֹּ֧ל אַבְרָהָ֛ם עַל־פָּנָ֖יו וַיִּצְחָ֑ק וַיֹּ֣אמֶר בְּלִבּ֗וֹ הַלְּבֶ֤ן מֵאָֽה־שָׁנָה֙ יִוָּלֵ֔ד וְאִ֨ם־שָׂרָ֔ה הֲבַת־תִּשְׁעִ֥ים שָׁנָ֖ה תֵּלֵֽד:

יחוַיֹּ֤אמֶר אַבְרָהָם֙ אֶל־הָ֣אֱלֹהִ֔ים ל֥וּ יִשְׁמָעֵ֖אל יִחְיֶ֥ה לְפָנֶֽיךָ:

יטוַיֹּ֣אמֶר אֱלֹהִ֗ים אֲבָל֙ שָׂרָ֣ה אִשְׁתְּךָ֗ יֹלֶ֤דֶת לְךָ֙ בֵּ֔ן וְקָרָ֥אתָ אֶת־שְׁמ֖וֹ יִצְחָ֑ק וַהֲקִמֹתִ֨י אֶת־בְּרִיתִ֥י אִתּ֛וֹ לִבְרִ֥ית עוֹלָ֖ם לְזַרְע֥וֹ אַחֲרָֽיו:

כוּֽלְיִשְׁמָעֵאל֮ שְׁמַעְתִּ֒יךָ֒ הִנֵּ֣ה | בֵּרַ֣כְתִּי אֹת֗וֹ וְהִפְרֵיתִ֥י אֹת֛וֹ וְהִרְבֵּיתִ֥י אֹת֖וֹ בִּמְאֹ֣ד מְאֹ֑ד שְׁנֵים־עָשָׂ֤ר נְשִׂיאִם֙ יוֹלִ֔יד וּנְתַתִּ֖יו לְג֥וֹי גָּדֽוֹל:

כאוְאֶת־בְּרִיתִ֖י אָקִ֣ים אֶת־יִצְחָ֑ק אֲשֶׁר֩ תֵּלֵ֨ד לְךָ֤ שָׂרָה֙ לַמּוֹעֵ֣ד הַזֶּ֔ה בַּשָּׁנָ֖ה הָאַחֶֽרֶת:

כבוַיְכַ֖ל לְדַבֵּ֣ר אִתּ֑וֹ וַיַּ֣עַל אֱלֹהִ֔ים מֵעַ֖ל אַבְרָהָֽם:

כגוַיִּקַּ֨ח אַבְרָהָ֜ם אֶת־יִשְׁמָעֵ֣אל בְּנ֗וֹ וְאֵ֨ת כָּל־יְלִידֵ֤י בֵיתוֹ֙ וְאֵת֙ כָּל־מִקְנַ֣ת כַּסְפּ֔וֹ כָּל־זָכָ֕ר בְּאַנְשֵׁ֖י בֵּ֣ית אַבְרָהָ֑ם וַיָּ֜מָל אֶת־בְּשַׂ֣ר עָרְלָתָ֗ם בְּעֶ֨צֶם֙ הַיּ֣וֹם הַזֶּ֔ה כַּאֲשֶׁ֛ר דִּבֶּ֥ר אִתּ֖וֹ אֱלֹהִֽים:

כדוְאַ֨בְרָהָ֔ם בֶּן־תִּשְׁעִ֥ים וָתֵ֖שַׁע שָׁנָ֑ה בְּהִמֹּל֖וֹ בְּשַׂ֥ר עָרְלָתֽוֹ:

כהוְיִשְׁמָעֵ֣אל בְּנ֔וֹ בֶּן־שְׁלֹ֥שׁ עֶשְׂרֵ֖ה שָׁנָ֑ה בְּהִ֨מֹּל֔וֹ אֵ֖ת בְּשַׂ֥ר עָרְלָתֽוֹ:

כובְּעֶ֙צֶם֙ הַיּ֣וֹם הַזֶּ֔ה נִמּ֖וֹל אַבְרָהָ֑ם וְיִשְׁמָעֵ֖אל בְּנֽוֹ:

כזוְכָל־אַנְשֵׁ֤י בֵיתוֹ֙ יְלִ֣יד בָּ֔יִת וּמִקְנַת־כֶּ֖סֶף מֵאֵ֣ת בֶּן־נֵכָ֑ר נִמֹּ֖לוּ אִתּֽוֹ:

1 And Abram was ninety-nine years old, and God appeared to Abram, and He said to him, "I am the Almighty God; walk before Me and be perfect. 2 And I will place My covenant between Me and between you, and I will multiply you very greatly." 3 And Abram fell upon his face, and God spoke with him, saying, 4 "As for Me, behold My covenant is with you, and you shall become the father of a multitude of nations. 5 And your name shall no longer be called Abram, but your name shall be Abraham, for I have made you the father of a multitude of nations. 6 And I will make you exceedingly fruitful, and I will make you into nations, and kings will emerge from you. 7 And I will establish My covenant between Me and between you and between your seed after you throughout their generations as an everlasting covenant, to be to you for a God and to your seed after you. 8 And I will give you and your seed after you the land of your sojournings, the entire land of Canaan for an everlasting possession, and I will be to them for a God." 9 And God said to Abraham, "And you shall keep My covenant, you and your seed after you throughout their generations. 10 This is My covenant, which you shall observe between Me and between you and between your seed after you, that every male among you be circumcised. 11 And you shall circumcise the flesh of your foreskin, and it shall be as the sign of a covenant between Me and between you. 12 And at the age of eight days, every male shall be circumcised to you throughout your generations, one that is born in the house, or one that is purchased with money, from any foreigner, who is not of your seed. 13 Those born in the house and those purchased for money shall be circumcised, and My covenant shall be in your flesh as an everlasting covenant. 14 And an uncircumcised male, who will not circumcise the flesh of his foreskin-that soul will be cut off from its people; he has broken My covenant." 15 And God said to Abraham, "Your wife Sarai-you shall not call her name Sarai, for Sarah is her name. 16 And I will bless her, and I will give you a son from her, and I will bless her, and she will become [a mother of] nations; kings of nations will be from her. " 17 And Abraham fell on his face and rejoiced, and he said to himself, "Will [a child] be born to one who is a hundred years old, and will Sarah, who is ninety years old, give birth?" 18 And Abraham said to God, "If only Ishmael will live before You!" 19 And God said, "Indeed, your wife Sarah will bear you a son, and you shall name him Isaac, and I will establish My covenant with him as an everlasting covenant for his seed after him. 20 And regarding Ishmael, I have heard you; behold I have blessed him, and I will make him fruitful, and I will multiply him exceedingly; he will beget twelve princes, and I will make him into a great nation. 21 But My covenant I will establish with Isaac, whom Sarah will bear to you at this time next year." 22 And He finished speaking with him, and God went up from above Abraham. 23 And Abraham took Ishmael his son and all those born in his house and all those purchased with his money, every male of the people of Abraham's household, and he circumcised the flesh of their foreskin on that very day, as God had spoken with him. 24 And Abraham was ninety-nine years old,

when he was circumcised of the flesh of his foreskin. 25
And Ishmael his son was thirteen years old, when he was
circumcised of the flesh of his foreskin. 26 On that very
day, Abraham was circumcised, and [so was] Ishmael his
son. 27 And all the people of his household, those born in
his house and those bought with money from foreigners,
were circumcised with him.

Book of Bereshit(Genesis) 18:1-33

אוַיֵּרָ֤א אֵלָיו֙ יְהֹוָ֔ה בְּאֵלֹנֵ֖י מַמְרֵ֑א וְה֛וּא יֹשֵׁ֥ב פֶּֽתַח־הָאֹ֖הֶל כְּחֹ֥ם
הַיּֽוֹם׃

בוַיִּשָּׂ֤א עֵינָיו֙ וַיַּ֔רְא וְהִנֵּה֙ שְׁלֹשָׁ֣ה אֲנָשִׁ֔ים נִצָּבִ֖ים עָלָ֑יו וַיַּ֗רְא וַיָּ֤רׇץ
לִקְרָאתָם֙ מִפֶּ֣תַח הָאֹ֔הֶל וַיִּשְׁתַּ֖חוּ אָֽרְצָה׃

גוַיֹּאמַ֑ר אֲדֹנָ֗י אִם־נָ֨א מָצָ֤אתִי חֵן֙ בְּעֵינֶ֔יךָ אַל־נָ֥א תַעֲבֹ֖ר מֵעַ֥ל
עַבְדֶּֽךָ׃

דיֻקַּֽח־נָ֣א מְעַט־מַ֔יִם וְרַחֲצ֖וּ רַגְלֵיכֶ֑ם וְהִֽשָּׁעֲנ֖וּ תַּ֥חַת הָעֵֽץ׃

הוְאֶקְחָ֨ה פַת־לֶ֜חֶם וְסַעֲד֤וּ לִבְּכֶם֙ אַחַ֣ר תַּעֲבֹ֔רוּ כִּֽי־עַל־כֵּ֥ן עֲבַרְתֶּ֖ם
עַֽל־עַבְדְּכֶ֑ם וַיֹּ֣אמְר֔וּ כֵּ֥ן תַּעֲשֶׂ֖ה כַּאֲשֶׁ֥ר דִּבַּֽרְתָּ׃

ווַיְמַהֵ֧ר אַבְרָהָ֛ם הָאֹ֖הֱלָה אֶל־שָׂרָ֑ה וַיֹּ֗אמֶר מַהֲרִ֞י שְׁלֹ֤שׁ סְאִים֙
קֶ֣מַח סֹ֔לֶת ל֖וּשִׁי וַעֲשִׂ֥י עֻגֽוֹת׃

זוְאֶל־הַבָּקָ֖ר רָ֣ץ אַבְרָהָ֑ם וַיִּקַּ֨ח בֶּן־בָּקָ֜ר רַ֤ךְ וָטוֹב֙ וַיִּתֵּ֣ן אֶל־הַנַּ֔עַר
וַיְמַהֵ֖ר לַעֲשׂ֥וֹת אֹתֽוֹ׃

חוַיִּקַּ֨ח חֶמְאָ֜ה וְחָלָ֗ב וּבֶן־הַבָּקָר֙ אֲשֶׁ֣ר עָשָׂ֔ה וַיִּתֵּ֖ן לִפְנֵיהֶ֑ם וְהֽוּא־
עֹמֵ֧ד עֲלֵיהֶ֛ם תַּ֥חַת הָעֵ֖ץ וַיֹּאכֵֽלוּ׃

ט וַיֹּאמְרוּ אֵלָיו אַיֵּה שָׂרָה אִשְׁתֶּךָ וַיֹּאמֶר הִנֵּה בָאֹהֶל:

י וַיֹּאמֶר שׁוֹב אָשׁוּב אֵלֶיךָ כָּעֵת חַיָּה וְהִנֵּה־בֵן לְשָׂרָה אִשְׁתֶּךָ וְשָׂרָה שֹׁמַעַת פֶּתַח הָאֹהֶל וְהוּא אַחֲרָיו:

יא וְאַבְרָהָם וְשָׂרָה זְקֵנִים בָּאִים בַּיָּמִים חָדַל לִהְיוֹת לְשָׂרָה אֹרַח כַּנָּשִׁים:

יב וַתִּצְחַק שָׂרָה בְּקִרְבָּהּ לֵאמֹר אַחֲרֵי בְלֹתִי הָיְתָה־לִּי עֶדְנָה וַאדֹנִי זָקֵן:

יג וַיֹּאמֶר יְהוָה אֶל־אַבְרָהָם לָמָּה זֶּה צָחֲקָה שָׂרָה לֵאמֹר הַאַף אֻמְנָם אֵלֵד וַאֲנִי זָקַנְתִּי:

יד הֲיִפָּלֵא מֵיְהוָה דָּבָר לַמּוֹעֵד אָשׁוּב אֵלֶיךָ כָּעֵת חַיָּה וּלְשָׂרָה בֵן:

טו וַתְּכַחֵשׁ שָׂרָה | לֵאמֹר לֹא צָחַקְתִּי כִּי | יָרֵאָה וַיֹּאמֶר | לֹא כִּי צָחָקְתְּ:

טז וַיָּקֻמוּ מִשָּׁם הָאֲנָשִׁים וַיַּשְׁקִפוּ עַל־פְּנֵי סְדֹם וְאַבְרָהָם הֹלֵךְ עִמָּם לְשַׁלְּחָם:

יז וַיהוָה אָמָר הַמְכַסֶּה אֲנִי מֵאַבְרָהָם אֲשֶׁר אֲנִי עֹשֶׂה:

יח וְאַבְרָהָם הָיוֹ יִהְיֶה לְגוֹי גָּדוֹל וְעָצוּם וְנִבְרְכוּ־בוֹ כֹּל גּוֹיֵי הָאָרֶץ:

יט כִּי יְדַעְתִּיו לְמַעַן אֲשֶׁר יְצַוֶּה אֶת־בָּנָיו וְאֶת־בֵּיתוֹ אַחֲרָיו וְשָׁמְרוּ דֶּרֶךְ יְהוָה לַעֲשׂוֹת צְדָקָה וּמִשְׁפָּט לְמַעַן הָבִיא יְהוָה עַל־אַבְרָהָם אֵת אֲשֶׁר־דִּבֶּר עָלָיו:

כ וַיֹּאמֶר יְהוָה זַעֲקַת סְדֹם וַעֲמֹרָה כִּי־רָבָּה וְחַטָּאתָם כִּי כָבְדָה מְאֹד:

כאאֵרֲדָה־נָּא וְאֶרְאֶה הַכְּצַעֲקָתָהּ הַבָּאָה אֵלַי עָשׂוּ | כָּלָה וְאִם־לֹא
אֵדָעָה:

כבוַיִּפְנוּ מִשָּׁם הָאֲנָשִׁים וַיֵּלְכוּ סְדֹמָה וְאַבְרָהָם עוֹדֶנּוּ עֹמֵד לִפְנֵי
יְהוָה::

כגוַיִּגַּשׁ אַבְרָהָם וַיֹּאמַר הַאַף תִּסְפֶּה צַדִּיק עִם־רָשָׁע:

כדאוּלַי יֵשׁ חֲמִשִּׁים צַדִּיקִם בְּתוֹךְ הָעִיר הַאַף תִּסְפֶּה וְלֹא־תִשָּׂא
לַמָּקוֹם לְמַעַן חֲמִשִּׁים הַצַּדִּיקִם אֲשֶׁר בְּקִרְבָּהּ:

כההָחָלִלָה לְּךָ מֵעֲשֹׂת | כַּדָּבָר הַזֶּה לְהָמִית צַדִּיק עִם־רָשָׁע וְהָיָה
כַצַּדִּיק כָּרָשָׁע חָלִלָה לָּךְ הֲשֹׁפֵט כָּל־הָאָרֶץ לֹא יַעֲשֶׂה מִשְׁפָּט:

כווַיֹּאמֶר יְהוָה אִם־אֶמְצָא בִסְדֹם חֲמִשִּׁים צַדִּיקִם בְּתוֹךְ הָעִיר
וְנָשָׂאתִי לְכָל־הַמָּקוֹם בַּעֲבוּרָם:

כזוַיַּעַן אַבְרָהָם וַיֹּאמַר הִנֵּה־נָא הוֹאַלְתִּי לְדַבֵּר אֶל־אֲדֹנָי וְאָנֹכִי
עָפָר וָאֵפֶר:

כחאוּלַי יַחְסְרוּן חֲמִשִּׁים הַצַּדִּיקִם חֲמִשָּׁה הֲתַשְׁחִית בַּחֲמִשָּׁה
אֶת־כָּל־הָעִיר וַיֹּאמֶר לֹא אַשְׁחִית אִם־אֶמְצָא שָׁם אַרְבָּעִים
וַחֲמִשָּׁה:

כטוַיֹּסֶף עוֹד לְדַבֵּר אֵלָיו וַיֹּאמַר אוּלַי יִמָּצְאוּן שָׁם אַרְבָּעִים וַיֹּאמֶר
לֹא אֶעֱשֶׂה בַּעֲבוּר הָאַרְבָּעִים:

לוַיֹּאמֶר אַל־נָא יִחַר לַאדֹנָי וַאֲדַבֵּרָה אוּלַי יִמָּצְאוּן שָׁם שְׁלֹשִׁים
וַיֹּאמֶר לֹא אֶעֱשֶׂה אִם־אֶמְצָא שָׁם שְׁלֹשִׁים:

לאוַיֹּאמֶר הִנֵּה־נָא הוֹאַלְתִּי לְדַבֵּר אֶל־אֲדֹנָי אוּלַי יִמָּצְאוּן שָׁם
עֶשְׂרִים וַיֹּאמֶר לֹא אַשְׁחִית בַּעֲבוּר הָעֶשְׂרִים:

לבַוַּּיֹאמֶר אַל־נָא יִחַר לַאדֹנָי וַאֲדַבְּרָה אַךְ־הַפַּעַם אוּלַי יִמָּצְאוּן
שָׁם עֲשָׂרָה וַיֹּאמֶר לֹא אַשְׁחִית בַּעֲבוּר הָעֲשָׂרָה:

לגוַיֵּלֶךְ יְהֹוָה כַּאֲשֶׁר כִּלָּה לְדַבֵּר אֶל־אַבְרָהָם וְאַבְרָהָם שָׁב
לִמְקֹמוֹ:

*1 Now the Lord appeared to him in the plains of Mamre,
and he was sitting at the entrance of the tent when the
day was hot. 2 And he lifted his eyes and saw, and
behold, three men were standing beside him, and he saw
and he ran toward them from the entrance of the tent,
and he prostrated himself to the ground. 3 And he said,
"My lords, if only I have found favor in your eyes, please
do not pass on from beside your servant. 4 Please let a
little water be taken, and bathe your feet, and recline
under the tree. 5 And I will take a morsel of bread, and
sustain your hearts; after[wards] you shall pass on,
because you have passed by your servant." And they
said, "So shall you do, as you have spoken." 6 And
Abraham hastened to the tent to Sarah, and he said,
"Hasten three seah of meal [and] fine flour; knead and
make cakes." 7 And to the cattle did Abraham run, and
he took a calf, tender and good, and he gave it to the
youth, and he hastened to prepare it. 8 And he took cream
and milk and the calf that he had prepared, and he placed
[them] before them, and he was standing over them under
the tree, and they ate. 9 And they said to him, "Where is
Sarah your wife?" And he said, "Behold in the tent." 10*

And he said, "I will surely return to you at this time next year, and behold, your wife Sarah will have a son." And Sarah heard from the entrance of the tent, and it was behind him. 11 Now Abraham and Sarah were old, coming on in years; Sarah had ceased to have the way of the women. 12 And Sarah laughed within herself, saying, "After I have become worn out, will I have smooth flesh? And also, my master is old." 13 And the Lord said to Abraham, "Why did Sarah laugh, saying, 'Is it really true that I will give birth, although I am old?' 14 Is anything hidden from the Lord? At the appointed time, I will return to you, at this time next year and Sarah will have a son." 15 And Sarah denied, saying, "I did not laugh," because she was afraid. And He said, "No, but you laughed." 16 And the men arose from there, and they looked upon Sodom, and Abraham went with them to escort them, 17 And the Lord said, "Shall I conceal from Abraham what I am doing? 18 And Abraham will become a great and powerful nation, and all the nations of the world will be blessed in him. 19 For I have known him because he commands his sons and his household after him, that they should keep the way of the Lord to perform righteousness and justice, in order that the Lord bring upon Abraham that which He spoke concerning him." 20 And the Lord said, "Since the cry of Sodom and Gomorrah has become great, and since their sin has become very grave, 21 I will descend now and see, *whether according to her cry, which has come to Me, they have done; [I will wreak] destruction [upon them]; and if not, I will know." 22 And the men turned from there and went to Sodom, and Abraham was still standing before the Lord. 23 And Abraham approached and said, "Will You even destroy the righteous with the wicked? 24 Perhaps there are fifty righteous men in the midst of the city; will You even destroy and not forgive the place for the sake of the fifty righteous men who are in its midst? 25 Far be it from You to do a thing such as this, to put to death the righteous with the wicked so that the righteous should be like the wicked. Far be it from You! Will the Judge of the entire earth not perform justice?" 26 And the Lord said, "If I find in Sodom fifty righteous men within the city, I will forgive the entire place for their sake." 27 And Abraham answered and said, "Behold now I have commenced to speak to the Lord, although I am dust and ashes. 28 Perhaps the fifty righteous men will be missing five. Will You destroy the entire city because of five?" And He said, "I will not destroy if I find there forty-five." 29 And he continued further to speak to Him, and he said, "Perhaps forty will be found there." And He said, "I will not do it for the sake of the forty." 30 And he said, "Please, let the Lord's wrath not be kindled, and I will speak. Perhaps thirty will be found there." And He said, "I will not do it if I find thirty there." 31 And he said, "Behold now I have desired to speak to the Lord,* perhaps twenty will be found there." And He said, "I will not destroy for the sake of the twenty." 32 And he said, "Please, let the Lord's wrath not be kindled, and I will speak yet this time, perhaps ten will be found there." And He said, "I will not destroy for the sake of the ten." 33 And the Lord departed when He finished speaking to Abraham, and Abraham returned to his place.

Book of Bereshit(Genesis) 19:27-29

כזוַיַּשְׁכֵּ֥ם אַבְרָהָ֖ם בַּבֹּ֑קֶר אֶ֨ל־הַמָּק֔וֹם אֲשֶׁר־עָ֥מַד שָׁ֖ם אֶת־פְּנֵ֥י יְהֹוָֽה:

כחוַיַּשְׁקֵ֗ף עַל־פְּנֵ֤י סְדֹם֙ וַעֲמֹרָ֔ה וְעַ֥ל כָּל־פְּנֵ֖י אֶ֣רֶץ הַכִּכָּ֑ר וַיַּ֗רְא וְהִנֵּ֤ה עָלָה֙ קִיטֹ֣ר הָאָ֔רֶץ כְּקִיטֹ֖ר הַכִּבְשָֽׁן:

כטוַיְהִ֗י בְּשַׁחֵ֤ת אֱלֹהִים֙ אֶת־עָרֵ֣י הַכִּכָּ֔ר וַיִּזְכֹּ֥ר אֱלֹהִ֖ים אֶת־אַבְרָהָ֑ם וַיְשַׁלַּ֤ח אֶת־לוֹט֙ מִתּ֣וֹךְ הַהֲפֵכָ֔ה בַּהֲפֹךְ֙ אֶת־הֶ֣עָרִ֔ים אֲשֶׁר־יָשַׁ֥ב בָּהֵ֖ן לֽוֹט:

27 And Abraham arose early in the morning to the place where he had stood before the Lord. 28 And he looked over the face of Sodom and Gomorrah and over the entire face of the land of the plain, and he saw, and behold, the smoke of the earth had risen like the smoke of a furnace. 29 And it came to pass, when God destroyed the cities of the plain, that God remembered Abraham, and He sent Lot out of the midst of the destruction when He overturned the cities in which Lot had dwelt.

Book of Bereshit(Genesis) 20:1-18

אוַיִּסַּע מִשָּׁם אַבְרָהָם אַרְצָה הַנֶּגֶב וַיֵּשֶׁב בֵּין־קָדֵשׁ וּבֵין שׁוּר וַיָּגָר
בִּגְרָר:

בוַיֹּאמֶר אַבְרָהָם אֶל־שָׂרָה אִשְׁתּוֹ אֲחֹתִי הִוא וַיִּשְׁלַח אֲבִימֶלֶךְ
מֶלֶךְ גְּרָר וַיִּקַּח אֶת־שָׂרָה:

גוַיָּבֹא אֱלֹהִים אֶל־אֲבִימֶלֶךְ בַּחֲלוֹם הַלָּיְלָה וַיֹּאמֶר לוֹ הִנְּךָ מֵת
עַל־הָאִשָּׁה אֲשֶׁר־לָקַחְתָּ וְהִוא בְּעֻלַת בָּעַל:

דוַאֲבִימֶלֶךְ לֹא קָרַב אֵלֶיהָ וַיֹּאמַר אֲדֹנָי הֲגוֹי גַּם־צַדִּיק תַּהֲרֹג:

הֲלֹא הוּא אָמַר־לִי אֲחֹתִי הִוא וְהִיא־גַם־הִוא אָמְרָה אָחִי הוּא
בְּתָם־לְבָבִי וּבְנִקְיֹן כַּפַּי עָשִׂיתִי זֹאת:

ווַיֹּאמֶר אֵלָיו הָאֱלֹהִים בַּחֲלֹם גַּם אָנֹכִי יָדַעְתִּי כִּי בְתָם־לְבָבְךָ
עָשִׂיתָ זֹּאת וָאֶחְשֹׂךְ גַּם־אָנֹכִי אוֹתְךָ מֵחֲטוֹ־לִי עַל־כֵּן לֹא־נְתַתִּיךָ
לִנְגֹּעַ אֵלֶיהָ:

זוְעַתָּה הָשֵׁב אֵשֶׁת־הָאִישׁ כִּי־נָבִיא הוּא וְיִתְפַּלֵּל בַּעַדְךָ וֶחְיֵה
וְאִם־אֵינְךָ מֵשִׁיב דַּע כִּי־מוֹת תָּמוּת אַתָּה וְכָל־אֲשֶׁר־לָךְ:

חוַיַּשְׁכֵּם אֲבִימֶלֶךְ בַּבֹּקֶר וַיִּקְרָא לְכָל־עֲבָדָיו וַיְדַבֵּר אֶת־כָּל־
הַדְּבָרִים הָאֵלֶּה בְּאָזְנֵיהֶם וַיִּירְאוּ הָאֲנָשִׁים מְאֹד:

טוַיִּקְרָא אֲבִימֶלֶךְ לְאַבְרָהָם וַיֹּאמֶר לוֹ מֶה־עָשִׂיתָ לָּנוּ וּמֶה־חָטָאתִי
לָךְ כִּי־הֵבֵאתָ עָלַי וְעַל־מַמְלַכְתִּי חֲטָאָה גְדֹלָה מַעֲשִׂים אֲשֶׁר לֹא־
יֵעָשׂוּ עָשִׂיתָ עִמָּדִי:

יוַיֹּאמֶר אֲבִימֶלֶךְ אֶל־אַבְרָהָם מָה רָאִיתָ כִּי עָשִׂיתָ אֶת־הַדָּבָר
הַזֶּה:

יאוַיֹּאמֶר אַבְרָהָם כִּי אָמַרְתִּי רַק אֵין־יִרְאַת אֱלֹהִים בַּמָּקוֹם הַזֶּה
וַהֲרָגוּנִי עַל־דְּבַר אִשְׁתִּי:

יבוְגַם־אָמְנָ֗ה אֲחֹתִ֤י בַת־אָבִי֙ הִ֔וא אַ֖ךְ לֹ֣א בַת־אִמִּ֑י וַתְּהִי־לִ֖י לְאִשָּֽׁה:

יגוַיְהִ֞י כַּאֲשֶׁ֧ר הִתְע֣וּ אֹתִ֗י אֱלֹהִים֮ מִבֵּ֣ית אָבִי֒ וָאֹמַ֣ר לָ֔הּ זֶ֣ה חַסְדֵּ֔ךְ אֲשֶׁ֥ר תַּעֲשִׂ֖י עִמָּדִ֑י אֶ֤ל כָּל־הַמָּקוֹם֙ אֲשֶׁ֣ר נָב֣וֹא שָׁ֔מָּה אִמְרִי־לִ֖י אָחִ֥י הֽוּא:

ידוַיִּקַּ֨ח אֲבִימֶ֜לֶךְ צֹ֣אן וּבָקָ֗ר וַעֲבָדִים֙ וּשְׁפָחֹ֔ת וַיִּתֵּ֖ן לְאַבְרָהָ֑ם וַיָּ֣שֶׁב ל֔וֹ אֵ֖ת שָׂרָ֥ה אִשְׁתּֽוֹ:

טווַיֹּ֣אמֶר אֲבִימֶ֔לֶךְ הִנֵּ֥ה אַרְצִ֖י לְפָנֶ֑יךָ בַּטּ֥וֹב בְּעֵינֶ֖יךָ שֵֽׁב:

טזוּלְשָׂרָ֣ה אָמַ֗ר הִנֵּ֨ה נָתַ֜תִּי אֶ֤לֶף כֶּ֨סֶף֙ לְאָחִ֔יךְ הִנֵּ֤ה הוּא־לָךְ֙ כְּס֣וּת עֵינַ֔יִם לְכֹ֖ל אֲשֶׁ֣ר אִתָּ֑ךְ וְאֵ֥ת כֹּ֖ל וְנֹכָֽחַת:

יזוַיִּתְפַּלֵּ֥ל אַבְרָהָ֖ם אֶל־הָאֱלֹהִ֑ים וַיִּרְפָּ֨א אֱלֹהִ֜ים אֶת־אֲבִימֶ֧לֶךְ וְאֶת־אִשְׁתּ֛וֹ וְאַמְהֹתָ֖יו וַיֵּלֵֽדוּ:

יחכִּֽי־עָצֹ֨ר עָצַ֤ר יְהֹוָה֙ בְּעַ֣ד כָּל־רֶ֔חֶם לְבֵ֖ית אֲבִימֶ֑לֶךְ עַל־דְּבַ֥ר שָׂרָ֖ה אֵ֥שֶׁת אַבְרָהָֽם:

1 And Abraham traveled from there to the land of the south, and he dwelt between Kadesh and between Shur, and he sojourned in Gerar. 2 And Abraham said about Sarah his wife, "She is my sister," and Abimelech the king of Gerar sent and took Sarah. 3 And God came to Abimelech in a dream of the night, and He said to him, "Behold you are going to die because of the woman whom you have taken, for she is a married woman." 4 And Abimelech had not come near to her, and he said, "O Lord, will You kill even a righteous nation? 5 Did he not say to me, 'She is my sister'? And she, even she said, 'He is my brother.' With the innocence of my heart and with the purity of my hands have I done this." 6 And God said to him in a dream, "I too know that you did this with the innocence of your heart, and I too have withheld you from sinning to Me; therefore, I did not let you touch her. 7 And now, return the man's wife, because he is a prophet, and he will pray for you and [you will] live; but if you do not return [her], know that you will surely die, you and all that is yours." 8 And Abimelech arose early in the morning, and he summoned all his servants, and he spoke all these words in their ears; and the men were very frightened. 9 And Abimelech summoned Abraham and said to him, "What have you done to us, and what have I sinned against you, that you have brought upon me and upon my kingdom a great sin? Deeds that are not done, you have done to me." 10 And Abimelech said to Abraham, "What did you see, that you did this thing?" 11 And Abraham said, "For I said, 'Surely, there is no fear of God in this place, and they will kill me because of my wife. 12 And also, indeed, she is my sister, the daughter of my father, but not the daughter of my mother, and she became my wife. 13 And it came to pass, when God caused me to wander from my father's house, that I said to her: This is your kindness, which you shall do with me: whither we come, say about me, 'He is my brother.'" 14 And Abimelech took flocks and cattle and menservants and maidservants, and he gave [them] to Abraham, and he restored to him his wife Sarah. 15 And Abimelech said, "Here is my land before you; wherever it pleases you, you may dwell." 16 And to Sarah he said, "Behold I have given a thousand pieces of silver to your brother; behold it is to you a covering of the eyes for all who are with you, and with all you shall contend." 17 And Abraham prayed to God, and God healed Abimelech and his wife and his handmaids, and they gave birth. 18 For the Lord had shut every womb of Abimelech's household, because of Sarah, Abraham's wife.

Book of Bereshit(Genesis) 21:2-34

בוַתַּ֨הַר וַתֵּ֧לֶד שָׂרָ֛ה לְאַבְרָהָ֖ם בֵּ֣ן לִזְקֻנָ֑יו לַמּוֹעֵ֕ד אֲשֶׁר־דִּבֶּ֥ר אֹת֖וֹ אֱלֹהִֽים:

גוַיִּקְרָ֨א אַבְרָהָ֜ם אֶֽת־שֶׁם־בְּנ֧וֹ הַנּֽוֹלַד־ל֛וֹ אֲשֶׁר־יָֽלְדָה־לּ֥וֹ שָׂרָ֖ה יִצְחָֽק:

דוַיָּ֤מָל אַבְרָהָם֙ אֶת־יִצְחָ֣ק בְּנ֔וֹ בֶּן־שְׁמֹנַ֖ת יָמִ֑ים כַּֽאֲשֶׁ֛ר צִוָּ֥ה אֹת֖וֹ אֱלֹהִֽים:

הוְאַבְרָהָ֖ם בֶּן־מְאַ֣ת שָׁנָ֑ה בְּהִוָּ֣לֶד ל֔וֹ אֵ֖ת יִצְחָ֥ק בְּנֽוֹ:

ווַתֹּ֣אמֶר שָׂרָ֔ה צְחֹ֕ק עָ֥שָׂה לִ֖י אֱלֹהִ֑ים כָּל־הַשֹּׁמֵ֖עַ יִֽצְחַק־לִֽי:

זוַתֹּ֗אמֶר מִ֤י מִלֵּל֙ לְאַבְרָהָ֔ם הֵינִ֥יקָה בָנִ֖ים שָׂרָ֑ה כִּֽי־יָלַ֥דְתִּי בֵ֖ן לִזְקֻנָֽיו:

חוַיִּגְדַּ֥ל הַיֶּ֖לֶד וַיִּגָּמַ֑ל וַיַּ֤עַשׂ אַבְרָהָם֙ מִשְׁתֶּ֣ה גָד֔וֹל בְּי֖וֹם הִגָּמֵ֥ל אֶת־יִצְחָֽק:

ח וַתֵּרֶא שָׂרָה אֶת־בֶּן־הָגָר הַמִּצְרִית אֲשֶׁר־יָלְדָה לְאַבְרָהָם מְצַחֵק:

ט וַתֹּאמֶר לְאַבְרָהָם גָּרֵשׁ הָאָמָה הַזֹּאת וְאֶת־בְּנָהּ כִּי לֹא יִירַשׁ בֶּן־הָאָמָה הַזֹּאת עִם־בְּנִי עִם־יִצְחָק:

י וַיֵּרַע הַדָּבָר מְאֹד בְּעֵינֵי אַבְרָהָם עַל אוֹדֹת בְּנוֹ:

יב וַיֹּאמֶר אֱלֹהִים אֶל־אַבְרָהָם אַל־יֵרַע בְּעֵינֶיךָ עַל־הַנַּעַר וְעַל־אֲמָתֶךָ כֹּל אֲשֶׁר תֹּאמַר אֵלֶיךָ שָׂרָה שְׁמַע בְּקֹלָהּ כִּי בְיִצְחָק יִקָּרֵא לְךָ זָרַע:

יג וְגַם אֶת־בֶּן־הָאָמָה לְגוֹי אֲשִׂימֶנּוּ כִּי זַרְעֲךָ הוּא:

יד וַיַּשְׁכֵּם אַבְרָהָם | בַּבֹּקֶר וַיִּקַּח־לֶחֶם וְחֵמַת מַיִם וַיִּתֵּן אֶל־הָגָר שָׂם עַל־שִׁכְמָהּ וְאֶת־הַיֶּלֶד וַיְשַׁלְּחֶהָ וַתֵּלֶךְ וַתֵּתַע בְּמִדְבַּר בְּאֵר שָׁבַע:

טו וַיִּכְלוּ הַמַּיִם מִן־הַחֵמֶת וַתַּשְׁלֵךְ אֶת־הַיֶּלֶד תַּחַת אַחַד הַשִּׂיחִם:

טז וַתֵּלֶךְ וַתֵּשֶׁב לָהּ מִנֶּגֶד הַרְחֵק כִּמְטַחֲוֵי קֶשֶׁת כִּי אָמְרָה אַל־אֶרְאֶה בְּמוֹת הַיֶּלֶד וַתֵּשֶׁב מִנֶּגֶד וַתִּשָּׂא אֶת־קֹלָהּ וַתֵּבְךְּ:

יז וַיִּשְׁמַע אֱלֹהִים אֶת־קוֹל הַנַּעַר וַיִּקְרָא מַלְאַךְ אֱלֹהִים | אֶל־הָגָר מִן־הַשָּׁמַיִם וַיֹּאמֶר לָהּ מַה־לָּךְ הָגָר אַל־תִּירְאִי כִּי־שָׁמַע אֱלֹהִים אֶל־קוֹל הַנַּעַר בַּאֲשֶׁר הוּא־שָׁם:

יח קוּמִי שְׂאִי אֶת־הַנַּעַר וְהַחֲזִיקִי אֶת־יָדֵךְ בּוֹ כִּי־לְגוֹי גָּדוֹל אֲשִׂימֶנּוּ:

יט וַיִּפְקַח אֱלֹהִים אֶת־עֵינֶיהָ וַתֵּרֶא בְּאֵר מָיִם וַתֵּלֶךְ וַתְּמַלֵּא אֶת־הַחֵמֶת מַיִם וַתַּשְׁקְ אֶת־הַנָּעַר:

כ וַיְהִי אֱלֹהִים אֶת־הַנַּעַר וַיִּגְדָּל וַיֵּשֶׁב בַּמִּדְבָּר וַיְהִי רֹבֶה קַשָּׁת

כאוַיֵּשֶׁב בְּמִדְבַּר פָּארָן וַתִּקַּח־לֹו אִמֹּו אִשָּׁה מֵאֶרֶץ מִצְרָיִם:

כבוַיְהִי בָּעֵת הַהִוא וַיֹּאמֶר אֲבִימֶלֶךְ וּפִיכֹל שַׂר־צְבָאֹו אֶל־אַבְרָהָם לֵאמֹר אֱלֹהִים עִמְּךָ בְּכֹל אֲשֶׁר־אַתָּה עֹשֶׂה:

כגוְעַתָּה הִשָּׁבְעָה לִּי בֵאלֹהִים הֵנָּה אִם־תִּשְׁקֹר לִי וּלְנִינִי וּלְנֶכְדִּי כַּחֶסֶד אֲשֶׁר־עָשִׂיתִי עִמְּךָ תַּעֲשֶׂה עִמָּדִי וְעִם־הָאָרֶץ אֲשֶׁר־גַּרְתָּה בָּהּ:

כדוַיֹּאמֶר אַבְרָהָם אָנֹכִי אִשָּׁבֵעַ:

כהוְהֹוכִחַ אַבְרָהָם אֶת־אֲבִימֶלֶךְ עַל־אֹדֹות בְּאֵר הַמַּיִם אֲשֶׁר גָּזְלוּ עַבְדֵי אֲבִימֶלֶךְ:

כווַיֹּאמֶר אֲבִימֶלֶךְ לֹא יָדַעְתִּי מִי עָשָׂה אֶת־הַדָּבָר הַזֶּה וְגַם־אַתָּה לֹא־הִגַּדְתָּ לִּי וְגַם אָנֹכִי לֹא שָׁמַעְתִּי בִּלְתִּי הַיֹּום:

כזוַיִּקַּח אַבְרָהָם צֹאן וּבָקָר וַיִּתֵּן לַאֲבִימֶלֶךְ וַיִּכְרְתוּ שְׁנֵיהֶם בְּרִית:

כחוַיַּצֵּב אַבְרָהָם אֶת־שֶׁבַע כִּבְשֹׂת הַצֹּאן לְבַדְּהֶן:

כטוַיֹּאמֶר אֲבִימֶלֶךְ אֶל־אַבְרָהָם מָה הֵנָּה שֶׁבַע כְּבָשֹׂת הָאֵלֶּה אֲשֶׁר הִצַּבְתָּ לְבַדָּנָה:

לוַיֹּאמֶר כִּי אֶת־שֶׁבַע כְּבָשֹׂת תִּקַּח מִיָּדִי בַּעֲבוּר תִּהְיֶה־לִּי לְעֵדָה כִּי חָפַרְתִּי אֶת־הַבְּאֵר הַזֹּאת:

לאעַל־כֵּן קָרָא לַמָּקֹום הַהוּא בְּאֵר שָׁבַע כִּי שָׁם נִשְׁבְּעוּ שְׁנֵיהֶם:

לבוַיִּכְרְתוּ בְרִית בִּבְאֵר שָׁבַע וַיָּקָם אֲבִימֶלֶךְ וּפִיכֹל שַׂר־צְבָאֹו וַיָּשֻׁבוּ אֶל־אֶרֶץ פְּלִשְׁתִּים:

לגוַיִּטַּע אֶשֶׁל בִּבְאֵר שָׁבַע וַיִּקְרָא־שָׁם בְּשֵׁם יְהוָה אֵל עֹולָם:

לְדֹנָ֑י גָּ֤ר אַבְרָהָם֙ בְּאֶ֣רֶץ פְּלִשְׁתִּ֔ים יָמִ֥ים רַבִּֽים׃

2 And Sarah conceived and bore a son to Abraham in his old age, at the time of which God had spoken to him. 3 And Abraham named his son who had been born to him, whom Sarah had borne to him, Isaac. 4 And Abraham circumcised his son Isaac when he was eight days old, as God had commanded him. 5 And Abraham was a hundred years old, when his son Isaac was born to him. 6 And Sarah said, "God has made joy for me; whoever hears will rejoice over me." 7 And she said, "Who would have said to Abraham that Sarah would nurse children, for I have borne a son to his old age!" 8 And the child grew and was weaned, and Abraham made a great feast on the day that Isaac was weaned. 9 And Sarah saw the son of Hagar the Egyptian, whom she had borne to Abraham, making merry. 10 And Sarah said to Abraham, "Drive out this handmaid and her son, for the son of this handmaid shall not inherit with my son, with Isaac." 11 But the matter greatly displeased Abraham, concerning his son. 12 And God said to Abraham, "Be not displeased concerning the lad and concerning your handmaid; whatever Sarah tells you, hearken to her voice, for in Isaac will be called your seed. 13 But also the son of the handmaid I will make into a nation, because he is your seed." 14 And Abraham arose early in the morning, and he took bread and a leather pouch of water, and he gave [them] to Hagar, he placed [them] on her shoulder, and the child, and he sent her away; and she went and wandered in the desert of Beer sheba. 15 And the water was depleted from the leather pouch, and she cast the child under one of the bushes. 16 And she went and sat down from afar, at about the distance of two bowshots, for she said, "Let me not see the child's death." And she sat from afar, and she raised her voice and wept. 17 And God heard the lad's voice, and an angel of God called to Hagar from heaven, and said to her, "What is troubling you, Hagar? Fear not, for God has heard the lad's voice in the place where he is. 18 Rise, pick up the lad and grasp your hand upon him, for I shall make him into a great nation." 19 And God opened her eyes, and she saw a well of water, and she went and filled the pouch with water and gave the lad to drink. 20 And God was with the lad, and he grew, and he dwelt in the desert, and he became an archer. 21 And he dwelt in the desert of Paran, and his mother took for him a wife from the land of Egypt. 22 Now it came to pass at that time, that Abimelech and Phicol his general said to Abraham, saying, "God is with you in all that you do. 23 And now, swear to me here by God, that you will not lie to me or to my son or to my grandson; according to the kindness that I have done with you, you shall do with me, and with the land wherein you have sojourned." 24 And Abraham said, "I will swear." 25 And Abraham contended with Abimelech about the well of water that the servants of

Abimelech had forcibly seized. 26 And Abimelech said, "I do not know who did this thing, neither did you tell me, nor did I hear [of it] until today. " 27 And Abraham took flocks and cattle, and gave them to Abimelech, and they both formed a covenant. 28 And Abraham placed seven ewe lambs by themselves. 29 And Abimelech said to Abraham, "What are these seven ewe lambs, which you have placed by themselves?" 30 And he said, "For these seven ewe lambs you shall take from my hand, in order that it be to me for a witness that I dug this well." 31 Therefore, he named that place Beer sheba, for there they both swore. 32 And they formed a covenant in Beer-sheba, and Abimelech and Phicol his general arose, and they returned to the land of the Philistines. 33 And he planted an eishel in Beer-Sheba, and he called there in the name of the Lord, the God of the world. 34 And Abraham dwelt in the land of the Philistines for many days.

Book of Bereshit(Genesis) 22:1-19

אוַיְהִ֗י אַחַר֙ הַדְּבָרִ֣ים הָאֵ֔לֶּה וְהָ֣אֱלֹהִ֔ים נִסָּ֖ה אֶת־אַבְרָהָ֑ם וַיֹּ֣אמֶר אֵלָ֔יו אַבְרָהָ֖ם וַיֹּ֥אמֶר הִנֵּֽנִי:

בוַיֹּ֡אמֶר קַח־נָ֠א אֶת־בִּנְךָ֨ אֶת־יְחִֽידְךָ֤ אֲשֶׁר־אָהַ֙בְתָּ֙ אֶת־יִצְחָ֔ק וְלֶךְ־לְךָ֔ אֶל־אֶ֖רֶץ הַמֹּרִיָּ֑ה וְהַעֲלֵ֤הוּ שָׁם֙ לְעֹלָ֔ה עַ֚ל אַחַ֣ד הֶֽהָרִ֔ים אֲשֶׁ֖ר אֹמַ֥ר אֵלֶֽיךָ:

גוַיַּשְׁכֵּ֨ם אַבְרָהָ֜ם בַּבֹּ֗קֶר וַֽיַּחֲבֹשׁ֙ אֶת־חֲמֹר֔וֹ וַיִּקַּ֞ח אֶת־שְׁנֵ֤י נְעָרָיו֙ אִתּ֔וֹ וְאֵ֖ת יִצְחָ֣ק בְּנ֑וֹ וַיְבַקַּע֙ עֲצֵ֣י עֹלָ֔ה וַיָּ֣קָם וַיֵּ֔לֶךְ אֶל־הַמָּק֖וֹם אֲשֶׁר־אָֽמַר־ל֥וֹ הָאֱלֹהִֽים:

דבַּיּוֹם הַשְּׁלִישִׁי וַיִּשָּׂא אַבְרָהָם אֶת־עֵינָיו וַיַּרְא אֶת־הַמָּקוֹם
מֵרָחֹק:

הוַיֹּאמֶר אַבְרָהָם אֶל־נְעָרָיו שְׁבוּ־לָכֶם פֹּה עִם־הַחֲמוֹר וַאֲנִי
וְהַנַּעַר נֵלְכָה עַד־כֹּה וְנִשְׁתַּחֲוֶה וְנָשׁוּבָה אֲלֵיכֶם:

ווַיִּקַּח אַבְרָהָם אֶת־עֲצֵי הָעֹלָה וַיָּשֶׂם עַל־יִצְחָק בְּנוֹ וַיִּקַּח בְּיָדוֹ
אֶת־הָאֵשׁ וְאֶת־הַמַּאֲכֶלֶת וַיֵּלְכוּ שְׁנֵיהֶם יַחְדָּו:

זוַיֹּאמֶר יִצְחָק אֶל־אַבְרָהָם אָבִיו וַיֹּאמֶר אָבִי וַיֹּאמֶר הִנֶּנִּי בְנִי
וַיֹּאמֶר הִנֵּה הָאֵשׁ וְהָעֵצִים וְאַיֵּה הַשֶּׂה לְעֹלָה:

חוַיֹּאמֶר אַבְרָהָם אֱלֹהִים יִרְאֶה־לּוֹ הַשֶּׂה לְעֹלָה בְּנִי וַיֵּלְכוּ שְׁנֵיהֶם
יַחְדָּו:

טוַיָּבֹאוּ אֶל־הַמָּקוֹם אֲשֶׁר אָמַר־לוֹ הָאֱלֹהִים וַיִּבֶן שָׁם אַבְרָהָם
אֶת־הַמִּזְבֵּחַ וַיַּעֲרֹךְ אֶת־הָעֵצִים וַיַּעֲקֹד אֶת־יִצְחָק בְּנוֹ וַיָּשֶׂם אֹתוֹ
עַל־הַמִּזְבֵּחַ מִמַּעַל לָעֵצִים:

יוַיִּשְׁלַח אַבְרָהָם אֶת־יָדוֹ וַיִּקַּח אֶת־הַמַּאֲכֶלֶת לִשְׁחֹט אֶת־בְּנוֹ:

יאוַיִּקְרָא אֵלָיו מַלְאַךְ יְהוָה מִן־הַשָּׁמַיִם וַיֹּאמֶר אַבְרָהָם | אַבְרָהָם
וַיֹּאמֶר הִנֵּנִי:

יבוַיֹּאמֶר אַל־תִּשְׁלַח יָדְךָ אֶל־הַנַּעַר וְאַל־תַּעַשׂ לוֹ מְאוּמָה כִּי |
עַתָּה יָדַעְתִּי כִּי־יְרֵא אֱלֹהִים אַתָּה וְלֹא חָשַׂכְתָּ אֶת־בִּנְךָ אֶת־
יְחִידְךָ מִמֶּנִּי:

יגוַיִּשָּׂא אַבְרָהָם אֶת־עֵינָיו וַיַּרְא וְהִנֵּה־אַיִל אַחַר נֶאֱחַז בַּסְּבַךְ
בְּקַרְנָיו וַיֵּלֶךְ אַבְרָהָם וַיִּקַּח אֶת־הָאַיִל וַיַּעֲלֵהוּ לְעֹלָה תַּחַת בְּנוֹ:

ידוַיִּקְרָא אַבְרָהָם שֵׁם־הַמָּקוֹם הַהוּא יְהוָה | יִרְאֶה אֲשֶׁר יֵאָמֵר
הַיּוֹם בְּהַר יְהוָה יֵרָאֶה:

טו וַיִּקְרָ֠א מַלְאַ֨ךְ יְהֹוָ֤ה אֶל־אַבְרָהָם֙ שֵׁנִ֔ית מִן־הַשָּׁמָֽיִם:

טז וַיֹּ֕אמֶר בִּ֥י נִשְׁבַּ֖עְתִּי נְאֻם־יְהֹוָ֑ה כִּ֗י יַ֚עַן אֲשֶׁ֤ר עָשִׂ֙יתָ֙ אֶת־הַדָּבָ֣ר הַזֶּ֔ה וְלֹ֥א חָשַׂ֖כְתָּ אֶת־בִּנְךָ֥ אֶת־יְחִידֶֽךָ:

יז כִּֽי־בָרֵ֣ךְ אֲבָרֶכְךָ֗ וְהַרְבָּ֨ה אַרְבֶּ֤ה אֶֽת־זַרְעֲךָ֙ כְּכֽוֹכְבֵ֣י הַשָּׁמַ֔יִם וְכַח֕וֹל אֲשֶׁ֖ר עַל־שְׂפַ֣ת הַיָּ֑ם וְיִרַ֣שׁ זַרְעֲךָ֔ אֵ֖ת שַׁ֥עַר אֹיְבָֽיו:

יח וְהִתְבָּרֲכ֣וּ בְזַרְעֲךָ֔ כֹּ֖ל גּוֹיֵ֣י הָאָ֑רֶץ עֵ֕קֶב אֲשֶׁ֥ר שָׁמַ֖עְתָּ בְּקֹלִֽי:

יט וַיָּ֤שָׁב אַבְרָהָם֙ אֶל־נְעָרָ֔יו וַיָּקֻ֛מוּ וַיֵּלְכ֥וּ יַחְדָּ֖ו אֶל־בְּאֵ֣ר שָׁ֑בַע וַיֵּ֥שֶׁב אַבְרָהָ֖ם בִּבְאֵ֥ר שָֽׁבַע:

1 And it came to pass after these things, that God tested Abraham, and He said to him, "Abraham," and he said, "Here I am." 2 And He said, "Please take your son, your only one, whom you love, yea, Isaac, and go away to the land of Moriah and bring him up there for a burnt offering on one of the mountains, of which I will tell you." 3 And Abraham arose early in the morning, and he saddled his donkey, and he took his two young men with him and Isaac his son; and he split wood for a burnt offering, and he arose and went to the place of which God had told him. 4 On the third day, Abraham lifted up his eyes and saw the place from afar. 5 And Abraham said to his young men, "Stay here with the donkey, and I and the lad will go yonder, and we will prostrate ourselves and return to you." 6 And Abraham took the wood for the burnt offering, and he placed [it] upon his son Isaac, and he took into his hand the fire and the knife, and they both went together. 7 And Isaac spoke to Abraham his father, and he said, "My father!" And he said, "Here I am, my son." And he said, "Here are the fire and the wood, but where is the lamb for the burnt offering?" 8 And Abraham said, "God will provide for Himself the lamb for the burnt offering, my son." And they both went together. 9 And they came to the place of which God had spoken to him, and Abraham built the altar there and arranged the wood, and he bound Isaac his son and placed him on the altar upon the wood. 10 And Abraham stretched forth his hand and took the knife, to slaughter his son. 11 And an angel of God called to him from heaven and said, "Abraham! Abraham!" And he said, "Here I am." 12 And he said, "Do not stretch forth your hand to the lad, nor do the slightest thing to him, for now I know that you are a God fearing man, and you did not withhold your son, your only one, from Me." 13 And Abraham lifted up his eyes, and he saw, and lo! there was a ram, [and] after [that] it was caught in a tree by its horns. And Abraham went and took the ram and offered it up as a burnt offering instead of his son. 14 And Abraham named that place, The Lord will see, as it is said to this day: On the mountain, the Lord will be seen. 15 And an angel of the Lord called to Abraham a second time from heaven. 16 And he said, "By Myself have I sworn, says the Lord, that because you have done this thing and you did not withhold your son, your only one,

17 That I will surely bless you, and I will greatly multiply your seed as the stars of the heavens and as the sand that is on the seashore, and your descendants will inherit the cities of their enemies. 18 And through your children shall be blessed all the nations of the world, because you hearkened to My voice." 19 And Abraham returned to his young men, and they arose and went together to Beer sheba; and Abraham remained in Beer sheba.

Book of Bereshit(Genesis) 23:1-20

אוַיִּהְיוּ חַיֵּי שָׂרָה מֵאָה שָׁנָה וְעֶשְׂרִים שָׁנָה וְשֶׁבַע שָׁנִים שְׁנֵי חַיֵּי שָׂרָה:

בוַתָּמָת שָׂרָה בְּקִרְיַת אַרְבַּע הִוא חֶבְרוֹן בְּאֶרֶץ כְּנָעַן וַיָּבֹא אַבְרָהָם לִסְפֹּד לְשָׂרָה וְלִבְכֹּתָהּ:

גוַיָּקָם אַבְרָהָם מֵעַל פְּנֵי מֵתוֹ וַיְדַבֵּר אֶל־בְּנֵי־חֵת לֵאמֹר:

דגֵּר־וְתוֹשָׁב אָנֹכִי עִמָּכֶם תְּנוּ לִי אֲחֻזַּת־קֶבֶר עִמָּכֶם וְאֶקְבְּרָה מֵתִי מִלְּפָנָי:

הוַיַּעֲנוּ בְנֵי־חֵת אֶת־אַבְרָהָם לֵאמֹר לוֹ:

ושְׁמָעֵנוּ | אֲדֹנִי נְשִׂיא אֱלֹהִים אַתָּה בְּתוֹכֵנוּ בְּמִבְחַר קְבָרֵינוּ קְבֹר אֶת־מֵתֶךָ אִישׁ מִמֶּנּוּ אֶת־קִבְרוֹ לֹא־יִכְלֶה מִמְּךָ מִקְּבֹר מֵתֶךָ:

זוַיָּקָם אַבְרָהָם וַיִּשְׁתַּחוּ לְעַם־הָאָרֶץ לִבְנֵי־חֵת:

חוַיְדַבֵּר אִתָּם לֵאמֹר אִם־יֵשׁ אֶת־נַפְשְׁכֶם לִקְבֹּר אֶת־מֵתִי מִלְּפָנַי שְׁמָעוּנִי וּפִגְעוּ־לִי בְּעֶפְרוֹן בֶּן־צֹחַר:

ט וְיִתֶּן־לִ֞י אֶת־מְעָרַ֤ת הַמַּכְפֵּלָה֙ אֲשֶׁר־ל֔וֹ אֲשֶׁ֖ר בִּקְצֵ֣ה שָׂדֵ֑הוּ
בְּכֶ֧סֶף מָלֵ֛א יִתְּנֶ֥נָּה לִּ֖י בְּתוֹכְכֶ֥ם לַאֲחֻזַּת־קָֽבֶר׃

י וְעֶפְר֥וֹן יֹשֵׁ֖ב בְּת֣וֹךְ בְּנֵי־חֵ֑ת וַיַּעַן֩ עֶפְר֨וֹן הַחִתִּ֤י אֶת־אַבְרָהָם֙ בְּאָזְנֵ֣י
בְנֵי־חֵ֔ת לְכֹ֛ל בָּאֵ֥י שַֽׁעַר־עִיר֖וֹ לֵאמֹֽר׃

יא לֹֽא־אֲדֹנִ֣י שְׁמָעֵ֔נִי הַשָּׂדֶה֙ נָתַ֣תִּי לָ֔ךְ וְהַמְּעָרָ֥ה אֲשֶׁר־בּ֖וֹ לְךָ֣
נְתַתִּ֑יהָ לְעֵינֵ֧י בְנֵי־עַמִּ֛י נְתַתִּ֥יהָ לָ֖ךְ קְבֹ֥ר מֵתֶֽךָ׃

יב וַיִּשְׁתַּ֙חוּ֙ אַבְרָהָ֔ם לִפְנֵ֖י עַם־הָאָֽרֶץ׃

יג וַיְדַבֵּ֨ר אֶל־עֶפְר֜וֹן בְּאָזְנֵ֤י עַם־הָאָ֙רֶץ֙ לֵאמֹ֔ר אַ֛ךְ אִם־אַתָּ֥ה ל֖וּ
שְׁמָעֵ֑נִי נָתַ֜תִּי כֶּ֤סֶף הַשָּׂדֶה֙ קַ֣ח מִמֶּ֔נִּי וְאֶקְבְּרָ֥ה אֶת־מֵתִ֖י שָֽׁמָּה׃

יד וַיַּ֧עַן עֶפְר֛וֹן אֶת־אַבְרָהָ֖ם לֵאמֹ֥ר לֽוֹ׃

טו אֲדֹנִ֣י שְׁמָעֵ֗נִי אֶרֶץ֩ אַרְבַּ֨ע מֵאֹ֧ת שֶֽׁקֶל־כֶּ֛סֶף בֵּינִ֥י וּבֵֽינְךָ֖ מַה־הִ֑וא
וְאֶת־מֵתְךָ֖ קְבֹֽר׃

טז וַיִּשְׁמַ֣ע אַבְרָהָם֮ אֶל־עֶפְרוֹן֒ וַיִּשְׁקֹ֤ל אַבְרָהָם֙ לְעֶפְרֹ֔ן אֶת־הַכֶּ֕סֶף
אֲשֶׁ֥ר דִּבֶּ֖ר בְּאָזְנֵ֣י בְנֵי־חֵ֑ת אַרְבַּ֤ע מֵאוֹת֙ שֶׁ֣קֶל כֶּ֔סֶף עֹבֵ֖ר לַסֹּחֵֽר׃

יז וַיָּ֣קָם ׀ שְׂדֵ֣ה עֶפְר֗וֹן אֲשֶׁר֙ בַּמַּכְפֵּלָ֔ה אֲשֶׁ֖ר לִפְנֵ֣י מַמְרֵ֑א הַשָּׂדֶה֙
וְהַמְּעָרָ֣ה אֲשֶׁר־בּ֔וֹ וְכָל־הָעֵץ֙ אֲשֶׁ֣ר בַּשָּׂדֶ֔ה אֲשֶׁ֥ר בְּכָל־גְּבֻל֖וֹ סָבִֽיב׃

יח לְאַבְרָהָ֥ם לְמִקְנָ֖ה לְעֵינֵ֣י בְנֵי־חֵ֑ת בְּכֹ֖ל בָּאֵ֥י שַֽׁעַר־עִירֽוֹ׃

יט וְאַחֲרֵי־כֵן֩ קָבַ֨ר אַבְרָהָ֜ם אֶת־שָׂרָ֣ה אִשְׁתּ֗וֹ אֶל־מְעָרַ֞ת שְׂדֵ֧ה
הַמַּכְפֵּלָ֛ה עַל־פְּנֵ֥י מַמְרֵ֖א הִ֣וא חֶבְר֑וֹן בְּאֶ֖רֶץ כְּנָֽעַן׃

כ וַיָּ֨קָם הַשָּׂדֶ֜ה וְהַמְּעָרָ֧ה אֲשֶׁר־בּ֛וֹ לְאַבְרָהָ֖ם לַאֲחֻזַּת־קָ֑בֶר מֵאֵ֖ת
בְּנֵי־חֵֽת׃

1 And the life of Sarah was one hundred years and twenty years and seven years; [these were] the years of the life of Sarah. 2 And Sarah died in Kiriath arba, which is Hebron, in the land of Canaan, and Abraham came to eulogize Sarah and to bewail her. 3 And Abraham arose from before his dead, and he spoke to the sons of Heth, saying, 4 "I am a stranger and an inhabitant with you. Give me burial property with you, so that I may bury my dead from before me." 5 And the sons of Heth answered Abraham, saying to him, 6 "Listen to us, my lord; you are a prince of God in our midst; in the choicest of our graves bury your dead. None of us will withhold his grave from you to bury your dead." 7 And Abraham arose and prostrated himself to the people of the land, to the sons of Heth. 8 And he spoke with them, saying, "If it is your will that I bury my dead from before me, listen to me and entreat for me to Ephron the son of Zohar. 9 That he may give me the Machpelah (double) Cave, which belongs to him, which is at the end of his field; for a full price let him give it to me in your midst for burial property." 10 Now Ephron was sitting in the midst of the sons of Heth, and Ephron the Hittite answered Abraham in the hearing of the sons of Heth, of all those who had come into the gate of his city, saying, 11 "No, my lord, listen to me. I have given you the field, and the cave that is in it, I have given it to you. Before the eyes of the sons of my people, I have given it to you; bury your dead." 12

And Abraham prostrated himself before the people of the land. 13 And he spoke to Ephron in the hearing of the people of the land, saying, "But, if only you would listen to me. I am giving the money for the field; take [it] from me, and I will bury my dead there." 14 And Ephron replied to Abraham, saying to him, 15 "My lord, listen to me; a [piece of] land worth four hundred shekels of silver, what is it between me and you? Bury your dead." 16 And Abraham listened to Ephron, and Abraham weighed out to Ephron the silver that he had named in the hearing of the sons of Heth, four hundred shekels of silver, accepted by the merchant. 17 And so the field of Ephron which was in Machpelah, facing Mamre, was established (as Abraham's possession). [This included] the field and the cave that was in it, and all the trees that were in the field, which were within its entire border around. 18 [It was] to Abraham as a possession before the eyes of the sons of Heth, in the presence of all who had come within the gate of his city. 19 And afterwards, Abraham buried Sarah his wife in the cave of the field of Machpelah, facing Mamre, which is Hebron, in the land of Canaan. 20 And the field and the cave within it were established to Abraham as burial property, [purchased] from the sons of Heth.

Book of Bereshit(Genesis) 24:1-9

אוֹאַבְרָהָם זָקֵן בָּא בַּיָּמִים וַיהוָה בֵּרַךְ אֶת־אַבְרָהָם בַּכֹּל:

בוַיֹּאמֶר אַבְרָהָם אֶל־עַבְדּוֹ זְקַן בֵּיתוֹ הַמֹּשֵׁל בְּכָל־אֲשֶׁר־לֶוֹ שִׂים־
נָא יָדְךָ תַּחַת יְרֵכִי:

גוְאַשְׁבִּיעֲךָ בַּיהֹוָה אֱלֹהֵי הַשָּׁמַיִם וֵאלֹהֵי הָאָרֶץ אֲשֶׁר לֹא־תִקַּח
אִשָּׁה לִבְנִי מִבְּנוֹת הַכְּנַעֲנִי אֲשֶׁר אָנֹכִי יוֹשֵׁב בְּקִרְבּוֹ:

דכִּי אֶל־אַרְצִי וְאֶל־מוֹלַדְתִּי תֵּלֵךְ וְלָקַחְתָּ אִשָּׁה לִבְנִי לְיִצְחָק:

הוַיֹּאמֶר אֵלָיו הָעֶבֶד אוּלַי לֹא־תֹאבֶה הָאִשָּׁה לָלֶכֶת אַחֲרַי אֶל־
הָאָרֶץ הַזֹּאת הֶהָשֵׁב אָשִׁיב אֶת־בִּנְךָ אֶל־הָאָרֶץ אֲשֶׁר־יָצָאתָ
מִשָּׁם:

ווַיֹּאמֶר אֵלָיו אַבְרָהָם הִשָּׁמֶר לְךָ פֶּן־תָּשִׁיב אֶת־בְּנִי שָׁמָּה:

זיְהֹוָה | אֱלֹהֵי הַשָּׁמַיִם אֲשֶׁר לְקָחַנִי מִבֵּית אָבִי וּמֵאֶרֶץ מוֹלַדְתִּי
וַאֲשֶׁר דִּבֶּר־לִי וַאֲשֶׁר נִשְׁבַּע־לִי לֵאמֹר לְזַרְעֲךָ אֶתֵּן אֶת־הָאָרֶץ
הַזֹּאת הוּא יִשְׁלַח מַלְאָכוֹ לְפָנֶיךָ וְלָקַחְתָּ אִשָּׁה לִבְנִי מִשָּׁם:

חוְאִם־לֹא תֹאבֶה הָאִשָּׁה לָלֶכֶת אַחֲרֶיךָ וְנִקִּיתָ מִשְּׁבֻעָתִי זֹאת רַק
אֶת־בְּנִי לֹא תָשֵׁב שָׁמָּה:

טוַיָּשֶׂם הָעֶבֶד אֶת־יָדוֹ תַּחַת יֶרֶךְ אַבְרָהָם אֲדֹנָיו וַיִּשָּׁבַע לוֹ עַל־
הַדָּבָר הַזֶּה:

1 And Abraham was old, advanced in days, and the Lord
had blessed Abraham with everything. 2 And Abraham
said to his servant, the elder of his house, who ruled over
all that was his, "Please place your hand under my thigh.
3 And I will adjure you by the Lord, the God of the
heaven and the God of the earth, that you will not take a
wife for my son from the daughters of the Canaanites, in
whose midst I dwell. 4 But you shall go to my land and

to my birthplace, and you shall take a wife for my son, for Isaac." 5 And the servant said to him, "Perhaps the woman will not wish to go after me to this land. Shall I return your son to the land from which you came?" 6 And Abraham said to him, "Beware, lest you return my son back there. 7 The Lord, God of the heavens, Who took me from my father's house and from the land of my birth, and Who spoke about me, and Who swore to me, saying, 'To your seed will I give this land' He will send His angel before you, and you shall take a wife for my son from there. 8 And if the woman will not wish to go after you, you will be absolved of this, my oath; only do not return my son back there." 9 And the servant placed his hand under the thigh of Abraham his master, and he swore to him concerning this matter.

Book of Bereshit(Genesis) 25:1-10

אוַיֹּסֶף אַבְרָהָם וַיִּקַּח אִשָּׁה וּשְׁמָהּ קְטוּרָה:

בוַתֵּלֶד לוֹ אֶת־זִמְרָן וְאֶת־יָקְשָׁן וְאֶת־מְדָן וְאֶת־מִדְיָן וְאֶת־יִשְׁבָּק וְאֶת־שׁוּחַ:

גוְיָקְשָׁן יָלַד אֶת־שְׁבָא וְאֶת־דְּדָן וּבְנֵי דְדָן הָיוּ אַשּׁוּרִם וּלְטוּשִׁם וּלְאֻמִּים:

דוּבְנֵי מִדְיָן עֵיפָה וָעֵפֶר וַחֲנֹךְ וַאֲבִידָע וְאֶלְדָּעָה כָּל־אֵלֶּה בְּנֵי קְטוּרָה:

הוַיִּתֵּן אַבְרָהָם אֶת־כָּל־אֲשֶׁר־לוֹ לְיִצְחָק:

וְלִבְנֵי הַפִּילַגְשִׁים אֲשֶׁר לְאַבְרָהָם נָתַן אַבְרָהָם מַתָּנֹת וַיְשַׁלְּחֵם מֵעַל יִצְחָק בְּנוֹ בְּעוֹדֶנּוּ חַי קֵדְמָה אֶל־אֶרֶץ קֶדֶם:

זוְאֵלֶּה יְמֵי שְׁנֵי־חַיֵּי אַבְרָהָם אֲשֶׁר־חָי מְאַת שָׁנָה וְשִׁבְעִים שָׁנָה וְחָמֵשׁ שָׁנִים:

חוַיִּגְוַע וַיָּמָת אַבְרָהָם בְּשֵׂיבָה טוֹבָה זָקֵן וְשָׂבֵעַ וַיֵּאָסֶף אֶל־עַמָּיו:

טוַיִּקְבְּרוּ אֹתוֹ יִצְחָק וְיִשְׁמָעֵאל בָּנָיו אֶל־מְעָרַת הַמַּכְפֵּלָה אֶל־שְׂדֵה עֶפְרֹן בֶּן־צֹחַר הַחִתִּי אֲשֶׁר עַל־פְּנֵי מַמְרֵא:

יהַשָּׂדֶה אֲשֶׁר־קָנָה אַבְרָהָם מֵאֵת בְּנֵי־חֵת שָׁמָּה קֻבַּר אַבְרָהָם וְשָׂרָה אִשְׁתּוֹ:

1 And Abraham took another wife and her name was Keturah. 2 And she bore him Zimran and Jokshan and Medan and Midian and Jishbak and Shuah. 3 And Jokshan begot Sheba and Dedan, and the sons of Dedan were Ashurim, Letushim, and Leumim. 4 And the sons of Midian [were] Ephah and Epher and Enoch and Abida and Elda'ah; all these were the sons of Keturah. 5 And Abraham gave all that he possessed to Isaac. 6 And to the sons of Abraham's concubines, Abraham gave gifts, and he sent them away from his son Isaac while he [Abraham] was still alive, eastward to the land of the East. 7 And these are the days of the years of Abraham's life that he lived: one hundred years and seventy years and five years. 8 And Abraham expired and died in a good old age, old and satisfied, and he was gathered to his people. 9 And Isaac and Ishmael his sons buried him in the Cave

of Machpelah in the field of Ephron the son of Zohar the Hittite, which faces Mamre, 10 The field that Abraham had bought from the sons of Heth there Abraham and his wife Sarah were buried.

What you have just read is practically everything Jews have regarding Abraham and in totality we learned very little about the actual religion of Abraham. We learned more about his commercial business dealings than his creed or doctrines. The scarcity is so shocking that I almost abandoned this book altogether because the Jews have so little data. I was dismayed at how can a comparative religious study occur when the Jews have nearly nothing of substance to contribute to their claim of Abrahamic tradition? Essentially the focus of Jewish information is that God loved Abraham specially more than other Prophets for reasons never made apparent and as such made promises to him that would also extend to his offspring. These promises are very political in nature regarding real estate property. Additionally we learn that Abraham initiated the practice of circumcision, nearly scarified one of his sons, cleverly lied to royalty to protect his life when his beautiful wife was courted by said royalty and used to prostrate often putting his head on the ground. Abraham invoked the one unique God who was the Creator of humans, as evidenced by his deity unexpectedly creating Abraham's children in his old age. We also learn that the God of Abraham communicates either directly to the prophet or via angelic messengers and punishes those who are corrupt disbelieving sinners. However if we were to take this Jewish Abrahamic data we don't have enough to concoct a religion out of this because there isn't enough knowledge about God to identify him or do acts of worship. Hence many scholars have stated this Jewish source material was written long after Abraham as a political history narrative to justify conquests of the readers for whom the texts were written by and for. Truly more importance is given in the Jewish Abrahamic narrative to stakes of land grabbing than spirituality or facts of faith. So if these were the only texts that were ever available regarding Abraham we would be clueless as to what his religion was and couldn't imitate him regarding it. Unless religion is merely circumcision and putting your head on the ground when grateful the Jews have little to support their claim to be following Abraham because there isn't even a footprint they have amongst them to follow. So why is there such Jewish devotion to a man whose religion is not described in their books? Because without the alleged promise of land to Abraham's descendants there is no justification for Jewish military warfare over such territory. Hence politics plays a greater role in Jewish allegiance to Abraham than anything else. It is to attain the Abrahamic entitlement instead of the Abrahamic enlightenment that Jews choose to lay claim to following Abraham.

Regarding the alleged Abrahamic sacrifice the Hebrew Bible states Abraham took his "only son" to be sacrificed, but then the angel stopped him as he passed the test God had given him. Both Ishmael and Isaac were alive at the time Abraham died and present to bury him together according to Genesis 25:8-9, so since Ishmael was born first Ishmael is the only one who could ever have been considered the "only son" of Abraham. Yet many Christians and Jews will say Ishmael wasn't legitimate because his mother Hagar was a slave and Sarah was Abraham's wife. However in the bible Genesis 16:3 says "*So after Abram had been living in Canaan ten years, Sarai his wife took her Egyptian slave Hagar and gave her to her husband to be his wife.*" So biblically speaking Hagar was the wife of Abraham too. The bible says Abraham had 2 wives at the same time, and it was his wife's idea for him to marry her slave

Hagar. Genesis 16:15-16 continues "*So Hagar bore Abram a son, and Abram gave the name Ishmael to the son she had borne.* [16] **_Abram was eighty-six years old when Hagar bore him Ishmael._**" While Genesis 21:13 confirms that Ishmael was indeed the legitimate son of Abraham when it says God said "*I will make the son of the slave into a nation also, because he is your offspring.*" Genesis 21:11 "*The matter distressed Abraham greatly because it concerned his son.*" This shows the biblical text considers and states that Ishmael is a legitimate son of Abraham. So since biblically Ishmael is indeed Abraham's son and his firstborn son, who then could possibly be Abraham's "only son" who was almost sacrificed? Linguistically it can only be Ishmael. The circumcision was to be the sign of an everlasting covenant with Abraham and all of his descendants. However why is circumcision so important? Frequently today people will cite medical benefits but keep in mind Abraham did not know about the medical benefits and he also did it as an old man who was promised future children by God. Now imagine that you are an elderly man living thousands of years ago and God says you are miraculously going to be a father. After hearing such news you wouldn't naturally be inclined to start cutting off a piece of your penis. Logically that would be a very foolish thing to do, especially when nobody else is circumcised, meaning nobody knows how to safely do that operation including Abraham who learned by doing it on himself first. Whereas circumcising yourself isn't something you can afford to "mess up the first few times and try again until you get it right". Yet despite how crazy it may seem on the surface there really is a reason for God to have commanded it be done. Do you remember the Phallic idols? Where for thousands of years people worshipped penis idols? What do you think such penis worshippers would think about a religion that says men have to have their penis partially cut off? They would think that to be a "anti-penis" religion that goes against everything they hold sacred. As Christians commonly preach "Your body is a temple"(since they think they got the Holy Ghost or the Eucharist in them, or are made "in the image of God") the phallic pagans taught that a penis is a fleshly idol. To circumcise was a declaration of war against the phallic faiths. It would also prove to phallic worshippers that the penis doesn't produce life but God the Creator does regardless of one's penis. Plus circumcision would act as a permanent sign of hatred for phallicism and a physical opposition to the belief in phallicism. It was simply impossible for a believing man to be accused of worshipping phallic idols since his own organ was physically altered, which would not have been done if he considered the penis to be sacred. Also this ensured that when phallic worshippers converted to the true religion, it was genuine because you can't go from worshipping penis to getting circumcised unless you really don't worship penis anymore. So circumcision is a permanent disavowal and disassociation from the popular idolatrous promiscuous phallicism that was prevalent in Abraham's time.

From Genesis 17 verses 23-27 we are told "*On that very day*" Abraham circumcised Ishmael , thereby establishing the covenant with him when he was 13 years old and Abraham was 99. Together those sections of 1-14 and 23-27 make complete sense and flow smoothly. However in between there is another paragraph of verses 15-22 where we are told God renamed Abraham's wife and informed him she will bear a son. In response Abraham uncharacteristically laughs at God and asks how he can have a son when he is "*a hundred years old*". God says it will happen and that his covenant will only be with that son named Isaac who will be born the next year when Abraham is 101 years old. But then in verse 23 we get told "*On that very day*" "*Abraham was 99 years old*". So we have a problem in that biblically Abraham went from being 99 to being 100 back to being 99 years old all in one day. Or else someone has corrupted the text and put things out of order. But why would they or God do that, if this is indeed divine revelation? Well lets imagine the bible was in chronological order and a person read that the covenant is made with Abraham and his descendants at age 99 and he only has 1 kid at that time. The sign of the covenant is circumcision and he circumcises himself and his only son Ishmael "*on that very day*" he is told of the covenant. Everyone would understand biblically the covenant is made with Ishmael, it doesn't mean it's only with Ishmael, but it was undeniably made with Ishmael when he was 13 years old. Likewise when God makes a covenant, according to the bible, it's never an exclusively genetic covenant. This is evident by the biblical covenants God made with Noah and David of which their descendants were listed as being part of the covenant. Yet then the bible curses those very same descendants of Noah and David because of their disobedience. Although some of these biblical curses again seem due to racist Jews, such as Canaan (Noah's grandson) being cursed by

Noah before he is born because his father Ham allegedly walked in on Noah when he was passed out drunk and naked. Whereas I don't think that post-flood Noah would've drunk himself into such a stupor that he passed out naked and then when he wakes up he curses his unborn grandson whom God already made a covenant with. It's more likely that Israelites just wanted to wage war with Canaanites so they put this curse of Canaanites in the bible to justify their war policies. Anyway just because God makes a covenant doesn't mean it's a free pass or irrevocable, it's more of a contract that can be broken if humans don't fulfill their part. Although if we go into covenants being legitimately broken and we say God made a covenant with Abraham and his descendants, it's clear that not all of the descendants kept their part of the covenant until modern times. If we get genetic and say Ishmaelites and Israelites both had the covenant then it's easy to see examples of Israelites breaking the covenant but when did the Ishmaelites? Also just because individuals or a collective people may break God's covenant that doesn't mean that covenant isn't still available to their race. A covenant with God is more like a special contract only offered to certain people, that is different from the offer God gives to the whole world. So when a covenant is made with people that means an offer is on the table, if the people accept that offer there are conditions to be fulfilled and if they don't fulfill those conditions there are consequences. Covenants are high risk/high reward contracts with God but then again nobody ever refuses a covenant because it's truly a gift, similar to a prestigious job offer. Few will turn down a job offer even though they know it will require work and could cause bigger trouble for them if they mess up on the job. The point is that biblically the covenant was made with Ishmael too and not just Isaac the father of Jacob/Israel.

The bible's next chapter Genesis 18 relates a version of what happened when angels appeared to Abraham in the form of men to announce the destruction of Sodom and the birth of Isaac. The points relevant to us are Genesis 18:9-15, ""*Where is your wife Sarah?" they asked him. "There, in the tent,"* he said. [10] *Then* ___*one of them said, "I will surely return to you about this time next year, and Sarah your wife will have a son."*___ *Now Sarah was listening at the entrance to the tent, which was behind him.* [11] *Abraham and Sarah were already very old, and Sarah was past the age of childbearing.* [12] *So Sarah laughed to herself as she* *thought, "After I am worn out and my lord is old, will I now have this pleasure?"* ¹³ *Then the Lord said to Abraham, "**Why did Sarah laugh** and say, 'Will I really have a child, now that I am old?' ¹⁴ Is anything too hard for the Lord? **I will return to you at the appointed time next year, and Sarah will have a son.**"* ¹⁵ *Sarah was afraid, so she lied and said, "I did not laugh." But he said, "Yes, you did laugh."*

Lots can be learned from this. Firstly we should note that Sarah was clearly surprised at the news of her having a child and she laughed as a result. Yet pages before in Genesis 17 we were told that God already informed Abraham that his wife Sarah would have a child. In that version Abraham laughed at the news. Why then would God tell him again and why didn't Sarah already know? Did Abraham just keep the news a secret and not tell Sarah that God blessed her and she would give birth to a kid with an everlasting covenant that was exclusive for her kid and not given to his already existing kid Ishamael? It's very unlikely Abraham would keep Genesis 17:15-22 a secret from his wife especially if as it says God would make a covenant with Sarah's son and not Ishmael. Although if we do pretend Abraham kept God's revelations and good news a secret from his beloved wife then why would God in Genesis 18 give Sarah such a hard time for laughing when Genesis 17 says Abraham laughed and it was no problem? Genesis 18 chastises Sarah for laughing but when Abraham laughs in Genesis 17 it's ok? I do say something is very funny about this biblical narrative and it is not the funny kind of funny. It actually seems that whoever wrote Genesis 18 didn't know about the verses in Genesis 17:15-22 which coincidentally happen to list Abraham as 100 even though verses 1-14 and 23-27 have him at age 99. Yet these suspicious verses also happen to be the ones which say the covenant is only with Isaac/Israelites and they specifically say it's not with Ishmael despite other parts of the bible indicating that it is with Ishmael too. Sadly it seems somebody made up some racist verses and put them into the bible and it has been passed off as revelation for many generations and modern Jews have been fooled. Furthermore Genesis 18 says that Sarah lied about laughing whereas the bible says God hates liars. So biblically God hates Sarah for lying but then blesses those he hates? And if Sarah could lie to the prophet Abraham and/or God then isn't it possible the author(s) of Genesis was lying when they wrote? The majority of Jews and Christians would be appalled at such a question but just look at the bible verses of Genesis 19:30-38,

"Lot and his two daughters left Zoar and settled in the mountains, for he was afraid to stay in Zoar. He and his two daughters lived in a cave. 31 One day the older daughter said to the younger, "Our father is old, and there is no man around here to give us children – as is the custom all over the earth. 32 Let's get our father to drink wine and then sleep with him and preserve our family line through our father." 33 That night they got their father to drink wine, and the older daughter went in and slept with him. He was not aware of it when she lay down or when she got up. 34 The next day the older daughter said to the younger, "Last night I slept with my father. Let's get him to drink wine again tonight, and you go in and sleep with him so we can preserve our family line through our father." 35 So they got their father to drink wine that night also, and the younger daughter went in and slept with him. Again he was not aware of it when she lay down or when she got up. So both of Lot's daughters became pregnant by their father. 37 The older daughter had a son, and she named him Moab; he is the father of the Moabites of today. 38 The younger daughter also had a son, and she named him Ben-Ammi; he is the father of the Ammonites of today."

These bible verses say that the prophet Lot, the same who condemned homosexuality in Sodom who fled it with his 2 daughters, later on impregnated those same daughters via drunken sex. As bad and slanderous as this is Christians and Jews say that Moses wrote this about Lot. Of course it is written in narrative fashion and is not an eye witness account, as evidenced by the phrases "of today". Biblically one of Lot's incestuous sons was the father of the Moabites and the other was the father of the Ammonites. Both these nations were enemies of the nation of Israel so it wouldn't be surprising if Israel lied about them being of incestuous lineage simply due to war propaganda. Both Moabites and Ammonites did indeed exist during the time Moses is said to have existed so there is no issue there, he could've written about them. However Moabites arose in the late 14th century while Ammonites arose in the 13th century before common era timeline. So the problem with these bible verses is that Moabites existed about 100-200 years before the Ammonites existed. It'd be a reasonable mistake for someone in the nation of Israel to make if they were to say Moabites and Ammonites came to prominence at the same time because ancient historical records were spotty and inaccessible, especially the records of the enemies. Yet the bible says the father of the Moabites was conceived only one day before the father of the Ammonites. So God could not have gotten this wrong and Moses couldn't have gotten it wrong either. Thus Moses could not possibly have written that Lot got drunk and had sex with both of his daughters who gave birth to the Moabites and Ammonites. Furthermore it is impossible that the Moabites and Ammonites could have been brother nations because the Moabites preceded the Ammonites by 100-200 years. Unless of course one of Lot's daughters was pregnant for 100-200 years longer than her sister was, but we know that isn't the case. Afterall if she was they would've put that detail in the bible right? Or are important details needed for a story to be true just not included in the bible for some special reason? Could people writing religious fiction be that "special reason"? These are some of my most disliked bible verses because they not only accuse Lot of being a drunkard and incestuous but they also blame this slander on Moses and or God. To put this in perspective it'd be liking saying that Jesus called Moses a drug dealing sodomite rapist. Anyone would say that's extremely disrespectful to both

Jesus and Moses, but Christians and Jews still maintain this double slander concerning Moses and Lot because it's in the bible. Even if a Jew or Christian tries to put polish on the story and say Lot didn't really know what was going on because he was drunk(which is sinful to say in itself) then they are still saying that Lot's daughters raped him on 2 consecutive nights. So their way of trying to say the bible doesn't say Lot was incestuous but was just drunk also requires them to say that the bible says the believing daughters of Lot raped their prophet! As you've seen the bible says that a prophet of God who condemned sodomy, later got drunk and was raped by his daughters. The bible says it's good for girls to rape their father and that it's good for girls to rape their prophet. Not quite a child friendly book, unless you want your kids to rape you. But lets go back to the biblical narrative concerning Abraham's kids who were actually related to Lot and his daughters because historically Lot and Abraham were cousins. Fortunately the bible does not say they were "kissing cousins", as far as I know. Maybe that plot twist will be revealed in next year's edition. Although biblically according to Genesis 11:27, Abraham was the uncle of Lot. Meaning biblically 2 of the 2nd nieces of Abraham incestually raped the nephew of Abraham. However the biblical story gets even worse as in the New Testament Matthew 1:5 lists Ruth as the grandmother of David and the ancestor of Jesus. Why do I say that makes the story worse? Because this Ruth was a Moabite (Ruth 2:2) slave who married her master/relative Boaz, according to the book of Ruth in the bible. So this biblical incestual rape of Lot led to the direct progeny of David's Moabite grandmother and by extension every prophet who descended from David, such as Solomon and Jesus. The bible says that prophets David, Solomon and Jesus descended from a rapist who raped her father/prophet Lot despite both being relatives of the friend of God, known as Abraham. All this filthy slander against such persons exist in the bible despite God praising the family of Abraham and singling them out for a special covenant with him.

The bible says Abraham sent Hagar and Ishmael away because of his wife Sarah being jealous Ishmael was getting attention over Isaac. The bible literally says it was all Sarah's plan to just "get rid of them" and God agreed with her. Yet that seems very uncharacteristic since Sarah was the one who got Abraham married to Hagar to begin with, but conveniently this part of the bible just refers to Hagar as a "slave woman" instead of Abraham's wife like Genesis 16:3 says. While Genesis 21:11 says Hagar wasn't even a concern for Abraham, despite being his wife, and he was only distressed because it concerned Ishmael. So again it's like whoever wrote Genesis 21 didn't read Genesis 16, or Genesis 17 or Genesis 18. This is because Genesis 21 refers to Sarah laughing and asking " *Who would have said to Abraham that Sarah would nurse children? Yet I have borne him a son in his old age.*" Whereas biblically speaking all kinds of beings said this to Abraham and her well before the birth took place, you had God say it several times, the angels, Abraham but the Sarah in Genesis 21 seems to have forgotten all these beings who said the very thing she thinks none would have said. The bible even says she got in trouble and interrogated for laughing when she heard Abraham get told. So first of all it's unlikely she'd laugh after getting in trouble for laughing before AND it's insane for her to say what Genesis 21 says she said after giving birth. It almost makes you wonder if this is the same Sarah. Did she have memory loss or a split personality? If so I don't think Abraham would've obeyed the inhumane demands of such a wife who is so prone to forget things. Honestly if they made a movie about this we would be all confused and say what kind of movie is this where the actors don't remember the plot that they were a part of. Anyways in biblical context Sarah has a baby and basically says to her husband "*Get rid of your other wife who gave birth to your first son, and get your firstborn son out of here too because I don't want him to get any inheritance from you which would make my baby boy possibly get less.*" It sounds unrealistic to me but since Christians and Jews believe, let's examine it. Chronologically this story is impossible because at the time Ishmael and Hagar went into the desert Ishmael was a baby and Isaac wasn't born until long after Ishmael, so Sarah didn't have kids at the time. Now I know that's not what Genesis 21 says, but I'm taking the full context of the story. The bible repeatedly refers to Ishmael being a helpless boy when the incident in the desert took place. If Abraham sent away his firstborn and at that time only son, as well as the boy's mother, into the desolate desert because of his wife that would have been sinful and tantamount to murder. Sarah was rewarded with Isaac by God for being pious, for her to advocate murdering Ishmael in the desert out of envy for her miraculous child is uncharacteristically hypocritical. Sarah and Abraham are role models not murderous racist child abusers. Rather God had specially commanded Abraham to do this, possibly to prevent any issue of jealousy from arising between Sarah and Hagar which would cause Abraham difficulty. Now what reason could I give for insisting Ishmael was the only son of Abraham when the desert fiasco took place? Well I use the reason that the Genesis 21 version of events is impossible according to the bible itself. According to the Bible in Genesis 16:16, Abraham was 86 years old when Ishmael was born. While according to Gensis 21:5 Abraham was 100 years old when Isaac was born. This means biblically Ishmael was 14 years older than Isaac. In Genesis 21:8 the expulsion of Ishmael and Hagar is alleged to have occurred after Isaac was weaned. Biblically the babies weren't weaned until the age of 3. So biblically Ishmael would've been 17 when Sarah tells Abraham to get rid of his wife(Hagar) and her "boy" (Ishmael) . He's clearly described as if he were a baby who's too weak to carry anything, or help his mother and just lays down crying his eyes out because he's thirsty and there's no water, which saddens his mother so much she goes away from him not being able to bear to watch him die. Now for a baby that's appropriate behavior, however for a 17 year old in the time of Abraham who was the son of the prophet Abraham? I don't think so. And if Ishmael acted like that I don't think God would bless him the way the bible says God blessed him. Also do you think a 17 year old son of Abraham is going to mock his 3 year old brother who was miraculously born to a woman well past child-bearing age, whose birth was foretold by God and angels? And then after doing so Sarah tells Abraham to expel his wife and her/his 17 year old son abandoning them to the desert? Don't you think the son will just walk right back to his home? Also Genesis 21:15 says "*When the water in the skin was gone, she put the boy under one of the bushes.*" Biblically Ishmael was 17 years old when "*she put the boy(Ishmael) under one of the bushes*". Now call me skeptical, or heretical, but I simply do not believe that Hagar put her 17 year old son under a bush! Even a 2 year old can't fit under a bush! This is just a biblical impossibility. I challenge every Jew and Christian in the world to go to the desert of Paran and demonstrate how a woman can put her 17 year old son, who is dying of thirst, under a single bush. In fact this would be a miracle if it happened. So either the bible has some seriously false information or else Hagar and Ishmael performed a miracle, simply because Hagar didn't want to see Ishmael die of thirst. Which also if true would point to the noble character of Ishmael. Because if you are a 17 year old boy stranded in the desert to die with your elderly mother, what 17 year old is going to let his mother drink the water and choose to die of thirst first? You'd have to say Ishmael was quite a great 17 year old if he did that. Yet that doesn't mesh with the biblical narrative of a 17 year old Ishmael mocking his 3 year old brother who is the son of his prophet. Furthermore Genesis 21:18 says God told Hagar "*Lift the boy up*". Now explain to me how this old woman was able to lift up her 17 year old son, despite being on the brink of death via malnutrition and dehydration? That would be another miracle God helped biblical Hagar do with Ishmael. And again I challenge every Jew and Christian to replicate this event in the desert of Paran today. If I'm supposed to believe it's possible and they did it then show me how they did it yourself, otherwise one must credit Hagar and Ishmael with many miracles. But Christians and Jews say God hated Hagar and Ishmael so much Ishmael was excluded from the covenant despite being the firstborn son of Abraham. Thus this biblical tale is unrealistic for many reasons and nobody really believes in it, as evident by bible believers holding antagonistic views towards both Hagar and Ishmael with some even claiming they were cursed for all eternity along with their offspring. Also note that biblically Abraham was 103 years old at the time. Do you think a 103 year old man is just going to be able to abandon a strong 17 year old man in the desert with his elderly mother, no questions asked? Realistically you'd expect the 17 year old to physically take over and leave the 103 year old and the 93 year old Sarah and the 3 year old Isaac in the desert to die. That's more probable, but that didn't happen either. Also how many 103 year old guys do you know who are pushovers when their 93 year old wife tells them to basically kill their other wife and son who they prayed to God to give them? But what's even more shocking is that then Christians and Jews will say that when Isaac was a teenager, Abraham took him out to sacrifice him because of a vision/dream he had. Yet the bible doesn't mention the age of Abraham at the time, nor the age of Isaac nor does it mention anything at all of what Abraham thought of allegedly going to kill Isaac. Whereas obviously those are very important details that would be included if this incident took place since the bible says Isaac was weaned and specifies many other ages and dates. Anyways do you think Sarah would be ok with Abraham trying to kill Isaac? Biblically Sarah was the type who ordered murder out of love for her son, so I don't think she would tolerate a biblical Abraham going out to kill her teenage son. According to Genesis 23:1 Sarah was 127 years old when she died. Whereas the alleged near sacrifice of Isaac is related in Genesis 22, so Sarah was biblically alive at the time the biblical Abraham was alleged to be going to slaughter Isaac, at least chronologically. But we could make the case that Sarah's opinions are not mentioned regarding the attempted alleged slaughter of Isaac because perhaps she was dead and the bible is out of chronological order. However in Genesis 17:17 the bible says Isaac will be born when Abraham is 100 and Sarah is 90. Now Genesis 21:5 confirms Isaac was born when Abraham was 100. Therefore in order for the bible to get away with not mentioning Sarah's views on Abraham allegedly attempting to kill her son, which she was willing to order the death of 2 others to ensure a larger share of inheritance for, then she would've had to be dead when the near sacrifice took place. Biblically this would mean that Isaac was 37 years old when Abraham allegedly tried to sacrifice him. It goes without saying that is completely unrealistic and as such the Jewish and Christian notion that Isaac was almost sacrificed is also unrealistic and doesn't fit the biblical narrative even though Genesis 22 says explicitly that Isaac was the one Abraham attempted to slaughter. Which may offend Jews and Christians, but Genesis 22 also says Isaac was Abraham's "only son" and we know that is just not true. However the person who wrote Genesis 22 might not have known that or wanted his readers to know that, which is why they wrote what they wrote. Also regarding all these promises the biblical God is said to have made with Isaac then during the attempted sacrifice it is interesting to note that Abraham never once bothers to ask God "*What about all those promises you made about Isaac and his offspring? How will this everlasting covenant come true if I sacrifice Isaac?*" Also from a logical biblical perspective, if Abraham boots Ishmael out of his life and then God tells him to kill Isaac, logically Abraham would wonder if he was being punished by God for expelling Ishmael and that maybe he'd be better off had he expelled Isaac instead of Ishmael. On top of that when biblical God tells Abraham that Isaac is his "only son",

Abraham goes along with it and doesn't object or ask what is meant by that or anything, almost as if the Abraham in Genesis 22 really thought he only had one biological son. The only other explanations to justify this odd Abraham in Genesis 22 is to say he knew he had another son and was trying to fool God by playing along thinking that if he told God he had 2 then he might get told to kill both or the sacrifice might not get him as many points with God. Either that or Ishmael was a disbeliever in God and the prophethood of Abraham and that is why neither God nor Abraham in Genesis 22 remember that Ishmael is a son too. But the apostate theory doesn't hold up when we consider the time biblical Ishmael spent with Abraham, and the miracles God facilitated with Ishmael in the desert and that Abraham kept in contact with Ishmael throughout his life and was on good terms with him, as was Isaac when the bible says both Ishmael and Isaac buried Abraham together when he died. So it's really a big slip up in the biblical narrative that makes it seem like a fictional story because it's so unrealistic without suspense or stress. Romantic Science Fiction Horror Comedies are more realistic than this biblical narrative. No realistic logical rationale is ever expressed in this biblical narrative. Thus either the Abraham who Christians and Jews say nearly killed Isaac must have not known about the biblical Abraham whom God apparently made all these promises to in regards to Isaac and his offspring, or the author of the biblical narrative didn't know what the other parts of the bible said. So again we have the problem of biblical characters not knowing their own life story which the bible narrates. The bible characters have practically no character development at all and don't even seem human because they just act so fake and unrealistic. These prophets were sent to be real live human role models, but their biblical portrayals make them seem more mythical than man, especially in regards to Jesus. In reality at the time of the attempted sacrifice Ishmael was Abraham's only son, which made this sacrifice more difficult for Abraham since he had prayed to have offspring for years. To say that Ishmael was hated by Abraham is a lie because Abraham kept in contact with Ishmael. Likewise Hagar couldn't have been hated by God, especially if the bible is true in saying that "God opened her eyes" and sent an angel to speak to her. There aren't many ladies who can claim such honors like the honors the bible gives to Hagar, yet Christians and

Jews slander her saying awful things despite what the bible says. The birth of Abraham's son Isaac by Sarah wasn't announced to Abraham until the angels came to inform him they were going to destroy the sodomites where his cousin Lot lived, which was after Ishmael and Hagar had already settled away from Abraham. The angels announced the birth of Isaac to Abraham specifically as a reward for having nearly sacrificed his "only son", thus it's impossible the birth of Isaac could be the reward for nearly sacrificing Isaac. This is an instance where the biblical verses contradict the biblical timeline and alerts us to an interpolated textual addition by Israelites. I know it might've been confusing to go through and analyze the biblical narrative, because corrupted texts are confusing. That's why Christians make movies and put on plays imitating the pagan Greeks because otherwise nobody can follow the biblical plot, which is why most people don't read the bible and if they do they read it very very slowly so they forget the plot as they read along. Many Jews and Christians will say Ishmael was an illegitimate son of Abraham and only Isaac was a prophet. But if we are to talk about possible illegitimacy Genesis 20:11-12 depicts what Abraham thought of Sarah:

"*Abraham replied, "I said to myself, 'There is surely no fear of God in this place, and they will kill me because of my wife.'* [12] *Besides, <u>she really is my sister, the daughter of my father though not of my mother; and she became my wife</u>.*" Biblically Sarah was the half-sister of Abraham, this is what the bible says. So biblically Isaac was the son of an incestual relationship, married his first cousin, and Isaac's son Jacob (aka Israel) married 2 of his first cousins. According to Jewish, Christian and Muslim standards the biblical depiction of Abraham and Sarah is incest, thus Isaac is biblically a product of a sinful sexual act that involved a miracle from God. Whereas according to Christian standards Isaac committed incest by marrying his first cousin Rebekah. So honestly tell me does God say incest is good? Because the bible says Abraham did it and his favorite/best/blessed child came out of that incestual sexual relationship. On the other hand Ishmael was not born of incest, didn't marry his cousins and as far as I know only had 1 wife at a time his whole life. If anyone between Ishmael and Isaac were to be disqualified from the covenant one would think it'd be Isaac and not Ishmael. Afterall Ishmael was the firstborn son of an elderly friend of God and no sins of his are known to us. Biblically in Genesis 17:25 Abraham even circumcised Ishmael when he was 13 years old. Whereas since circumcision is the very sign of the covenant that means Ishmael is part of the covenant and chose to be circumcised as compared to Isaac who was involuntarily circumcised at 8 days old. It is evident from Genesis 21 that God had a special relationship with Ishmael and provided a miraculous well for him to drink from in the middle of the desert. The specific desert of Paran is named as the place of the well and where Ishmael lived. Paran is another name for Mecca and that well, known as ZamZam, is flowing there to this day, everyday thousands of gallons come forth every hour. The miraculous water is known as ZamZam water and has miraculous curative effects for those who drink it, for both believers and disbelievers alike. The water itself is free due to its special history, but the bottles the water comes in can be very expensive if you don't get the water from the well yourself. All the historians of that region agree the ZamZam well today is the same one God created for Hagar and Ishmael. The historians of Arabia also unanimously agree Abraham and Ishmael built the Kaba in Mecca. It is rare for historians to unanimously agree on anything, usually there is one or two different opinions, but all the records of all historians in the region say there is no dispute that Abraham and Ishmael built the Kaba and the ZamZam well is the well God made for Hagar and Ishmael. The surprising thing is that Jews and Christians don't care in the slightest to see, visit or drink from this well. This well is a literal miracle people can witness today. It's on par with the miracle of Moses striking a rock and having water gush forth, which we don't know where that took place or if those streams of water even exist today. Yet this is a past and present miraculous well with miraculous water which the bible itself mentions yet Jews and Christians don't care and most don't even know about it. Why is that? Because it's Ishmael and Hagar and subconsciously they hate them. They might try to avoid admitting this but eventually they'll say God himself hates them so that's why they hate or don't like them. But there is no such thing as God "doesn't like someone", either God loves you a little or a lot or hates you a little or a lot. So God either loved Hagar and Ishmael or he hated them, but the fact is God performed a miracle on their behalf which still exists today for all to see, feel and drink from so that action alone is quite a strong indication of love, possibly even everlasting love. This is a serious topic because to love who God hates is disbelief and makes God hate the lover, while to hate who God loves is disbelief and makes God hate the hater. So both love and hate must be for God's sake.

Since Ishmael was biblically 14 years older than Isaac (Genesis 16:16 and Genesis 21:5) there was a significant time frame when Ishmael would be considered the "only son" of Abraham. Now some may say the whole age issue can be explained away by saying copiers and translators wrote down the wrong numbers when saying the age of Abraham when each kid was born. This argument is invalid because in the text the numbers are written in letter format in word form. If it were a valid argument then it means the words written in the bible are the wrong words and thus cannot be the word of God or inspired by God. Also if this argument were valid then one could say well maybe they also made a mistake in saying there is only one God, and they might've meant a different number and all kinds of crazy things which basically would mean any mention of a number in the bible can be claimed to be the wrong number. Such as God creating things in 6 days, creating 1 man and 1 woman, the 3 day theory, 40 years or 40 days or with all the 40s it might not really be 40 but just 4 or maybe 0 or 250 trillion; one can literally make up any number they want with this argument. Instead Christians and Jews should just accept the truth that Ishmael was the only son nearly sacrificed by Abraham, there is no doubt about it. That the bible says Isaac was Abraham's "only son" and was almost sacrificed is an impossibility, either it was Isaac or Abraham's only son, Isaac was never the "only son" of Abraham. Thus the biblical version of what happened isn't correct and something has been tampered with. Plus Genesis 17:23 and Genesis 25:8-9 say Ishmael was Abraham's son AND in the same exact capacity as Isaac was Abraham's son, they are equal in their sonship. And if "only son" doesn't really mean only literal son but just favorite or blessed or chosen then you tell Christians that if so then John 3:16 must not really mean that Jesus is the "only son" or "only begotten son" of God and that maybe God had lots of literal sons born of virgin women throughout history, but they all turned evil. Or maybe they were good guys that God liked but they just didn't make the cut. Or maybe Jesus went and killed them all so he was the last one left, or maybe they mocked Jesus the way the bible says Ishmael mocked Isaac so that's why they weren't considered sons of God anymore. You know maybe the virgin Mary had more than one miraculously born son but the earlier ones mocked Jesus and got sent to go die in the desert? So this whole "only son" doesn't really mean "only son" excuse doesn't work either. Also since they will agree Ishmael and Isaac were both sons then the real difference is just with the word "only", and if "only" doesn't really mean "only 1" but means "only good 1" then I guess the bible really means there are many gods which exist but God is the "only good 1". So the more they try to argue their way out of it, they just dig themselves a deeper grave. They should just let their protests lie down and die already. But sadly some will as a last resort out of desperate loyalty to the bible and their faith say, "*it doesn't really matter who it was but the important thing is that it happened*", but the details matter. Imagine being an elderly Abraham and you are told by God to kill your son. Now if you only have one child that will be much harder to do than if you have two so it really does make a difference. Even if one were to go with the lie that Abraham didn't like Ishmael and God didn't like him, having 2 sons whoever they are and wherever they are makes a huge difference if God tells you to kill one of your sons, because you will know that you have a backup to continue your lineage and hang out with or get some help from someday if you need it; and Abraham was an old guy at the time too in a land where old people didn't survive. Also we don't want to be lying about who Abraham almost slaughtered either. Keep in mind that when God commanded Abraham to give a human sacrifice there was a specific way to do it and it wasn't crucifixion. Also if you know it happened then you must know who it happened to and this "who" really does matter for political, ethnic and religious reasons around the world today. The bible says it was Isaac, the Quran says Ishmael. So one of those 2 books is wrong and thus cannot be from God. This question of who is literally a Bible vs. Quran battle, then the Christian and Jew will brush it off and say *"it doesn't really matter who"*. No Muslims say that, but the Christians and Jews do. Why? Because they religiously can't let the bible be proven wrong because that would mean their religious beliefs are wrong. Thus when they give this argument of "it doesn't really matter" they don't even believe that, they just don't want to argue or debate it because they don't want to face the fact that the bible is wrong on something, and they know if they try to prove who it was or argue over it then it will damage their religious convictions. So in order to keep believing in their bible and religion they flee from the battlefield saying *"it doesn't really matter, let's not argue "*. Whereas this is the catchphrase of theological retreat upon fear of expected defeat. On the other hand there will still be some staunch firm devoutly committed Christians and Jews who say, *"If the bible says it then it's true. It was Isaac! I don't care what you say! "* I used to be one of those people, and I do hope that you currently aren't one but if you are then hear me out before cursing me out. I appeal to the bible itself in Deuteronomy 21:15-17, "***If a man has two wives, and he loves one but not the other, and both bear him sons but the firstborn is the son of the wife he does not love***, [16] *when he wills his property to his sons,* **he must not give the rights of the firstborn to the son of the wife he loves in preference to his actual firstborn, the son of the wife he does not love.** [17] **He must acknowledge the son of his unloved wife as the firstborn by giving him a double share of all he has.** *That son is the first sign of his father's strength.* _The right of the firstborn belongs to him."_

Therefore since Genesis 16:3 says *"So after Abram had been living in Canaan ten years, Sarai his wife took her Egyptian slave Hagar and gave her to her husband to be his wife."* Then biblically Ishmael cannot and never can be deprived of his biblical God-given rights as a firstborn son regardless of who his mother is. Likewise the children of Isaac, Jacob cannot and never can usurp the rights of the firstborn son Esau. Whereas the whole thing with Esau and Jacob doesn't even come close to comparison to the Ishmael and Isaac case because both Esau and Jacob had the same mother. Whereas the bible says Hagar was Abraham's wife. Now Muslims say she was a slave and not a wife and still legitimate, but the Christians and Jews say she was a slave and not a wife thus he is illegitimate. So anyway you look at it either the bible is wrong to say Hagar was the wife of Abraham so that would mean Jews and Christians are wrong to say their book is right, or the bible is right to say Hagar was Abraham's wife and Ishmael cannot be disinherited or considered illegitimate in any way. However let's say that Hagar wasn't Abraham's wife but just a slave. Maybe the "inspired word of God" in the bible just made Hagar a wife because of a typo? Then if she was a slave according to the bible, Jewish and Christian religions Ishmael would be illegitimate and deprived of inheritance and the covenant right?

Wrong! Do you know why that's wrong? Because biblically Jacob (also known as Israel who is the son of Isaac) had 2 wives, Leah and Rachel and he had 12 sons. Hence the 12 tribes of Israel. But guess what? Only 8 of those sons were born to Leah and Rachel. You see biblically Jacob had sex with Leah's slave Zilpah who gave birth to Gad and then Asher, and Jacob also had sex with Rachel's slave Bilhah who gave birth to Dan and Naphtali. So 4 of Jacob's 12 sons were born via sex with slaves. This is all related in Genesis 30. However a Jew or Christian will quickly point out how "well the english bible says the slaves became his wives", yet the dialogue doesn't say this. Genesis 30:3 says Rachel told Jacob *"Here is Bilhah, my servant. Sleep with her so that she can bear children for me and I too can build a family through her."* It's only after that in commentary which alleges Jacob took the slaves as wives. Yet Genesis 35:22 also mentions this very same Bilhah saying *"While Israel was living in that region, **__Reuben went in and slept with his father's concubine Bilhah__**, and Israel heard of it. Jacob had twelve sons:"* Now don't be tricked by the mentioning of Israel and Jacob in the same verse, Israel is Jacob. Who was Reuben? Well the next verse in Genesis 35:23 answers that, *"The sons of Leah: **__Reuben the firstborn of Jacob__**, Simeon, Levi, Judah, Issachar and Zebulun."*

What a story! Jacob/Israel had his firstborn son Reuben(son of Leah) have sex with his concubine Bilhah (slave of Rachel (Leah's sister/Reuben's aunt))! Actually if she's just a concubine, that's not really that bad, is it? It's kinda disrespectful but it's not that bad, it's just biblical. Always remember the difference between bad and biblical. Generally the Jewish and Christian rule is that if it's bad outside of the bible then when it's in the bible it's not because it's biblical. Or as the Christian may say *"Well that's the Old Testament, that's all pre-Jesus"* as if that makes bad things good things if they happened before Jesus came to earth. That despite Christian doctrine saying that bad things are worse during the pre-Jesus period because that's before the alleged atonement where you had to strictly follow all God's laws or go to hell. Apparently Christians think Jesus *"saved us from that super strict impossibly hard to follow moral standard"*. However remember Genesis 30 and how Christians insist that the bible says Bilhah was Jacob's wife? Well Genesis 35 says she was Jacob's concubine. If she was his wife then Reuben would've been guilty of Adultery with his father's and a prophet's wife. This same Reuben was the firstborn of Israel, essentially the head of the first tribe of Israel. And people think soap operas are full of sex drama? The bible's steamier than any soap opera on tv, they wouldn't even be able to put the bible's sex tales on tv because they're so scandalous. Now the truth of the matter is either Bilhah was Jacob's wife, or she was his concubine, or she was his wife and she got demoted to being a concubine by the time his son had his turn with her. Like father like son isn't that how it goes, or is that just in the pre-Jesus period? Who knows maybe the Christian will say Jacob the prophet divorced his wife so his son could have sex with her? If so when did that happen? Biblically there was no divorce, the only clue we have is in Genesis 33:1-2 which says, "*Jacob looked up and there was Esau, coming with his four hundred men; so he divided the children among* **_Leah, Rachel and the two female servants_**. *[2] He put* **_the female servants and their children in front_**, *Leah and her children next, and Rachel and Joseph in the rear.*" What happened to Jacob's 4 wives ? I guess the modern bible only counts them as wives when they were having sex. Or did I use the babies bible? Nope I used the adult version, it says "wives" in Genesis 30, "servants" in Genesis 33 and "concubine" in Genesis 35. Could it be that the adult bible is deliberately censored? What other explanation could there be for the same women having such different status' in those 3 biblical chapters? The sad thing is that bible believers will read these chapters and not even notice these contradictions because they have such a firm faith that it's all from God. Yet they insist it's not "blind faith", which it's probably best not to say "blind faith" lest we offend blind people. Realistically Bilhah was just a concubine and biblically legitimate children can be born from concubine slaves. Jews and Christians who insist this can't be only do so because they say Ishmael was the son of a slave women and is illegitimate due to that, thus they changed the bible; a lot. Yet the bible also says Abraham took Hagar as a wife. The reason the bibles say this is because in modern times if the bibles were printed saying that some guy had sex with his slaves who gave birth to his kids it would be scandalous. So the bible publishers add in the wife bits to make it more "decent". In the past the bible said different stuff, and American slave owners quoted the bible to justify everything they did to their African slaves from beatings, to whippings, to raping their slave girls. Some black slaves who escaped American plantations even wrote on how the reason they didn't become Christian was because their masters would bring them to Church every Sunday and they would get told all the bible verses that said all their masters did to them was the same as God commanded them to do to them. So if there were some biblical rule that prohibited men from having sex with their slaves, (rape is rape and that's different, I'm just talking about consensual sex) and if it were prohibited between a man and his female slaves then why did the devout Christian bible thumpers a few hundred years ago not know about it? They weren't ignorant folk, they knew and quoted everything the bible said about slaves and not once did they think of marrying their slaves prior to having sex with them. Now the Jew or Christian may say, no it's not like that they really were wives. Okay then if so that means Jacob had 4 wives at the same time AND they were all okay with it. Islam also allows men a maximum of 4 wives if they can afford it and be perfectly just between them all, but the Christians find this outrageous. Yet when it comes to Jacob, the progenitor of all the tribes of Israel, he can have 4 wives and it's okay? They'll say that was then and this is now. Well when did God ever say a change was made? Did God ever say it's one man for one women? Or was it a government and pop culture? Christians will say how in Genesis God originally made one man

Adam and one woman Eve, therefore 1 for 1. But then again the book of Genesis also says 4 for 1 according to bible verses in Genesis 30. So who knew better, Prophet Jacob or you? Also remember that Cain killed Abel because he wanted to marry the girl Abel was going to marry, so that means there was an extra woman in the 2nd generation of humanity. Meaning ever since the time of Adam and Eve, before they died there was an imbalance to the 1:1 male/female ratio so that it was no longer 1:1. Plus Adam and Eve got married in paradise, so one can't use marital examples of people in paradise when declaring marital rulings for people on earth. Was Adam's extra daughter just supposed to spend life single forever because 1 guy got killed so some woman had to be the odd one left single? Keep in mind prophets are never wrong about religious rulings, such as the number of wives a man can have. Anyways this bit about Jacob having 4 wives doesn't even really count because Genesis 30 says Jacob was given Rebekah's slave to be his wife because she couldn't have kids. Then it says Leah copied her sister and gave Jacob her slave to be his wife because she stopped having kids due to old age. Although then after Jacob's 2 allegedly sterile wives give him slaves to allegedly be his wives it turns out Leah starts having kids again and Rebekah gives birth to kids too. Interestingly both of these women giving birth to multiple kids after giving their slaves to be wives never make a big deal of this as though they were miraculous births. Sarah is recorded as making a big deal when she gave birth but Rebekah and Leah don't? Maybe that's because they never had an issue with childbirth and thus never had a reason to make their slaves co-wives and they were just slaves who had sex with their husband. The reason this is obvious is because in Genesis 30 both Leah and Rebekah name the children who their slaves give birth to. Biblically Hagar was Sarah's slave and Abraham's wife simultaneously, yet Sarah was not allowed to name the child Hagar gave birth to. Yet dozens of chapters later Leah and Rebekah get to name the children of their slaves/co-wives? Also from the biblical text one gets the impression that Rebekah and Leah considered the sons of their slaves to be literally their own sons. Now this could only theoretically be justified if they were slaves only and not wives. Because if you recall Sarah did not consider Ishmael her son in any way and if she did then she wouldn't have been surprised to hear she would have a son because she would have already considered herself as having given Abraham a son via her slave's son. Therefore the most reasonable thing we can conclude is that Jacob had sex with his slaves and they were not his wives and despite this those sons were legitimate in every way. On the other hand if a man having sex with his slave means those kids aren't legitimate we have to say there are only 8 tribes of Israel and that Jacob only had 8 sons. So I guess somebody better tell God there are only 8 tribes of Israel and that he miscounted and that Moses was only supposed to take out 8 tribes away from Egypt and not 12 and that when he struck the rock causing water to gush forth only 8 streams were supposed to come out and not 12. Whoopsie! Also, the bible has to get changed in many places to say there are only 8 tribes instead of 12 and many prophets who are considered Israeli prophets can no longer be considered Israeli, because of their tribes coming from the 33% of Jacob's sons who were born via sex with slave girls instead of his wives. Also even if one believes the modern translations which depict the slave girls as Jacob's wives then the bible also says Hagar was a wife, yet Christians and Jews maintain her son isn't legit because of slave status. Thus it's a bigoted double standard, where slave-wife kids count if they're Israeli but not if they aren't. Especially concerning the tribe of Dan, many illustrious biblical characters are members of the tribe of Dan, including many Judges of Israel. The famous Samson is from the tribe of Dan and the interbreeding is so extensive that Jesus himself probably had a little bit of Dan in him, or if not Dan then definitely some Gad, Asher or Naphtali. So if slave kids don't count in the covenant then many biblical prophets get excommunicated as a result. There is one little loophole that could fix all these issues up. Jews and Christians could just admit that Ishmael is a valid legitimate son and God made a covenant with him too, whether his mother was married to Abraham or not, regardless of what Sarah may or may not have said. Thus the only reason a Christian or Jew can give to think that Ishmael was not part of the covenant is because of their own personal prejudice, racism or their doctrine because the bible destroys that favoritistic Jewish and Christian belief. In context the bible supports the legitimacy of Ishmael and a covenant being made with him, out of context and with extra textual insertions it doesn't, but the main issue is just Jewish and Christian personal opinions based upon ancient racist traditions. Theologically racism has shaped Jewish and Christian doctrines. Their anti-Ishmaeli beliefs have no support from biblical context. The reason Abraham's son Ishmael is such a big deal is because Muhammad is a direct descendant of Ishmael and Abraham. A Jew or Christian who hated Muhammad would be motivated to cover up these facts and distort scripture in order to remove Ishmael as to diminish the closeness Muhammad has to Abraham. I suspect this has been done because other places of the bible explicitly state the covenant with Abraham and the descendants of Abraham does not apply to Ishmael despite the verse of the covenant clearly using all-inclusive language in the bible. A tale about Jacob usurping his older brother's birthright and deceptively getting blessed by their dying father by "*bearing false witness*" is also a likely insertion done by the racist Jews to try to eliminate non-Jew descendants of Ishmael from the covenant. It turns out that many pagans practice tying goat skin strips around their wrists and necks just as the bible said Jacob did to fool his allegedly poor sighted dad Isaac. Coincidentally the pagan tribes throughout the world did/do this considering it a way to be "born again" in order to legally transfer the children to adopted parents and give the children inheritance rights and to ratify a contract or covenant. Some pagans reenacted the birthing process pretending to be goats, involving goat guts and skins, mimicking goat births with the child playing along until the ritual ended and the adopted child is *"born-again"* as the new mothers "kid", since the children of goats are called "kids". Seems a bit too coincidental that the bible says Jacob stole his brother's blessing by utilizing a goat skin costume while pagans also use them in order to transfer inheritance rights. Let's face it, Judaism is another form of Racism. So if a progenitor of the Arabs was also part of the covenant Jews had with God then don't you think racist Jews would change the book of God to kick Arabs out of the picture as they had with so many other things they didn't like? It also seems unlikely a 100% divine scripture would say there is a covenant with all the descendants and then later on say that all doesn't really mean all but only means one of the two, it is a blatant contradiction and God isn't contradicting. The bible itself says in reference to Ishmael *"God heard the child crying"* and *"God was with the child as he grew up"* also when taking into account the fact that God created a well in the middle of the desert so this child and his mother could survive tells us that this Ishmael was indeed very special and had some important role to play for the future of the world if God cared about him so much. God saved Ishmael's life because he wanted him to live and reproduce bearing heirs, he wasn't a mistake, God created him. The name Ishmael itself means "God heard", which was the name given to Ishmael when God told Abraham that he answered his prayer for offspring. Ironically one meaning of the name "Israel" is *struggled with God* which is apt to describe this situation in which the nation of Israel struggled with the fact that Ishmael was part of the covenant and struggled to justify kicking the Arabs out of the picture until they made a story about Israel the prophet stealing a blessing and obtaining the older firstborn son's right. When you think about it the story in the bible of Jacob disguising himself as Esau to steal Isaac's blessing would mean Israel had broken 3 of the 10 commandments the nation of Israel would later receive; by stealing, bearing false witness and coveting the blessing intended for his brother. Plus the story just seems stupid. How can Prophet Isaac mistakenly bless the wrong son and then say, "*Whoops! I used up my blessing abilities on Jacob thinking it was you. Sorry I can't bless you Esau, your brother pulled a fast one on me and now God will never ever bless you."* If Isaac wanted to bless Esau, then he could have done it whenever he wanted, yet the bible story says he needed to be served his favorite dish before he could give his blessing. How else do Christians and Jews justify this stolen blessing? By quoting Genesis 25:29-34 which relates: *"Once when Jacob was cooking some stew, Esau came in from the open country, famished. [30] He said to Jacob, "Quick, let me have some of that red stew! I'm famished!" (That is why he was also called Edom.) [31] **Jacob replied, "First sell me your birthright." [32] "Look, I am about to die," Esau said.** "What good is the birthright to me?"[33] **But Jacob said, "Swear to me first." So he swore an oath to him, selling his birthright to Jacob.** [34] Then Jacob gave Esau some bread and some lentil stew. He ate and drank, and then got up and left. So Esau despised his birthright."*

Today this is called extortion and it is illegal. It was also illegal for believers to do and especially brothers. First of all Jacob was a prophet of God. No prophet of God would treat their brother the way the bible says Jacob treated Esau. If he did God would probably curse him rather than bless him. The bible clearly even says Esau told Jacob that if he didn't feed him he would literally die. Thus Esau was in a compulsive survival situation and any deal he made to survive is not legally binding, and most definitely not valid in the sight of God. Another issue I take with this is that its clearly written by men as evidenced by the "*(That is why he was also called Edom.)*" and "*So Esau despised his birthright.*" bits. God knows that Esau didn't and wouldn't have "despised his birthright". Realistically what would you do in that biblical situation? Your brother has food and if you don't get to eat it then you will die. He refuses to give it to you unless you promise him your entire share in the inheritance of your father. You could either beat up your brother and take his food by force, or you could say whatever he wanted you to say in order to keep on living, or you could just starve to death. Also keep in mind your father and grandfather are prophets of God who taught you to be a good big brother. Of course in such a situation every decent person would do what the bible says Esau did and none would think the deal counted and that God would hate Esau because of making a deal to get food from his brother in order to stay alive. If anything we'd say Jacob/Israel was a very bad guy to do what the bible falsely alleges, especially considering that his father was a prophet and his grandfather was a prophet and his grandfather Abraham even met him and taught him. So the way the bible portrays Jacob here is entirely unrealistic and uncharacteristic. Yet today much of the world believes the prophet Jacob acted this way. Why? Because the Bible, Jews and Christians say so. Whereas to me this seems like exactly the type of nonsense a racist Jew would make up to justify their immoral business ethics by saying a prophet made immoral deals and also in order to get away with excluding Ishmael and the Arabs from the covenant promised to Abraham's descendants. Because this Jacob and Esau incident is what's commonly used to justify the raw deal the bible gives to Ishmael and Jews/Christians will say "*Well Esau was the firstborn son too, and look God didn't give him part of the covenant.*" Yet the bible even says God said about Ishmael, "*I will make him into a great nation*". Whereas when God refers to "nations" he refers to groups of believers who follow a certain prophet and uses the word "people" to describe disbelievers. For example we have the people of Pharaoh vs. the nation of Moses which never held any territory despite being called a nation. Or the nation of Israel, which doesn't mean every ethnic Jew but everyone who followed the religion of Israel. Another very popular error many Jews and

Christians have is that they think all the prophets are Israeli, yet this is another anti-biblical belief. For instance the prophet Job is accepted as a prophet by Jews and Christians alike. But Job was a descendant of Esau and not Jacob/Israel. Meaning that Job was not an Israeli, yet the bible says he was a prophet. So you don't have to be a Jew to be a prophet and you don't have to be a descendant of Jacob to be a prophet either and if we believe the bible saying that all of Esau's birthright was given to Jacob, then I guess prophethood is NOT included in birthrights nor inheritance. God simply makes whoever he wants to be his prophet his prophet, whether people like it or not, regardless of their genealogical history. God is the one who picks his prophets, we don't. Thus in full biblical context when the biblical God promises to make a great nation of the Ishmaelites, this means with prophethood and belief. This promise of prophethood and belief to Ishmael also extends to his descendants. Therefore when Ishmael's descendant Muhammad claims to be a Prophet it warrants us to examine the claim and study it to see if he meets the criteria of a Prophet. Also in the name of fairness if God makes such a promise to 2 brothers, like Ishmael and Isaac, they will naturally wonder who's nation will be better than the other's because of competitive human and brotherly nature. Now God could either make one better and more numerous than the other, or give both nations equal numbers of prophets, books and believers, or God could give the bulk of prophets and books to the second born and give the firstborn son the last prophet and the last book to be sent. So that the firstborn son will get the last prophet who will lead the last nation of believers. The third option seems to be the most just and fair since having the last prophet and last book balances out, so that both brothers will feel equally as great as the other. Lastly the covenant God made with Abraham and his descendants must include Ishmael as well as Isaac or else the bible is false. This is because Genesis 17:7 says God told Abraham, *"I will establish my covenant as an **everlasting covenant between me and you and your descendants after you** for the generations to come, to be your God and the God of your descendants after you."* The covenant is everlasting, meaning will not end or be broken. However in regards to the covenant with Israel the bible says God said in Hosea 6:4-10,

"What can I do with you, Ephraim? What can I do with you, Judah? Your love is like the morning mist, like the

*early dew that disappears.*⁵ <u>*Therefore I cut you in pieces*</u> <u>*with my prophets,*</u> *I killed you with the words of my mouth — then my judgments go forth like the sun.* ⁶ *For I desire mercy, not sacrifice, and acknowledgment of God rather than burnt offerings.* ⁷ *As at Adam,* **<u>they have</u>** **<u>broken the covenant;</u>** *they were unfaithful to me there.* ⁸ *Gilead is a city of evildoers, stained with footprints of blood.* ⁹ *As marauders lie in ambush for a victim, so do bands of priests; they murder on the road to Shechem, carrying out their wicked schemes.* ¹⁰ *I have seen a horrible thing in Israel: There Ephraim is given to prostitution,* <u>*Israel is defiled.*</u>"

These bible verses inform the world that the covenant God had with Israel in the past was broken. Broken means "not everlasting". Thus if the covenant God made with Abraham was only through Isaac and the Israelites alone then God lied when calling it everlasting. However if the covenant God made with Abraham also included Ishmael then the covenant would still be considered everlasting and we would have one less biblical contradiction. So either Genesis 17:7 is false or the covenant is with Ishmael as well. Another important lesson from the covenant being broken with Israel is that this means their so-called "right to possession of the Holy Land" is null and void since they broke the covenant. This is why Orthodox Jews will publicly say they have no right to have a State, Palestine or the holy land the biblical God once promised to Israel because the covenant God had with Israel was broken according to the bible. Also by me claiming the covenant was broken and God rejected the Israelites don't think this is out of context either. The bible actually paints a vivid and ugly picture of how God displayed his disgust with Israel and their rejection in Hosea 1: 2-10,

*"**When the Lord began to speak through Hosea, the Lord said to him, "Go, marry a promiscuous woman and have children with her, for like an adulterous wife this land is guilty of unfaithfulness to the Lord."** ³ So he married Gomer daughter of Diblaim, and she conceived and bore him a son.⁴ Then the Lord said to Hosea, "Call him Jezreel, because I will soon punish the house of Jehu for the massacre at Jezreel, and I will put an end to the kingdom of Israel. ⁵ In that day I will break Israel's bow in the Valley of Jezreel." ⁶ Gomer conceived again and gave birth to a daughter. Then **the Lord said to Hosea, "Call her Lo-Ruhamah (which means "not loved"), for I will no longer show love to Israel, that I should at all forgive them.** ⁷ Yet I will show love to Judah; and I will save them — not by*

bow, sword or battle, or by horses and horsemen, but I, the Lord their God, will save them."

*8 After she had weaned Lo-Ruhamah, **Gomer had another son. 9 Then the Lord said, "Call him Lo-Ammi (which means "not my people"), for you are not my people, and I am not your God.** 10 "Yet the Israelites will be like the sand on the seashore, which cannot be measured or counted. In the place where it was said to them, 'You are not my people,' they will be called 'children of the living God.'*

These bible verses are very very stern, it says God told Hosea who Jews and Christians consider to be a prophet to go marry a promiscuous woman who commits adultery to symbolize the infidelity of Israel and their betrayal of the covenant. Then the biblical God even tells Hosea to give the kids bad names like "not loved" and "not my people" with the reason being that God wants to make it clear to Israel that they are not loved, not God's people and he is no longer their God despite them being called the children of God in the holy land where he declares that they are not his people. While Hosea 13:4-16 reiterates:

*"But I have been the Lord your God ever since you came out of Egypt. **You shall acknowledge no God but me, no Savior except me.** 5 I cared for you in the wilderness,*

in the land of burning heat. ⁶ When I fed them, they were satisfied; when they were satisfied, they became proud; then they forgot me. ⁷ So I will be like a lion to them, like a leopard I will lurk by the path. ⁸ Like a bear robbed of her cubs, <u>I will attack them and rip them open</u>; like a lion I will devour them – a wild animal will tear them apart. ⁹ "**<u>You are destroyed, Israel, because you are against me</u>**, against your helper. ¹⁰ Where is your king, that he may save you? Where are your rulers in all your towns, of whom you said, Give me a king and princes'? ¹¹ So in my anger I gave you a king, and in my wrath I took him away. ¹² The guilt of Ephraim is stored up, his sins are kept on record. ¹³ Pains as of a woman in childbirth come to him, but he is a child without wisdom; when the time arrives, he doesn't have the sense to come out of the womb. ¹⁴ "I will deliver this people from the power of the grave; I will redeem them from death. Where, O death, are your plagues? Where, O grave, is your destruction? "I will have no compassion, ¹⁵even though he thrives among his brothers. An east wind from the Lord will come, blowing in from the desert; his spring will fail and his well dry up. His storehouse will be plundered of all its treasures. ¹⁶ The people of Samaria must bear their guilt because they have rebelled against their God. They will fall by the sword; their little ones will be dashed to the ground, their pregnant women ripped open."

The reason given for God's extreme hatred towards Israel is because they did not acknowledge God as their exclusive deity and their exclusive savior. This puts Christians in the same boat, because they say Jesus is their savior and then some say he's God too while others say God is God but Jesus is their Lord and/or savior. Yet the bible is clear that the only God and the only savior is the very same being who was God since the Jews came out of Egypt and the very same who cared for them in the wilderness and fed them there, with manna and quail. Now Jesus didn't do any of that stuff so he cannot be a savior or God. The bible says God destroys them in brutal fashion, so much so that he will bring them back to life and the grave isn't going to save them from the punishment and death isn't going to save them from punishment either. The bible says God says "*I will have no compassion*" towards Israel and then the Christians say that God is all-loving and loves everybody for all time and Jesus saved everybody who came before him etc., etc., etc. So it makes you wonder what bible are Christians reading? The bible portrays God as one who gets pissed off at people he allegedly made an exclusive everlasting covenant with who he will never have compassion on even after they die and God is going to bring them back from their grave and state of death just to hurt them some more. But that's not all there is to the story. Ezekial, whom Jews and Christians believe is a prophet of God, also bore a severe load due to God's hatred of Israel as the bible says in Ezekial 3:22-27,

"The hand of the Lord was on me there, and he said to me, "Get up and go out to the plain, and there I will speak to you." 23 So I got up and went out to the plain. And the glory of the Lord was standing there, like the glory I had seen by the Kebar River, and I fell facedown.

24 Then the Spirit came into me and raised me to my feet. He spoke to me and said: "Go, shut yourself inside your house. 25 And you, son of man, they will tie with ropes; you will be bound so that you cannot go out among the people. 26 I will make your tongue stick to the roof of your mouth so that you will be silent and unable to rebuke them, for they are a rebellious people. 27 But when I speak to you, I will open your mouth and you shall say to them, 'This is what the Sovereign Lord says.' Whoever will listen let them listen, and whoever will refuse let them refuse; for they are a rebellious people."

Although the biblical God didn't just make Ezekial, a biblical prophet, mute and put him under house arrest. In the next book Ezekial 4:1-14 continues with the biblical God's instructions to a biblical prophet of Israel,

"Now, son of man, take a block of clay, put it in front of you and draw the city of Jerusalem on it. ² *Then lay siege to it: Erect siege works against it, build a ramp up to it, set up camps against it and put battering rams around it.* ³ *Then take an iron pan, place it as an iron wall between you and the city and turn your face toward it. It will be under siege, and you shall besiege it. This will be a sign to the people of Israel.*⁴ *"Then __lie on your left side__ and __put the sin of the people of Israel upon yourself. You are to bear their sin for the number of days you lie on your side.__* ⁵ *I have assigned you the same number of days as the years of their sin. So __for 390 days__ you will bear the sin of the people of Israel.*⁶ *"__After you have finished this, lie down again, this time on your right side, and bear the sin of the people of Judah. I have assigned you 40 days, a day for each year.__* ⁷ *Turn your face toward the siege of Jerusalem and with bared arm prophesy against her.* ⁸ *__I will tie you up with ropes so that you cannot turn from one side to the other until you have finished the days__ of your siege.* ⁹ *"Take wheat and barley, beans and lentils, millet and spelt; put them in a storage jar and use them to __make bread for yourself. You are to eat it during the 390 days you lie on your side.__*

¹⁰ Weigh out twenty shekels of food to eat each day and eat it at set times. ¹¹ Also measure out a sixth of a hin of water and drink it at set times. ¹² Eat the food as you would a loaf of barley bread; **bake it in the sight of the people, using human excrement for fuel.**" *¹³ The Lord said, "In this way the people of Israel will eat defiled food among the nations where I will drive them." ¹⁴ Then I said, "Not so, Sovereign Lord! I have never defiled myself. From my youth until now I have never eaten anything found dead or torn by wild animals. No impure meat has ever entered my mouth."¹⁵* **"Very well," he said, "I will let you bake your bread over cow dung instead of human excrement.""**

So biblically speaking God was so mad at Israel that he made their prophet lie on his left side for 390 days followed by 40 days of lieing on his right side, during which he was supposed to eat bread baked with human excrement (aka poop). Although merciful as God is, after negotiating he allowed the biblical Israeli prophet to use cow poop as a substitute for human poop because the Israeli prophet was a innocent good guy in God's view. This bible section is often misunderstood and taken out of context by people saying God made a prophet eat human poop. It wasn't actually human poop, it was cow poop and poop was only used as the cooking source instead of oil, but most importantly this was the biblical God and a biblical Israeli prophet; which are two important details to remember. Now just because the bible says this biblical prophet set the world record for lieing, on one's side, does not mean he was a liar or that the bible contains lies. The bit that makes me doubt the authenticity of this text is that it says Ezekial can bear the sins of Israel and Judah simply by lieing, on his side, for a certain number of days. However the thing about lieing on one's side for hundreds of days is that it is impossible to do without getting deadly bed sores and having one's organs get stuck together. This is why God makes us turn over when we sleep for extended periods, because we would get sores and die if we weren't turned over when sleeping for extremely long periods. Now someone who is familiar with the Quran may wonder what about the people of the Cave whom Allah says slept for hundreds of years? Well the Quran says Allah turned them over while they slept, and it said this thousands of years ago before people even knew humans would die if they didn't turn over when they slept or laid on their sides for long periods of time. Scientifically Ezekiel would've died had he laid on his side for 390 days or 40 days, he had to have turned over but the bible says he didn't and wasn't allowed to. Perhaps the authors didn't know what would happen if someone actually did this when they wrote it, and it can't be called a miracle because no Jew or Christian ever claimed such a thing before, if they do it now it would just be a excuse they made up all by themselves to justify their personal beliefs in the bible being 100% true. Anyways this concept of lieing sins away is unjust and impossible according to Islam but it also contradicts Christianity which teaches Jesus bore all sins via death on a cross, or stake, or whatever they are guessing nowadays. The bible says Ezekial bore a total of 430 years worth of sins, so that means Jesus couldn't have since they were already taken care of by Ezekial according to the bible. So is Ezekial the savior of centuries worth of Israelis? No, he's just some guy the bible says had to lie on his sides for 430 consecutive days and eat bread he cooked with cow poop, oh and God made this biblical prophet's tongue get stuck to the top of his throat except when he was inspired to speak, which I actually don't find any problem with. If only Christians and Jews could have such a policy where they only say what the bible says and don't add any extra stuff from other people. Another reason I don't believe Ezekiel bore 430 years worth of sins for Israel is because I've tried to transfer money from America to other countries and it almost can't be done. That's with money, consensually being digitally sent while paying people to do so. If that is so hard to do then there's no way sins can be transferred from Adam to us, or from us to Jesus , nor from Israel to Ezekial when that's unjust and nonconsensual. There would be too much paperwork and regulations. It can't be done. As regards Ezekial why does the bible say he was put through such a humiliating disgusting ordeal? Because God was mad at Israel for breaking the covenant. The bible says God was mad at them for hundreds of years. Yet then people say God made Israelis his chosen people for all time and has always loved them ever since Isaac was born. Now regardless of what else the bible says it is crystal clear that after Israel had a covenant, that covenant was broken beyond repair. Perhaps God could've made a new covenant but the covenant with the Israelites was not everlasting. So either God also included Ishmael in the covenant he made with Abraham or the Israelites made God break his promise to his friend Abraham. We know God is a great enemy but he is also a great friend who would never break a promise he made to Abraham and his descendants or a everlasting covenant.

Unfortunately pro-Israeli people quoting God's biblical favor of Israel to justify Zionism never get past the first few chapters or bother to take the bible in context, otherwise they'd know God's covenant was made with Ishmael too and Israelis broke the covenant a long time ago. For those who disagree ask them what if anything the Jewish people could do to break the Covenant? Most on this side of the argument will stubbornly insist that the text is clear when everlasting means everlasting, it means nothing Jews can do no matter if its blasphemy, genocide, even killing prophets of God and corrupting religion cannot disqualify Jews from this everlasting blessing of God. So they say God made a deal thousands of years ago and its impossible no matter how evil or bad Jews get they will always be better blessed than non-Jews all because of one man Abraham being such a good guy he basically did more for Jews than Christians claim Jesus did for Christians. Non-religious Jews who follow this racism disguised as religion will say Jews can do no wrong in God's sight because God loved Abraham so much they have a free pass to basically do anything they want. This attitude is evident in their practices in the Israeli Zionist state which has perfected criminal state sponsored oppression on every level but is protected from reprisal by this myth of shared tolerance among Abrahamic faiths. Yet this is not my book about "The History of the Zionist State", it is about the anti-interfaith Abrahamic faith.

It is crucial to keep perspective in mind. The only real reason we care about this everlasting covenant is because Abraham was such a great prophet. Otherwise instead of saying Abrahamic faiths we could say Noahide faiths or Adamic faiths to include everybody under one unified biological religious umbrella. The most important thing for Jews regarding Abraham is what God promised his descendants and many ignore the religion of the man himself. As you have seen for yourself the Jewish bible has very few religious teachings regarding the faith of Abraham. Whereas common sense dictates if you are not following the religion of Abraham to begin with then it doesn't matter even if you are genealogically related to Abraham because God cares about your religion more than your racial background. Surely God would not make religious guidance and blessings a genetic inheritance that equates to a divine mandate over earthly territory regardless of the religious character of the people in question. Also even if we say there is a permanent Jewish right to certain parts of land on earth, what about the rest of the planet? Does God say only a tiny part of earth is supposed to be inhabited by believers and ruled by prophetic law? Or is all of the world supposed to be ruled by God's laws? In summary Jews due to their scarce and racist data about Abraham have decisively failed the test of claiming adherence to the singular Abrahamic faith. Maybe they can claim to be following Moses' faith or some other prophet but they don't have enough information about Abraham to be following his religion. Also if as Jews claim that God's covenant with Abraham only applies to Israelis via the lineage of Isaac then clearly they disbelieve in the interfaith ideals of tolerance and cooperation and peace. So why do Jews participate in interfaith Abrahamic faith conferences if they believe they are the exclusively Abrahamic faithful and non-Israelis have nothing to do with Abraham's God even if they are Abraham's firstborn son Ishmael? Jews honestly believe they are closer to Abraham than his own son Ishmael is. Whereas if Ishmael isn't even a member of the

Abrahamic faith or covenant when he is the son of the prophet then how can three various categories of religions thousands of years later with hundreds of different denominations among them ever be considered as having equal standing in their claims to follow Abraham's religion? Thus it is very confusing as to how Jews who have such a arrogant attitude of exclusive divine favor due to their race can partake in interfaith religious functions in the name of Abrahamic commonality. Unless all of it is a deceptive theatrical ruse done for the greater Jewish political good as a war tactic to call for peace which results in a land grab benefitting them exclusively in opposition to all the rest, who as they say are not the special chosen people of Abraham. When outnumbered by such an extent as the Jewish population is then it makes sense to publicly lie about being tolerant of other "Abrahamic faiths" in order to prevent backlash that could turn catastrophically violent (as has happened in the past) or have severely negative political consequences. Yet this is two-faced hypocrisy which God will never bless. Instead this misrepresentation of adherence to Abraham's faith is likely to be divinely punished sooner or later, in this life and the next.

Lastly the Jewish bible says Abraham got remarried after Sarah died to a woman named Keturah and had six more additional kids as well as other kids born from concubines. Which admittedly if true causes another issue in that are all these extra kids included or excluded from the "everlasting Covenant" and the political promise of land which is attached to such a covenant. Yet when you contemplate this question of the many other kids of Abraham remember to answer the yes or no with a thorough explanation of why, if you can. I will abstain from delving into that question and limit myself to discussing Ismael and Isaac because both were textually blessed with miracles and scripturally blessed according to what was written. However it could be that the phrase "descendants" is mistranslated or miswritten or misunderstood or that "everlasting covenant" is mistranslated, miswritten or misunderstood. Or perhaps there was no such everlasting covenant as we imagine it to be that comes with holy land grants giving a permanent casus belli to wage war against any illegitimate occupiers. This book however is not about the promises God made to Abraham or who is intended to be included in those promises. It is about the faith of Abraham the man himself and so far based on just the Jewish claim we have hardly anything to identify this unique prestigious prophetic religion. Now let us examine what Abrahamic data Christians have to present from their Greek New Testament, Greek being a language neither Abraham nor John nor Jesus understood.

Abrahamic data from the Christian Greek New Testament

Matthew 3:1-10

Ἐν δὲ ταῖς ἡμέραις ἐκείναις παραγίνεται Ἰωάννης ὁ βαπτιστὴς κηρύσσων ἐν τῇ ἐρήμῳ τῆς Ἰουδαίας καὶ λέγων ·Μετανοεῖτε, ἤγγικεν γὰρ ἡ βασιλεία τῶν οὐρανῶν. οὗτος γάρ ἐστιν ὁ ῥηθεὶς διὰ Ἡσαΐου τοῦ προφήτου λέγοντος ·Φωνὴ βοῶντος ἐν τῇ ἐρήμῳ · Ἑτοιμάσατε τὴν ὁδὸν κυρίου, εὐθείας ποιεῖτε τὰς τρίβους αὐτοῦ. αὐτὸς δὲ ὁ Ἰωάννης εἶχεν τὸ ἔνδυμα αὐτοῦ ἀπὸ τριχῶν καμήλου καὶ ζώνην δερματίνην περὶ τὴν ὀσφὺν αὐτοῦ, ἡ δὲ τροφὴ ἦν αὐτοῦ ʾ ἀκρίδες καὶ μέλι ἄγριον. τότε ἐξεπορεύετο πρὸς αὐτὸν Ἰεροσόλυμα καὶ πᾶσα ἡ Ἰουδαία καὶ πᾶσα ἡ περίχωρος τοῦ Ἰορδάνου, καὶ ἐβαπτίζοντο ἐν τῷ Ἰορδάνῃ ποταμῷ ὑπ᾽ αὐτοῦ ἐξομολογούμενοι τὰς ἁμαρτίας αὐτῶν. Ἰδὼν δὲ πολλοὺς τῶν Φαρισαίων καὶ Σαδδουκαίων ἐρχομένους ἐπὶ τὸ βάπτισμα αὐτοῦ εἶπεν αὐτοῖς ·Γεννήματα ἐχιδνῶν, τίς ὑπέδειξεν ὑμῖν φυγεῖν ἀπὸ τῆς μελλούσης ὀργῆς; ποιήσατε οὖν καρπὸν ἄξιον τῆς μετανοίας καὶ μὴ δόξητε λέγειν ἐν ἑαυτοῖς ·Πατέρα ἔχομεν τὸν Ἀβραάμ, λέγω γὰρ ὑμῖν ὅτι δύναται ὁ θεὸς ἐκ τῶν λίθων τούτων ἐγεῖραι τέκνα τῷ Ἀβραάμ. ἤδη δὲ ἡ ἀξίνη πρὸς τὴν ῥίζαν τῶν δένδρων κεῖται ·πᾶν οὖν δένδρον μὴ ποιοῦν καρπὸν καλὸν ἐκκόπτεται καὶ εἰς πῦρ βάλλεται.

1 Now in those days John the Immerser comes, preaching in the wilderness of Judea, 2 and saying, Repent; for the kingdom of the heavens has drawn near. 3 For this one is he who was spoken of by Isaiah the prophet, saying, 'A voice is crying in the wilderness, prepare the way of the Lord, make his paths straight.' 4 Now John himself had his outer clothing made from camel's hair and a leather belt around his loin, and his nourishment was locusts and wild honey. 5 Then Jerusalem and everyone in Judea and everyone from the region around the Jordan were traveling out to him. 6 And they were being immersed by him in the Jordan, confessing their sins. 7 But after he saw many of the Pharisees and Sadducees coming upon his immersion, he said to them, Offsprings of vipers, who warned you to flee from the future wrath? 8 Therefore produce fruit worthy of repentance. 9 Do not think to say among yourselves, We have Abraham for our father; for I say to you, that God is able to lift up children out of these stones for Abraham. 10 But even already, the ax is laid to the root of the trees. Therefore every tree which is not producing good fruit is cut down and cast into the fire.

Luke 3:3-9

καὶ ἦλθεν εἰς πᾶσαν περίχωρον τοῦ Ἰορδάνου κηρύσσων βάπτισμα μετανοίας εἰς ἄφεσιν ἁμαρτιῶν, ὡς γέγραπται ἐν βίβλῳ λόγων Ἡσαΐου τοῦ προφήτου · Φωνὴ βοῶντος ἐν τῇ ἐρήμῳ · Ἑτοιμάσατε τὴν ὁδὸν κυρίου, εὐθείας ποιεῖτε τὰς τρίβους αὐτοῦ. πᾶσα φάραγξ πληρωθήσεται καὶ πᾶν ὄρος καὶ βουνὸς ταπεινωθήσεται, καὶ ἔσται τὰ σκολιὰ εἰς εὐθείαν καὶ αἱ τραχεῖαι εἰς ὁδοὺς λείας · καὶ ὄψεται πᾶσα σὰρξ τὸ σωτήριον τοῦ θεοῦ. Ἔλεγεν οὖν τοῖς ἐκπορευομένοις ὄχλοις βαπτισθῆναι ὑπ' αὐτοῦ · Γεννήματα ἐχιδνῶν, τίς ὑπέδειξεν ὑμῖν φυγεῖν ἀπὸ τῆς μελλούσης ὀργῆς; ποιήσατε οὖν καρποὺς ἀξίους τῆς μετανοίας · καὶ μὴ ἄρξησθε λέγειν ἐν ἑαυτοῖς · Πατέρα ἔχομεν τὸν Ἀβραάμ, λέγω γὰρ ὑμῖν ὅτι δύναται ὁ θεὸς ἐκ τῶν λίθων τούτων ἐγεῖραι τέκνα τῷ Ἀβραάμ. ἤδη δὲ καὶ ἡ ἀξίνη πρὸς τὴν ῥίζαν τῶν δένδρων κεῖται · πᾶν οὖν δένδρον μὴ ποιοῦν καρπὸν καλὸν ἐκκόπτεται καὶ εἰς πῦρ βάλλεται.

3 And he came into all the region around the Jordan, preaching the immersion of repentance into the forgiveness of sins; 4 as it has been written in the book of the words of Isaiah the prophet, saying, 'The voice of one crying in the wilderness, Prepare the way of the Lord. Make his paths straight. 5 Every valley will be filled and every mountain and hill will be humbled, and the crooked into straight and the rough ways into smooth. 6 And all flesh will be seeing the salvation of God.' 7 Therefore, he was saying to the crowds who travel out to be immersed by him, Offsprings of vipers! Who warned you to flee from the future wrath? 8 Therefore produce fruits worthy of repentance and do not begin to say among yourselves, We have Abraham as our father; for I say to you, that God is able to lift up children to Abraham from these stones. 9 Now the ax is also already reserved toward the root of the trees. Therefore, every tree which is not producing good fruit is cut down and cast into the fire.

Luke 16:19-31

Ἄνθρωπος δέ τις ἦν πλούσιος, καὶ ἐνεδιδύσκετο πορφύραν καὶ βύσσον εὐφραινόμενος καθ' ἡμέραν λαμπρῶς. πτωχὸς δέ τις ὀνόματι Λάζαρος ἐβέβλητο πρὸς τὸν πυλῶνα αὐτοῦ εἱλκωμένος καὶ ἐπιθυμῶν χορτασθῆναι ἀπὸ τῶν πιπτόντων ἀπὸ τῆς τραπέζης τοῦ πλουσίου · ἀλλὰ καὶ οἱ κύνες ἐρχόμενοι ἐπέλειχον τὰ ἕλκη αὐτοῦ. ἐγένετο δὲ ἀποθανεῖν τὸν πτωχὸν καὶ ἀπενεχθῆναι αὐτὸν ὑπὸ τῶν ἀγγέλων εἰς τὸν κόλπον Ἀβραάμ · ἀπέθανεν δὲ καὶ ὁ πλούσιος καὶ ἐτάφη. καὶ ἐν τῷ ᾅδῃ ἐπάρας τοὺς ὀφθαλμοὺς αὐτοῦ, ὑπάρχων ἐν βασάνοις, ὁρᾷ Ἀβραὰμ ἀπὸ μακρόθεν καὶ Λάζαρον ἐν τοῖς κόλποις αὐτοῦ. καὶ αὐτὸς φωνήσας εἶπεν · Πάτερ Ἀβραάμ, ἐλέησόν με καὶ πέμψον Λάζαρον ἵνα βάψῃ τὸ ἄκρον τοῦ δακτύλου αὐτοῦ ὕδατος καὶ καταψύξῃ τὴν γλῶσσάν μου, ὅτι ὀδυνῶμαι ἐν τῇ φλογὶ ταύτῃ. εἶπεν δὲ

Ἀβραάμ · Τέκνον, μνήσθητι ὅτι ἀπέλαβες τὰ ἀγαθά σου ἐν τῇ ζωῇ σου, καὶ Λάζαρος ὁμοίως τὰ κακά · νῦν δὲ ὧδε παρακαλεῖται σὺ δὲ ὀδυνᾶσαι. καὶ ἐν πᾶσι τούτοις μεταξὺ ἡμῶν καὶ ὑμῶν χάσμα μέγα ἐστήρικται, ὅπως οἱ θέλοντες διαβῆναι ἔνθεν πρὸς ὑμᾶς μὴ δύνωνται, μηδὲ ἐκεῖθεν πρὸς ἡμᾶς διαπερῶσιν. εἶπεν δὲ · Ἐρωτῶ σε οὖν, πάτερ, ἵνα πέμψῃς αὐτὸν εἰς τὸν οἶκον τοῦ πατρός μου, ἔχω γὰρ πέντε ἀδελφούς, ὅπως διαμαρτύρηται αὐτοῖς, ἵνα μὴ καὶ αὐτοὶ ἔλθωσιν εἰς τὸν τόπον τοῦτον τῆς βασάνου. λέγει δὲ Ἀβραάμ · Ἔχουσι Μωϋσέα καὶ τοὺς προφήτας · ἀκουσάτωσαν αὐτῶν. ὁ δὲ εἶπεν · Οὐχί, πάτερ Ἀβραάμ, ἀλλ᾽ ἐάν τις ἀπὸ νεκρῶν πορευθῇ πρὸς αὐτοὺς μετανοήσουσιν. εἶπεν δὲ αὐτῷ · Εἰ Μωϋσέως καὶ τῶν προφητῶν οὐκ ἀκούουσιν, οὐδ᾽ ἐάν τις ἐκ νεκρῶν ἀναστῇ πεισθήσονται.

19 Now there was a certain rich man and he was clothing himself in purple and fine-linen, having been radiantly joyous daily. 20 Now there was a certain poor man, Lazarus by name, who had been put before his gate, having been full of sores, 21 and desiring to be fully-fed from the falling crumbs of the rich man's table. But even the dogs, coming to him, were licking his sores. 22 Now it happened for the poor man to die and to be carried away by the messengers into Abraham's bosom, and the rich man also died and was buried. 23 And he lifted up his eyes in Hades, being in torments, and he sees Abraham from afar, and Lazarus at his bosoms. 24 And having shouted, he said, Father Abraham, show-mercy to me, and send Lazarus in order that he may dip the tip of his finger in water and may cool my tongue, because I am in anguish in this flame. 25 But Abraham said, Child, remember that you received your good things in your life and Lazarus likewise evil things, but now he is comforted here and you are in anguish. 26 And over all these things, a great chasm has been established between us and you, that those who wish to cross over from here to you may not be able, nor may they ferry over from there to us. 27 But he said, Therefore father, I am requesting him in order that you should send him to my father's house; 28 for I have five brethren; that he may thoroughly testify to them, in order that they may not even come into this place of torment. 29 But Abraham says to him, They have Moses and the prophets. Let them hear them. 30 But he said, No, father Abraham, but if someone travels to them from the dead, they will be repenting. 31 But he said to him, If they do not hear Moses and the prophets, neither will they be persuaded, if someone rises up from the dead.

John 8:38-59

ἃ ἐγὼ ˋ ἑώρακα παρὰ τῷ πατρὶ λαλῶ · καὶ ὑμεῖς οὖν ἃ ἠκούσατε ˋ παρὰ τοῦ πατρὸς ˋ ποιεῖτε.

Ἀπεκρίθησαν καὶ εἶπαν αὐτῷ · Ὁ πατὴρ ἡμῶν
Ἀβραάμ ἐστιν. λέγει αὐτοῖς ὁ Ἰησοῦς · Εἰ τέκνα τοῦ
Ἀβραάμ ἐστε, τὰ ἔργα τοῦ Ἀβραὰμ ἐποιεῖτε · νῦν δὲ
ζητεῖτέ με ἀποκτεῖναι, ἄνθρωπον ὃς τὴν ἀλήθειαν
ὑμῖν λελάληκα ἣν ἤκουσα παρὰ τοῦ θεοῦ · τοῦτο
Ἀβραὰμ οὐκ ἐποίησεν. ὑμεῖς ποιεῖτε τὰ ἔργα τοῦ
πατρὸς ὑμῶν. εἶπαν αὐτῷ · Ἡμεῖς ἐκ πορνείας οὐ
γεγεννήμεθα ` · ἕνα πατέρα ἔχομεν τὸν θεόν. εἶπεν
αὐτοῖς ὁ Ἰησοῦς · Εἰ ὁ θεὸς πατὴρ ὑμῶν ἦν ἠγαπᾶτε
ἂν ἐμέ, ἐγὼ γὰρ ἐκ τοῦ θεοῦ ἐξῆλθον καὶ ἥκω · οὐδὲ
γὰρ ἀπ᾽ ἐμαυτοῦ ἐλήλυθα, ἀλλ᾽ ἐκεῖνός με
ἀπέστειλεν. διὰ τί τὴν λαλιὰν τὴν ἐμὴν οὐ γινώσκετε;
ὅτι οὐ δύνασθε ἀκούειν τὸν λόγον τὸν ἐμόν. ὑμεῖς ἐκ
τοῦ πατρὸς τοῦ διαβόλου ἐστὲ καὶ τὰς ἐπιθυμίας τοῦ
πατρὸς ὑμῶν θέλετε ποιεῖν. ἐκεῖνος ἀνθρωποκτόνος
ἦν ἀπ᾽ ἀρχῆς, καὶ ἐν τῇ ἀληθείᾳ οὐκ ἔστηκεν, ὅτι οὐκ
ἔστιν ἀλήθεια ἐν αὐτῷ. ὅταν λαλῇ τὸ ψεῦδος, ἐκ τῶν
ἰδίων λαλεῖ, ὅτι ψεύστης ἐστὶν καὶ ὁ πατὴρ αὐτοῦ.
ἐγὼ δὲ ὅτι τὴν ἀλήθειαν λέγω, οὐ πιστεύετέ μοι. τίς
ἐξ ὑμῶν ἐλέγχει με περὶ ἁμαρτίας; εἰ ἀλήθειαν λέγω,
διὰ τί ὑμεῖς οὐ πιστεύετέ μοι; ὁ ὢν ἐκ τοῦ θεοῦ τὰ
ῥήματα τοῦ θεοῦ ἀκούει · διὰ τοῦτο ὑμεῖς οὐκ
ἀκούετε ὅτι ἐκ τοῦ θεοῦ οὐκ ἐστέ. Ἀπεκρίθησαν οἱ
Ἰουδαῖοι καὶ εἶπαν αὐτῷ · Οὐ καλῶς λέγομεν ἡμεῖς
ὅτι Σαμαρίτης εἶ σὺ καὶ δαιμόνιον ἔχεις; ἀπεκρίθη
Ἰησοῦς · Ἐγὼ δαιμόνιον οὐκ ἔχω, ἀλλὰ τιμῶ τὸν

πατέρα μου, καὶ ὑμεῖς ἀτιμάζετέ με. ἐγὼ δὲ οὐ ζητῶ
τὴν δόξαν μου · ἔστιν ὁ ζητῶν καὶ κρίνων. ἀμὴν
ἀμὴν λέγω ὑμῖν, ἐάν τις τὸν ἐμὸν λόγον ﹅ τηρήσῃ,
θάνατον οὐ μὴ θεωρήσῃ εἰς τὸν αἰῶνα. εἶπον αὐτῷ οἱ
Ἰουδαῖοι · Νῦν ἐγνώκαμεν ὅτι δαιμόνιον ἔχεις.
Ἀβραὰμ ἀπέθανεν καὶ οἱ προφῆται, καὶ σὺ λέγεις ·
Ἐάν τις τὸν λόγον μου τηρήσῃ, οὐ μὴ γεύσηται
θανάτου εἰς τὸν αἰῶνα · μὴ σὺ μείζων εἶ τοῦ πατρὸς
ἡμῶν Ἀβραάμ, ὅστις ἀπέθανεν; καὶ οἱ προφῆται
ἀπέθανον · τίνα σεαυτὸν ποιεῖς; ἀπεκρίθη Ἰησοῦς ·
Ἐὰν ἐγὼ δοξάσω ἐμαυτόν, ἡ δόξα μου οὐδέν ἐστιν ·
ἔστιν ὁ πατήρ μου ὁ δοξάζων με, ὃν ὑμεῖς λέγετε ὅτι
θεὸς ἡμῶν ἐστιν, καὶ οὐκ ἐγνώκατε αὐτόν, ἐγὼ δὲ
οἶδα αὐτόν · κἂν εἴπω ὅτι οὐκ οἶδα αὐτόν, ἔσομαι
ὅμοιος ὑμῖν ψεύστης · ἀλλὰ οἶδα αὐτὸν καὶ τὸν
λόγον αὐτοῦ τηρῶ.Ἀβραὰμ ὁ πατὴρ ὑμῶν
ἠγαλλιάσατο ἵνα ἴδῃ τὴν ἡμέραν τὴν ἐμήν, καὶ εἶδεν
καὶ ἐχάρη. εἶπον οὖν οἱ Ἰουδαῖοι πρὸς αὐτόν ·
Πεντήκοντα ἔτη οὔπω ἔχεις καὶ Ἀβραὰμ ἑώρακας;
εἶπεν αὐτοῖς Ἰησοῦς · Ἀμὴν ἀμὴν λέγω ὑμῖν, πρὶν
Ἀβραὰμ γενέσθαι ἐγὼ εἰμί. ἦραν οὖν λίθους ἵνα
βάλωσιν ἐπ᾽ αὐτόν · Ἰησοῦς δὲ ἐκρύβη καὶ ἐξῆλθεν
ἐκ τοῦ ἱεροῦ.

39 *They answered and said to him, Our father is*
Abraham. **_Jesus says to them, If you were Abraham's_**
children, were you ever practicing the works of

Abraham? 40 *But now you are seeking to kill me, <u>a man who has spoken the truth to you</u>, which I heard from God.* **<u>Abraham did not ever do this</u>***. 41 You are practicing the works of your father. Therefore they said to him, We have not been born from fornication; we have one Father-- God. 42 Therefore Jesus said to them, If God was your Father, you would love me; for I came out and am coming from God; for neither have I come from myself, but from that one who sent me. 43 Why do you not know my speech? Is it because you are not able to hear my word? 44* **<u>You are from your father, the devil, and you are willing to do the lusts of your father.</u>** *That one was a murderer from the beginning and is not standing in the truth, because there is no truth in him. Whenever he speaks a lie, he speaks from his own things, because he is a liar and the father of it. 45 But because I speak the truth, you do not believe me. 46 Which out of you convicts me concerning sin? But if I speak the truth, why are you not believing in me? 47 He who is from God hears the declarations of God, but because of this, you do not hear them, because you are not from God. 48 Therefore the Jews answered and said to him, Do we not say well that you are a Samaritan and you have a demon? 49 Jesus answered, I do not have a demon, but I am honoring my Father and you are dishonoring me. 50 But I am not seeking my own glory. There is one who is seeking and is judging. 51 Assuredly, assuredly, I am* *saying to you, If anyone keeps my word, he should never view his death forever. 52 Therefore the Jews said to him, Now we have known that you have a demon. Abraham died and the prophets, and you say, If anyone keeps my word, he should never taste of death forever. 53 You are not greater than our father Abraham, who died, are you? And the prophets died; whom are you making* yourself out to be? 54 Jesus answered, If I am glorifying myself, my glory is nothing; it is my Father who is glorifying me; of whom you say, that he is our God. 55 And you have not known him, but I know him, and if I say, I do not know him, I will be similar to you, a liar, but I know him and I am keeping his word. 56 Your father Abraham was glad that he might see my day, and he saw it and rejoiced. 57 Therefore the Jews said to him, You do not yet have fifty years in and you have seen Abraham? 58 Jesus said to them, Assuredly, assuredly, I am saying to you, Before Abraham is to be born, I am.*

As a sidenote I will explain two misunderstood points about this Christian passage attributed to Jesus, though Christian Biblical Scholars say it is misattributed, that say Jews are not the children of Abraham nor the children of God but are children of the devil. Before I do though I will say that clearly textual Jesus was opposed to the idea of Jews following the Abrahamic faith. So it is mindboggling how Christians today worshipping

Jesus can claim Jews are upon the Abrahamic faith just like them. The misunderstood bits are the term "Father" used by Jesus and the last statement of "before Abraham is to be born, I am." Everywhere the bible mentions God having a son it is in the figurative sense with this understanding of a *"son of God"* being a righteous person blessed or befriended by God who doesn't sin. Every time the bible labeled someone as a son of God it has always been understood to mean that the person was very righteous. The Jews in the preceding passage even claimed God was their Father to Jesus himself, using this understanding. Many sons of God are described in the bible elsewhere rendering null the essential creed of most Christian denominations of Jesus being the one and only son of God.

Genesis 6:1-4 *"When human beings began to increase in number on the earth and daughters were born to them, 2 **the sons of God** saw that the daughters of humans were beautiful, and they married any of them they chose.3 Then the Lord said, "My Spirit will not contend with humans forever, for they are mortal; their days will be a hundred and twenty years." 4 The Nephilim were on the earth in those days – and also afterward – when **the sons of God** went to the daughters of humans and had* *children by them. They were the heroes of old, men of renown."*

Exodus 4:22-23 "²² *Then say to Pharaoh, 'This is what* **the Lord says: Israel is my firstborn son**, *and I told you, "Let my son go, so he may worship me." But you refused to let him go; so I will kill your firstborn son.'"*"

According to the book of Exodus it is impossible for Jesus to have been the firstborn son of God, or his only son because Israel was the firstborn son according to the bible. However, this verse is clearly corrupted because the earlier book of Genesis mentions sons of God, so this is obviously a Jewish insertion to make Jews seem special despite the very notion contradicting their earlier Scripture. Also the word "firstborn" denotes that there will be more to come so biblically speaking there can never be an only son unless it is the first which is biblically labeled as Israel. So Jesus is not the first son since Genesis and Exodus have already mentioned numerous sons with Israel being the first. It's also biologically literal since in context it has God allegedly comparing his "firstborn son" with Pharaoh's literal "firstborn son". Or at least that is how Jews and Christians interpret it, but historically Pharaoh didn't have kids and that's why he adopted Moses. Biblical scholars have said the Jews invented this story about God killing the firstborn sons of Egyptians because they wanted to hide the shame of their own firstborn sons being killed by Pharaoh and themselves due to Pharaonic intimidation/orders. Other biblical scholars said the Jews killed their own kids as a sacrifice to God hoping for improved working conditions but that is incorrect as well. Some may have killed their own sons simply to avoid Pharaoh's soldiers killing them but Pharaoh never had kids, so then what does God mean when the bible says he said "son"? But we have more trouble when Jeremiah 31:9 says God said,

*They will come with weeping; they will pray as I bring them back. I will lead them beside streams of water on a level path where they will not stumble, because **I am Israel's father, and Ephraim is my firstborn son.***

So not only does the bible teach that God has many sons, but that biblical God himself says he has many "firstborn sons of God" as well. Yet something must be false because by definition there can only be one "firstborn son" unless a "son " doesn't mean son in the literal sense and "firstborn" doesn't mean "firstborn" but if all this stuff in the bible doesn't actually mean what it says then why would anyone think it means what it says when it says similar stuff about Jesus in a Greek language Jesus and his true disciples never even spoke or wrote in verses which Christian biblical scholars have said are false attributions anyways? Furthermore, on the subject of sonship Psalm 89:24-34,

"*My faithful love will be with him, and through my name his horn will be exalted.* ^{25} *I will set his hand over the sea, his right hand over the rivers.* ^{26} **He will call out to me, 'You are my Father, my God, the Rock my Savior.'** ^{27} *And* **I will appoint him to be my firstborn**, **the most exalted of the kings of the earth.** ^{28} *I will maintain my love to him forever, and* **my covenant with him will never fail.** ^{29} *I will establish his line forever, his throne as long as the heavens endure.* ^{30} **"If his sons forsake my law** *and do not follow my statutes,* ^{31} *if they violate my decrees and fail to keep my commands,* ^{32} **I will punish their sin** *with the rod, their iniquity with flogging;* ^{33} *but I will not take my love from him, nor will I ever betray my faithfulness.* ^{34} **I will not violate my covenant or alter what my lips have uttered**.*"

Here the Psalms contradict Genesis, Exodus and Jeremiah by saying this other person will be appointed as God's firstborn. If Israel is indeed the firstborn then either God is lying in the Psalms or the Psalms are not authentic revelation or he was lying in Exodus and Exodus is not authentic. These verses from the alleged Psalms of David are particularly interesting because it says "He", denoting a human male, will call out *"You are my Father, my God, the Rock my Savior"*. Some Christians may try to say this is all referencing Jesus, but if that's the case then how can Jesus be a savior if he considers God to be his savior? Some Christians will even blasphemously claim Jesus is God! Psalms also says "He" will be appointed to be " *the most exalted of the kings of the earth.*" whereas Israel was never a king. Since the Psalms are said to be revealed to David then it is unlikely David is the "he". If we examine who was " *the most exalted of the kings of the earth.*" we will recognize Solomon, the prophet king son of David, as having the strongest kingdom of all time. Solomon was given authority by God over the wind and was able to use it to make ships in his army travel faster than naturally possible which fulfills the prophesy in verse 23. Solomon is also renowned for his architecture which would make him the most exalted who has been known to man ever since. The army of Solomon included animals big and small, such as lions and elephants, to birds who would spy for him and drop stones on enemies from above. Although one thing Solomon had which none before him had nor any after him will ever have was the special ability given by God to have authority over the Jinn. Solomon was able to command the Jinn to do what he wanted. Some have said his authority over the Jinn means he was satanic, or a magician, but this is a false Jewish slander because Solomon actually outlawed magic throughout his kingdom since it is dangerous and makes its users disbelievers. Angels even descended from Heaven to teach magic to people as a test in response to the allegations that Solomon was a magician. Because since Solomon eradicated magic the people didn't know the difference between magic and a miracle. Once the people saw the angels demonstrate what magic was they knew the difference between miracles done by a prophet like Solomon and the magical spells done by sorcerers. Unfortunately, some didn't heed the warning of the angels that practicing magic is disbelief and will eliminate the chance of paradise for those who practice it and don't repent. Since then magic has continued to be practiced in the world and out of jealousy for his superiority the magicians and Jews have tried to slander Solomon and reduce him to the level of a petty magician, instead of the prophet who was "*the most exalted of the kings of the earth."* In fact, Scripturally Jews wrote that Solomon due to marrying a foreign born non-Israeli Queen of Sheba thereby disbelieved in the faith of Abraham and God so he had his share in the Abrahamic Covenant revoked and the promised land taken away from him. Thus Jews claim they are better than Prophet Solomon. But you don't have to believe my claim the verse in the Hebrew Psalms third or fourth firstborn son of God being about Solomon because 1 Chronicles 22:9-13 says God told David : *"But you will have a son who will be a man of peace and rest, and I will give him rest from all his enemies on every side. **His name will be Solomon**, and I will grant Israel peace and quiet during his reign. 10 He is the one who will build a house for my Name. **He will be my son, and I will be his father**. And I will establish the throne of his kingdom over Israel forever.' 11 "Now, **my son, the Lord be with you**, and may you have success and build the house of the Lord your God, as he said you would. 12 May the Lord give you discretion and understanding when he puts you in command over Israel, so that you may keep the law of the Lord your God. 13 Then you will have success if you are careful to observe the decrees and laws that the Lord gave Moses for Israel. Be strong and courageous. Do not be afraid or discouraged."*

Another reason the Psalms cannot be referring to Jesus' alleged sonship is because it explictly mentions what will happen *"If his sons forsake my law"*, at this time Jesus does not have any sons and Christians claim he never will. Ironically some support that claim by saying Jesus is God and God can't have sons, yet then when you ask them why Jesus is God they say because he is the only son of God with them uttering contradicting blasphemy not realizing these statements contradict the same bible they claim is the word of God, or inspired by God. This is called double think when a person holds 2 contradictory beliefs simultaneously while accepting both of them to be true at the same time. I'm not mentioning this to make fun of or insult anybody, I just don't want people to slander God or Jesus and make themselves disbelievers by uttering such blasphemy or lies while they think they are correct or doing good. If God is God and Jesus is God then how can there only be one God? Jesus cannot possibly be the son of himself and God does not worship anything. And God cannot have multiple sons and multiple firstborn sons if all these verses mean what they've been translated as or if they are authentic to begin with. In actuality Hebrew didn't even exist until long after Solomon so these Psalms are not the actual original Zabur scripture given to Prophet David by God. I just mention this as a sidenote to Christian Greek texts attributing Jesus using the terminology of Father and Son when mentioning Abraham and how the Jews are not sons of Abraham nor is he their Father. Essentially meaning that they are not upon the Abrahamic faith. Whereas the exclusive sonship claim Christians limit to Jesus also contradicts numerous Hebrew bible verses which Christians claim are revelation so they cannot be on solid ground either when they worship Jesus whom Abraham didn't worship.

Regarding the "Before Abraham was born, I am." the "I am" is a sentence fragment and doesn't of itself mean anything, the authenticity of which is also dubious. Nevertheless the true meaning is simple to understand. It means that before Abraham physically existed Jesus existed in the knowledge of God, just as Moses existed in the knowledge of God, as did you and I. Before Abraham was physically alive, we all existed. Biblically Jesus wasn't the only person after Abraham who existed before Abraham. In the Hebrew bible Jerimiah 1:4-5 says Jeremiah wrote about himself saying:

4 The word of the Lord came to me, saying,5 "__Before I formed you in the womb I knew you, before you were born I set you apart__; I appointed you as a prophet to the nations."

So Jeremiah claimed to be in existence before being conceived in the womb of his mother.

Proverbs 8:23-27 say the prophet Solomon wrote:

23 __I was formed long ages ago, at the very beginning, when the world came to be.__ 24 When there were no watery depths, I was given birth, when there were no springs overflowing with water;25 before the mountains were settled in place, before the hills, I was given birth,26 before he made the world or its fields or any of the dust of the earth. 27 __I was there when he set the heavens in place__, when he marked out the horizon on the face of the deep"

Since some Christians use the statement of Jesus found in John saying he existed before Abraham was on earth to mean he is God, then according to the same methodology the humans Jeremiah and Solomon are also God too. So does that mean God has 5 parts or 3 sons or what? Maybe these statements just mean what they say and don't mean what Christians want them to mean. The doctrine of the trinity, or of Jesus being a divinity, can never be accepted by a rational human being if they seriously think about it. Nor can it be accepted by anyone who actually reads the bible in context. Anyone who read the bible verses of Jeremiah and Proverbs and John would see that this alleged statement by Jesus is no different than what other 100% humans have said in the bible. The problem occurs because people don't read the bible, they get told Jesus is God because of X verse and don't realize lots of other humans in the bible said X too. Instead they will memorize the Jesus X verse, base their whole life on their incorrect understanding and expect that X verse is the reason why people believe Jesus is God forgetting that they already believed Jesus was God before they ever heard of the X verse of Jesus. Instead of having reasons to justify their belief, Christians use bible verses as excuses for why they believe something. The more you think about the trinity the less sense it makes and this is why religious Jews, while disqualified from being followers of the Abrahamic faith are correct in their position that Christians are also disqualified to an even greater degree and further from Abrahamic monotheism due to their anthropomorphism and demi-god Jesus triune deity fetish of polytheistic falsehood. So you have

Christians saying Jesus said the Jews are following nothing of Abraham's faith and the Jews saying the Christians are following nothing of Abraham's faith despite sharing belief in the same books that aren't even in the original language of prophets Abraham, Moses, David or Solomon.

Regarding the rest of the Christian material on Abraham it is mostly just references of people being descended from the seed of Abraham. I have not included the writings attributed to Paul the infamous terrorist, as the bible labels as a terrorist in Acts 21:38, who corrupted the teachings of Jesus according to many Christian denominations because Paul's writings and the rest of the New Testament are letters not purported to be Divine or Prophetic speech. It seemed best to only include Greek New Testament Abrahamic passages attributed to John and Jesus. Paul's material is a non-prophetic preacher speaking from his back-pocket freestyling about Abraham who he has no direct testimony concerning. Besides most of what Paul and the other letter writers say about Abraham is just praise without any details on his creed, doctrines or practices. I will however mention one Abrahamic passage from a Greek New Testament letter written by an anonymous unknown source, often misattributed to be Paul, known as Hebrews.

Hebrews 7:1-4

Οὗτος γὰρ ὁ Μελχισέδεκ, βασιλεὺς Σαλήμ, ἱερεὺς τοῦ θεοῦ τοῦ ὑψίστου, ὁ συναντήσας Ἀβραὰμ ὑποστρέφοντι ἀπὸ τῆς κοπῆς τῶν βασιλέων καὶ εὐλογήσας αὐτόν, ᾧ καὶ δεκάτην ἀπὸ πάντων ἐμέρισεν Ἀβραάμ, πρῶτον μὲν ἑρμηνευόμενος βασιλεὺς δικαιοσύνης ἔπειτα δὲ καὶ βασιλεὺς Σαλήμ, ὅ ἐστιν βασιλεὺς εἰρήνης, ἀπάτωρ, ἀμήτωρ, ἀγενεαλόγητος, μήτε ἀρχὴν ἡμερῶν μήτε ζωῆς τέλος ἔχων, ἀφωμοιωμένος δὲ τῷ υἱῷ τοῦ θεοῦ, μένει ἱερεὺς εἰς τὸ διηνεκές. Θεωρεῖτε δὲ πηλίκος οὗτος ᾧ δεκάτην Ἀβραὰμ ἔδωκεν ἐκ τῶν ἀκροθινίων ὁ πατριάρχης.

1 For this Melchizedek, King of Salem, priest of the Highest God, who met with Abraham returning from the butcher of the kings and blessed him, 2 to whom Abraham also divided a tenth away from all things. Being first indeed, by translation, King of righteousness and thereafter also King of Salem, which is King of peace; **3 he had no father, no mother, with no genealogy, having neither beginning of days nor end of life, but having been made similar to the Son of God, remains a continual priest.** *4 Now view how-great this* *man was, to whom even Abraham, the patriarch, gave a tenth out of the spoils.*

This biblical Greek letter adds some quite interesting blasphemous paranormal details to the previously mentioned story regarding Abraham in Genesis, though the author mistakenly called him Abraham while in Genesis' version he was still Abram at the time of the story. According to this biblical passage Melchizedek has a more miraculous genealogy than Jesus, without father or mother and has the immortality of God. This is a completely blasphemous statement to say that a person is immortal "*without beginning of days or end of life*" this is beyond most pagan beliefs even, yet it is in the Greek New Testament Christian bible in that anonymously written book of Hebrews. What's even worse is that some Christians will maintain that God inspired these blasphemous words about the unborn immortal Melchizedek. Fortunately this verse is verifiable. If this biblical verse were true then this Melchizedek who allegedly met Abram/Abraham who gave him 10% of the spoils of war, would still exist today and we should be able to meet him. Melchizedek could come forth and prove his existence and the truth of the bible so all would believe. He wouldn't have to worry about getting assassinated because as the bible says he has no "*end of life*". He cannot be worried about fame because the bible says "*he remains a priest forever*" so it would be his duty to come forth and guide mankind under his ministry. Obviously this hasn't happened nor will it, because this portion of the bible is false information and whoever believes in this verse or it having come from a divine source is in error. Believing in the 3rd verse would constitute blasphemy and again make one a disbeliever liable to eternal punishment in the hellfire. Seriously when people say they believe the bible is the word of God, or inspired by God, it's terrifying to me because they have no idea what that means when they say it and the blasphemous statements that are contained within it. Even according to their own doctrines believing in some biblical verses makes them disbelievers in their own religion. For instance let's say someone still believes in this Melchizedek without a mother or father, in that case they have to disbelieve in Genesis 3:20 "*Adam named his wife **Eve**, because she **would become the mother of all the living**.*" So thus Eve must be Melchizedek's mother but Hebrews says he has no mother, but technically speaking Genesis says of "all the living" which of course doesn't really mean "all the living" such as animals and plants but just means humans. Thus Melchizedek must not be human but since he resembles the "Son of God" then that would mean Jesus is 0% human if we take Christian's mistaken understanding of Jesus being the exclusive son of God disregarding all the other biblical sons, yet Melchizedek was a king of Salem and a priest. Therefore at one time in biblical history there was a non-human king and God has a non-human priest, or it's a human without father or mother and isn't of "the living". So what is it then? A zombie or monster? It's heartbreaking to think about the billions who have fallen into disbelief in this manner not realizing the torment that awaits them. If God doesn't guide us we could be just the same, repeating claims to follow Abraham's faith while oblivious to the mistaken reality of missing the goal through lack of prophetic guidance.

I apologize for not giving adequate attention to these interconnected religious issues and perhaps being too brisk and/or offensive. This is a book about Abraham and the claims of the three major religions to be following Abrahamic faiths. Perhaps I was sidetracked on the Jesus material and wrote things that might have been interpreted as insulting. Yet it would be too dangerous to mention the verses attributed to Jesus about a interfaith Abrahamic claim of the Jews without clarifying the widely misunderstood vocabulary terms used in the passage. So as a religious individual I had a duty to comment but I cannot change the subject of this book to Jesus or Christianity. For those interested in learning more about Prophet Jesus, I refer you to my book "The Collection of Quotes Credited to Prophet Jesus".

Now last but not least we will examine the Islamic/Muslim claim to be following the faith of Abraham based on data from the Arabic Quran attributed to Allah and the Hadith attributed to Prophet Muhammad.

Abrahamic data from the Arabic Quran and Hadith

Quran 6:74-89

۞ وَإِذْ قَالَ إِبْرَٰهِيمُ لِأَبِيهِ ءَازَرَ أَتَتَّخِذُ أَصْنَامًا ءَالِهَةً إِنِّى أَرَىٰكَ وَقَوْمَكَ فِى ضَلَٰلٍ مُّبِينٍ (٧٤) وَكَذَٰلِكَ نُرِى إِبْرَٰهِيمَ مَلَكُوتَ ٱلسَّمَٰوَٰتِ وَٱلْأَرْضِ وَلِيَكُونَ مِنَ ٱلْمُوقِنِينَ (٧٥) فَلَمَّا جَنَّ عَلَيْهِ ٱلَّيْلُ رَءَا كَوْكَبًا قَالَ هَٰذَا رَبِّى فَلَمَّا أَفَلَ قَالَ لَآ أُحِبُّ ٱلْءَافِلِينَ (٧٦) فَلَمَّا رَءَا ٱلْقَمَرَ بَازِغًا قَالَ هَٰذَا رَبِّى فَلَمَّا أَفَلَ قَالَ لَئِن لَّمْ يَهْدِنِى رَبِّى لَأَكُونَنَّ مِنَ ٱلْقَوْمِ ٱلضَّآلِّينَ (٧٧) فَلَمَّا رَءَا ٱلشَّمْسَ بَازِغَةً قَالَ هَٰذَا رَبِّى هَٰذَآ أَكْبَرُ فَلَمَّا أَفَلَتْ قَالَ يَٰقَوْمِ إِنِّى بَرِىٓءٌ مِّمَّا تُشْرِكُونَ (٧٨) إِنِّى وَجَّهْتُ وَجْهِىَ لِلَّذِى فَطَرَ ٱلسَّمَٰوَٰتِ وَٱلْأَرْضَ حَنِيفًا وَمَآ أَنَا۠ مِنَ ٱلْمُشْرِكِينَ (٧٩) وَحَآجَّهُۥ قَوْمُهُۥ قَالَ أَتُحَٰجُّوٓنِّى فِى ٱللَّهِ وَقَدْ هَدَىٰنِ وَلَآ أَخَافُ مَا تُشْرِكُونَ بِهِۦٓ إِلَّآ أَن يَشَآءَ رَبِّى شَيْـًٔا وَسِعَ رَبِّى كُلَّ شَىْءٍ عِلْمًا أَفَلَا تَتَذَكَّرُونَ (٨٠) وَكَيْفَ أَخَافُ مَآ أَشْرَكْتُمْ وَلَا تَخَافُونَ أَنَّكُمْ أَشْرَكْتُم بِٱللَّهِ مَا لَمْ يُنَزِّلْ بِهِۦ عَلَيْكُمْ سُلْطَٰنًا فَأَىُّ ٱلْفَرِيقَيْنِ أَحَقُّ بِٱلْأَمْنِ إِن كُنتُمْ تَعْلَمُونَ (٨١) ٱلَّذِينَ ءَامَنُوا۟ وَلَمْ يَلْبِسُوٓا۟ إِيمَٰنَهُم بِظُلْمٍ أُو۟لَٰٓئِكَ لَهُمُ ٱلْأَمْنُ وَهُم مُّهْتَدُونَ (٨٢) وَتِلْكَ حُجَّتُنَآ ءَاتَيْنَٰهَآ إِبْرَٰهِيمَ عَلَىٰ قَوْمِهِۦ نَرْفَعُ دَرَجَٰتٍ مَّن نَّشَآءُ إِنَّ رَبَّكَ حَكِيمٌ عَلِيمٌ (٨٣) وَوَهَبْنَا لَهُۥٓ إِسْحَٰقَ وَيَعْقُوبَ كُلًّا هَدَيْنَا وَنُوحًا هَدَيْنَا مِن قَبْلُ وَمِن ذُرِّيَّتِهِۦ دَاوُۥدَ وَسُلَيْمَٰنَ وَأَيُّوبَ وَيُوسُفَ وَمُوسَىٰ وَهَٰرُونَ وَكَذَٰلِكَ نَجْزِى ٱلْمُحْسِنِينَ (٨٤) وَزَكَرِيَّا وَيَحْيَىٰ وَعِيسَىٰ وَإِلْيَاسَ كُلٌّ مِّنَ ٱلصَّٰلِحِينَ (٨٥) وَإِسْمَٰعِيلَ وَٱلْيَسَعَ وَيُونُسَ وَلُوطًا وَكُلًّا فَضَّلْنَا عَلَى ٱلْعَٰلَمِينَ (٨٦) وَمِنْ ءَابَآئِهِمْ وَذُرِّيَّٰتِهِمْ وَإِخْوَٰنِهِمْ وَٱجْتَبَيْنَٰهُمْ وَهَدَيْنَٰهُمْ إِلَىٰ صِرَٰطٍ مُّسْتَقِيمٍ (٨٧) ذَٰلِكَ هُدَى ٱللَّهِ يَهْدِى بِهِۦ مَن يَشَآءُ مِنْ عِبَادِهِۦ وَلَوْ أَشْرَكُوا۟ لَحَبِطَ عَنْهُم مَّا كَانُوا۟ يَعْمَلُونَ (٨٨) أُو۟لَٰٓئِكَ ٱلَّذِينَ ءَاتَيْنَٰهُمُ ٱلْكِتَٰبَ وَٱلْحُكْمَ وَٱلنُّبُوَّةَ فَإِن يَكْفُرْ بِهَا هَٰٓؤُلَآءِ فَقَدْ وَكَّلْنَا بِهَا قَوْمًا لَّيْسُوا۟ بِهَا بِكَٰفِرِينَ (٨٩)

And [mention, O Muhammad], when Abraham said to his father Azar, "Do you take idols as deities? Indeed, I see you and your people to be in manifest error." (74) And thus did We show Abraham the realm of the heavens and the earth that he would be among the certain [in faith] (75) So when the night covered him [with darkness], he saw a star. He said, "This is my lord." But when it set, he said, "I like not those that disappear." (76) And when he saw the moon rising, he said, "This is my lord." But when it set, he said, "Unless my Lord guides me, I will surely be among the people gone astray." (77) And when he saw the sun rising, he said, "This is my lord; this is greater." But when it set, he said, "O my people, indeed I am free from what you associate with Allah. (78) Indeed, I have turned my face toward He who created the heavens and the earth, inclining toward truth, and I am not of those who associate others with Allah." (79) And his people argued with him. He said, "Do you argue with me concerning Allah while He has guided me? And I fear not what you associate with Him [and will not be harmed] unless my Lord should will something. My Lord encompasses all things in knowledge; then will you not remember? (80) And how should I fear what you associate while you do not fear that you have associated with Allah that for which He has not sent down to you any authority? So which of the two parties has more right to security, if you should know?

(81) They who believe and do not mix their belief with injustice - those will have security, and they are [rightly] guided. (82) And that was Our [conclusive] argument which We gave Abraham against his people. We raise by degrees whom We will. Indeed, your Lord is Wise and Knowing. (83) And We gave to Abraham, Isaac and Jacob - all [of them] We guided. And Noah, We guided before; and among his descendants, David and Solomon and Job and Joseph and Moses and Aaron. Thus do We reward the doers of good. (84) And Zechariah and John and Jesus and Elias - and all were of the righteous. (85) And Ishmael and Elisha and Jonah and Lot - and all [of them] We preferred over the worlds. (86) And [some] among their fathers and their descendants and their brothers - and We chose them and We guided them to a straight path. (87) That is the guidance of Allah by which He guides whomever He wills of His servants. But if they had associated others with Allah, then worthless for them would be whatever they were doing. (88) Those are the ones to whom We gave the Scripture and authority and prophethood. But if the disbelievers deny it, then We have entrusted it to a people who are not therein disbelievers. (89)

Quran 21:51-75

۞ وَلَقَدْ ءَاتَيْنَآ إِبْرَٰهِيمَ رُشْدَهُۥ مِن قَبْلُ وَكُنَّا بِهِۦ عَٰلِمِينَ (٥١) إِذْ قَالَ لِأَبِيهِ وَقَوْمِهِۦ مَا هَٰذِهِ ٱلتَّمَاثِيلُ ٱلَّتِىٓ أَنتُمْ لَهَا عَٰكِفُونَ (٥٢) قَالُوا۟ وَجَدْنَآ ءَابَآءَنَا لَهَا عَٰبِدِينَ (٥٣) قَالَ لَقَدْ كُنتُمْ أَنتُمْ وَءَابَآؤُكُمْ فِى ضَلَٰلٍ مُّبِينٍ (٥٤) قَالُوٓا۟

أَجِئْتَنَا بِٱلْحَقِّ أَمْ أَنتَ مِنَ ٱللَّـٰعِبِينَ (٥٥) قَالَ بَل رَّبُّكُمْ رَبُّ ٱلسَّمَـٰوَٰتِ وَٱلْأَرْضِ ٱلَّذِى فَطَرَهُنَّ وَأَنَا۠ عَلَىٰ ذَٰلِكُم مِّنَ ٱلشَّـٰهِدِينَ (٥٦) وَتَٱللَّهِ لَأَكِيدَنَّ أَصْنَـٰمَكُم بَعْدَ أَن تُوَلُّواْ مُدْبِرِينَ (٥٧) فَجَعَلَهُمْ جُذَٰذًا إِلَّا كَبِيرًا لَّهُمْ لَعَلَّهُمْ إِلَيْهِ يَرْجِعُونَ (٥٨) قَالُواْ مَن فَعَلَ هَـٰذَا بِـَٔالِهَتِنَا إِنَّهُۥ لَمِنَ ٱلظَّـٰلِمِينَ (٥٩) قَالُواْ سَمِعْنَا فَتًى يَذْكُرُهُمْ يُقَالُ لَهُۥٓ إِبْرَٰهِيمُ (٦٠) قَالُواْ فَأْتُواْ بِهِۦ عَلَىٰٓ أَعْيُنِ ٱلنَّاسِ لَعَلَّهُمْ يَشْهَدُونَ (٦١) قَالُوٓاْ ءَأَنتَ فَعَلْتَ هَـٰذَا بِـَٔالِهَتِنَا يَـٰٓإِبْرَٰهِيمُ (٦٢) قَالَ بَلْ فَعَلَهُۥ كَبِيرُهُمْ هَـٰذَا فَسْـَٔلُوهُمْ إِن كَانُواْ يَنطِقُونَ (٦٣) فَرَجَعُوٓاْ إِلَىٰٓ أَنفُسِهِمْ فَقَالُوٓاْ إِنَّكُمْ أَنتُمُ ٱلظَّـٰلِمُونَ (٦٤) ثُمَّ نُكِسُواْ عَلَىٰ رُءُوسِهِمْ لَقَدْ عَلِمْتَ مَا هَـٰٓؤُلَآءِ يَنطِقُونَ (٦٥) قَالَ أَفَتَعْبُدُونَ مِن دُونِ ٱللَّهِ مَا لَا يَنفَعُكُمْ شَيْـًٔا وَلَا يَضُرُّكُمْ (٦٦) أُفٍّ لَّكُمْ وَلِمَا تَعْبُدُونَ مِن دُونِ ٱللَّهِ أَفَلَا تَعْقِلُونَ (٦٧) قَالُواْ حَرِّقُوهُ وَٱنصُرُوٓاْ ءَالِهَتَكُمْ إِن كُنتُمْ فَـٰعِلِينَ (٦٨) قُلْنَا يَـٰنَارُ كُونِى بَرْدًا وَسَلَـٰمًا عَلَىٰٓ إِبْرَٰهِيمَ (٦٩) وَأَرَادُواْ بِهِۦ كَيْدًا فَجَعَلْنَـٰهُمُ ٱلْأَخْسَرِينَ (٧٠) وَنَجَّيْنَـٰهُ وَلُوطًا إِلَى ٱلْأَرْضِ ٱلَّتِى بَـٰرَكْنَا فِيهَا لِلْعَـٰلَمِينَ (٧١) وَوَهَبْنَا لَهُۥٓ إِسْحَـٰقَ وَيَعْقُوبَ نَافِلَةً وَكُلًّا جَعَلْنَا صَـٰلِحِينَ (٧٢) وَجَعَلْنَـٰهُمْ أَئِمَّةً يَهْدُونَ بِأَمْرِنَا وَأَوْحَيْنَآ إِلَيْهِمْ فِعْلَ ٱلْخَيْرَٰتِ وَإِقَامَ ٱلصَّلَوٰةِ وَإِيتَآءَ ٱلزَّكَوٰةِ وَكَانُواْ لَنَا عَـٰبِدِينَ (٧٣) وَلُوطًا ءَاتَيْنَـٰهُ حُكْمًا وَعِلْمًا وَنَجَّيْنَـٰهُ مِنَ ٱلْقَرْيَةِ ٱلَّتِى كَانَت تَّعْمَلُ ٱلْخَبَـٰٓئِثَ إِنَّهُمْ كَانُواْ قَوْمَ سَوْءٍ فَـٰسِقِينَ (٧٤) وَأَدْخَلْنَـٰهُ فِى رَحْمَتِنَآ إِنَّهُۥ مِنَ ٱلصَّـٰلِحِينَ (٧٥)

And We had certainly given Abraham his sound judgement before, and We were of him well-Knowing (51) When he said to his father and his people, "What are these statues to which you are devoted?" (52) They said, "We found our fathers worshippers of them." (53) He said, "You were certainly, you and your fathers, in manifest error." (54) They said, "Have you come to us with truth, or are you of those who jest?" (55) He said, "[No], rather, your Lord is the Lord of the heavens and the earth who created them, and I, to that, am of those who testify. (56) And [I swear] by Allah, I will surely plan against your idols after you have turned and gone away." (57) So he made them into fragments, except a large one among them, that they might return to it [and question]. (58) They said, "Who has done this to our gods? Indeed, he is of the wrongdoers." (59) They said, "We heard a young man mention them who is called Abraham." (60) They said, "Then bring him before the eyes of the people that they may testify." (61) They said, "Have you done this to our gods, O Abraham?" (62) He said, "Rather, this - the largest of them - did it, so ask them, if they should [be able to] speak." (63) So they returned to [blaming] themselves and said [to each other], "Indeed, you are the wrongdoers." (64) Then they reversed themselves, [saying], "You have already known that these do not speak!" (65) He said, "Then do you worship instead of Allah that which does not benefit you at all or harm you? (66) Uff to you and to what you worship instead of Allah. Then will you not use reason?" (67) They said, "Burn him and support your gods - if you are to act." (68) Allah said, "O fire, be coolness and safety upon Abraham." (69) And they intended for him harm, but We made them the greatest losers. (70) And We delivered him and Lot to the land which We had blessed for the worlds. (71) And We gave him Isaac and Jacob in addition, and all [of them] We made righteous. (72) And We made them leaders guiding by Our command. And We inspired to them the doing of good deeds, establishment of prayer, and giving of zakah(charity); and they were worshippers of Us. (73) And to Lot We gave judgement and knowledge, and We saved him from the city that was committing wicked deeds. Indeed, they were a people of evil, defiantly disobedient. (74) And We admitted him into Our mercy. Indeed, he was of the righteous. (75)

Quran 26:69-89

وَٱتْلُ عَلَيْهِمْ نَبَأَ إِبْرَاهِيمَ (٦٩) إِذْ قَالَ لِأَبِيهِ وَقَوْمِهِ مَا تَعْبُدُونَ (٧٠) قَالُواْ نَعْبُدُ أَصْنَامًا فَنَظَلُّ لَهَا عَاكِفِينَ (٧١) قَالَ هَلْ يَسْمَعُونَكُمْ إِذْ تَدْعُونَ (٧٢) أَوْ يَنفَعُونَكُمْ أَوْ يَضُرُّونَ (٧٣) قَالُواْ بَلْ وَجَدْنَا ءَابَاءَنَا كَذَٰلِكَ يَفْعَلُونَ (٧٤) قَالَ أَفَرَءَيْتُم مَّا كُنتُمْ تَعْبُدُونَ (٧٥) أَنتُمْ وَءَابَاؤُكُمُ ٱلْأَقْدَمُونَ (٧٦) فَإِنَّهُمْ عَدُوٌّ لِّى إِلَّا رَبَّ ٱلْعَٰلَمِينَ (٧٧) ٱلَّذِى خَلَقَنِى فَهُوَ يَهْدِينِ (٧٨) وَٱلَّذِى هُوَ يُطْعِمُنِى وَيَسْقِينِ (٧٩) وَإِذَا مَرِضْتُ فَهُوَ يَشْفِينِ (٨٠) وَٱلَّذِى يُمِيتُنِى ثُمَّ يُحْيِينِ (٨١) وَٱلَّذِى أَطْمَعُ أَن يَغْفِرَ لِى خَطِيئَتِى يَوْمَ ٱلدِّينِ (٨٢) رَبِّ هَبْ لِى حُكْمًا وَأَلْحِقْنِى بِٱلصَّٰلِحِينَ (٨٣) وَٱجْعَل لِّى لِسَانَ صِدْقٍ فِى ٱلْأَخِرِينَ (٨٤) وَٱجْعَلْنِى مِن وَرَثَةِ جَنَّةِ ٱلنَّعِيمِ (٨٥) وَٱغْفِرْ لِأَبِى إِنَّهُ كَانَ مِنَ ٱلضَّآلِّينَ (٨٦) وَلَا تُخْزِنِى يَوْمَ يُبْعَثُونَ (٨٧) يَوْمَ لَا يَنفَعُ مَالٌ وَلَا بَنُونَ (٨٨) إِلَّا مَنْ أَتَى ٱللَّهَ بِقَلْبٍ سَلِيمٍ (٨٩)

And recite to them the news of Abraham, (69) When he said to his father and his people, "What do you worship?" (70) They said, "We worship idols and remain to them devoted." (71) He said, "Do they hear you when you supplicate? (72) Or do they benefit you, or do they harm?" (73) They said, "But we found our fathers doing thus." (74) He said, "Then do you see what you have been worshipping, (75) You and your ancient forefathers? (76) Indeed, they are enemies to me, except the Lord of the worlds, (77) Who created me, and He [it is who] guides me. (78) And it is He who feeds me and gives me drink. (79) And when I am ill, it is He who cures me (80) And who will cause me to die and then bring me to life (81) And who I aspire that He will forgive me my sin on the Day of Recompense." (82) [And he said], "My Lord, grant me authority and join me with the righteous. (83) And grant me a reputation of honor among later generations. (84) And place me among the inheritors of the Garden of Pleasure. (85) And forgive my father. Indeed, he has been of those astray. (86) And do not disgrace me on the Day they are [all] resurrected - (87) The Day when there will not benefit [anyone] wealth or children (88) But only one who comes to Allah with a sound heart." (89)

Quran 29:16-17

وَإِبْرَٰهِيمَ إِذْ قَالَ لِقَوْمِهِ ٱعْبُدُواْ ٱللَّهَ وَٱتَّقُوهُ ذَٰلِكُمْ خَيْرٌ لَّكُمْ إِن كُنتُمْ تَعْلَمُونَ
(١٦) إِنَّمَا تَعْبُدُونَ مِن دُونِ ٱللَّهِ أَوْثَٰنًا وَتَخْلُقُونَ إِفْكًا إِنَّ ٱلَّذِينَ تَعْبُدُونَ مِن
دُونِ ٱللَّهِ لَا يَمْلِكُونَ لَكُمْ رِزْقًا فَٱبْتَغُواْ عِندَ ٱللَّهِ ٱلرِّزْقَ وَٱعْبُدُوهُ وَٱشْكُرُواْ لَهُ
إِلَيْهِ تُرْجَعُونَ (١٧)

And [We sent] Abraham, when he said to his people, "Worship Allah and fear Him. That is best for you, if you should know. (16) You only worship, besides Allah, idols, and you produce a falsehood. Indeed, those you worship besides Allah do not possess for you [the power of] provision. So seek from Allah provision and worship Him and be grateful to Him. To Him you will be returned." (17)

Quran 29:24-27

فَمَا كَانَ جَوَابَ قَوْمِهِ إِلَّا أَن قَالُوا اقْتُلُوهُ أَوْ حَرِّقُوهُ فَأَنجَىٰهُ اللَّهُ مِنَ النَّارِ إِنَّ فِى ذَٰلِكَ لَأَيَٰتٍ لِقَوْمٍ يُؤْمِنُونَ (٢٤) وَقَالَ إِنَّمَا اتَّخَذْتُم مِّن دُونِ اللَّهِ أَوْثَٰنًا مَّوَدَّةَ بَيْنِكُمْ فِى الْحَيَوٰةِ الدُّنْيَا ثُمَّ يَوْمَ الْقِيَٰمَةِ يَكْفُرُ بَعْضُكُم بِبَعْضٍ وَيَلْعَنُ بَعْضُكُم بَعْضًا وَمَأْوَىٰكُمُ النَّارُ وَمَا لَكُم مِّن نَّٰصِرِينَ (٢٥) ۞ فَآمَنَ لَهُ لُوطٌ وَقَالَ إِنِّى مُهَاجِرٌ إِلَىٰ رَبِّى إِنَّهُ هُوَ الْعَزِيزُ الْحَكِيمُ (٢٦) وَوَهَبْنَا لَهُ إِسْحَٰقَ وَيَعْقُوبَ وَجَعَلْنَا فِى ذُرِّيَّتِهِ النُّبُوَّةَ وَالْكِتَٰبَ وَءَاتَيْنَٰهُ أَجْرَهُ فِى الدُّنْيَا وَإِنَّهُ فِى الْآخِرَةِ لَمِنَ الصَّٰلِحِينَ (٢٧)

And the answer of Abraham's people was not but that they said, "Kill him or burn him," but Allah saved him from the fire. Indeed in that are signs for a people who believe. (24) And [Abraham] said, "You have only taken, other than Allah, idols as [a bond of] affection among you in worldly life. Then on the Day of Resurrection you will deny one another and curse one another, and your refuge will be the Fire, and you will not have any helpers." (25) And Lot believed him. [Abraham] said, "Indeed, I will emigrate to [the service of] my Lord. Indeed, He is the Exalted in Might, the Wise." (26) And We gave to Him Isaac and Jacob and placed in his descendants prophethood and scripture. And We gave him his reward *in this world, and indeed, he is in the Hereafter among the righteous. (27)*

Quran 19:41-50

وَٱذْكُرْ فِى ٱلْكِتَـٰبِ إِبْرَٰهِيمَ إِنَّهُ ۥ كَانَ صِدِّيقًا نَّبِيًّا (٤١) إِذْ قَالَ لِأَبِيهِ يَـٰٓأَبَتِ لِمَ تَعْبُدُ مَا لَا يَسْمَعُ وَلَا يُبْصِرُ وَلَا يُغْنِى عَنكَ شَيْـًٔا (٤٢) يَـٰٓأَبَتِ إِنِّى قَدْ جَآءَنِى مِنَ ٱلْعِلْمِ مَا لَمْ يَأْتِكَ فَٱتَّبِعْنِىٓ أَهْدِكَ صِرَٰطًا سَوِيًّا (٤٣) يَـٰٓأَبَتِ لَا تَعْبُدِ ٱلشَّيْطَـٰنَ إِنَّ ٱلشَّيْطَـٰنَ كَانَ لِلرَّحْمَـٰنِ عَصِيًّا (٤٤) يَـٰٓأَبَتِ إِنِّىٓ أَخَافُ أَن يَمَسَّكَ عَذَابٌ مِّنَ ٱلرَّحْمَـٰنِ فَتَكُونَ لِلشَّيْطَـٰنِ وَلِيًّا (٤٥) قَالَ أَرَاغِبٌ أَنتَ عَنْ ءَالِهَتِى يَـٰٓإِبْرَٰهِيمُ لَئِن لَّمْ تَنتَهِ لَأَرْجُمَنَّكَ وَٱهْجُرْنِى مَلِيًّا (٤٦) قَالَ سَلَـٰمٌ عَلَيْكَ سَأَسْتَغْفِرُ لَكَ رَبِّىٓ إِنَّهُ ۥ كَانَ بِى حَفِيًّا (٤٧) وَأَعْتَزِلُكُمْ وَمَا تَدْعُونَ مِن دُونِ ٱللَّهِ وَأَدْعُواْ رَبِّى عَسَىٰٓ أَلَّآ أَكُونَ بِدُعَآءِ رَبِّى شَقِيًّا (٤٨) فَلَمَّا ٱعْتَزَلَهُمْ وَمَا يَعْبُدُونَ مِن دُونِ ٱللَّهِ وَهَبْنَا لَهُ ۥٓ إِسْحَـٰقَ وَيَعْقُوبَ ۖ وَكُلًّا جَعَلْنَا نَبِيًّا (٤٩) وَوَهَبْنَا لَهُم مِّن رَّحْمَتِنَا وَجَعَلْنَا لَهُمْ لِسَانَ صِدْقٍ عَلِيًّا (٥٠)

And mention in the Book [the story of] Abraham. Indeed, he was a man of truth and a prophet. (41) [Mention] when he said to his father, "O my father, why do you worship that which does not hear and does not see and will not benefit you at all? (42) O my father, indeed there has come to me of knowledge that which has not come to you, so follow me; I will guide you to an even path. (43) O my father, do not worship Satan. Indeed Satan has ever been, to the Most Merciful, disobedient. (44) O my father, indeed I fear that there will touch you a punishment from the Most Merciful so you would be to Satan a companion [in Hellfire]." (45) [His father] said, "Have you no desire for my gods, O Abraham? If you do not desist, I will surely stone you, so avoid me a prolonged time." (46) [Abraham] said, "Peace will be upon you. I will ask forgiveness for you of my Lord. Indeed, He is ever gracious to me. (47) And I will leave you and those you invoke other than Allah and will invoke my Lord. I expect that I will not be in invocation to my Lord unhappy." (48) So when he had left them and those they worshipped other than Allah, We gave him Isaac and Jacob, and each [of them] We made a prophet. (49) And We gave them of Our mercy, and we made for them a reputation of high honor. (50)

Quran 43:26-28

وَإِذْ قَالَ إِبْرَاهِيمُ لِأَبِيهِ وَقَوْمِهِۦ إِنَّنِى بَرَآءٌ مِّمَّا تَعْبُدُونَ (٢٦) إِلَّا ٱلَّذِى فَطَرَنِى فَإِنَّهُۥ سَيَهْدِينِ (٢٧) وَجَعَلَهَا كَلِمَةً بَاقِيَةً فِى عَقِبِهِۦ لَعَلَّهُمْ يَرْجِعُونَ (٢٨)

And [mention, O Muhammad], when Abraham said to his father and his people, "Indeed, I am disassociated from that which you worship (26) Except for He who created me; and indeed, He will guide me." (27) And he made it a word remaining among his descendants that they might return [to it]. (28)

Quran 9:113-115

مَا كَانَ لِلنَّبِىِّ وَٱلَّذِينَ ءَامَنُوٓا۟ أَن يَسْتَغْفِرُوا۟ لِلْمُشْرِكِينَ وَلَوْ كَانُوٓا۟ أُو۟لِى قُرْبَىٰ مِنۢ بَعْدِ مَا تَبَيَّنَ لَهُمْ أَنَّهُمْ أَصْحَـٰبُ ٱلْجَحِيمِ (١١٣) وَمَا كَانَ ٱسْتِغْفَارُ إِبْرَاهِيمَ لِأَبِيهِ إِلَّا عَن مَّوْعِدَةٍ وَعَدَهَآ إِيَّاهُ فَلَمَّا تَبَيَّنَ لَهُۥٓ أَنَّهُۥ عَدُوٌّ لِّلَّهِ تَبَرَّأَ مِنْهُ

إِنَّ إِبْرَٰهِيمَ لَأَوَّٰهٌ حَلِيمٌ (١١٤) وَمَا كَانَ ٱللَّهُ لِيُضِلَّ قَوْمًۢا بَعْدَ إِذْ هَدَىٰهُمْ حَتَّىٰ يُبَيِّنَ لَهُم مَّا يَتَّقُونَ إِنَّ ٱللَّهَ بِكُلِّ شَىْءٍ عَلِيمٌ (١١٥)

It is not for the Prophet and those who have believed to ask forgiveness for the polytheists, even if they were relatives, after it has become clear to them that they are companions of Hellfire. (113) And the request of forgiveness of Abraham for his father was only because of a promise he had made to him. But when it became apparent to Abraham that his father was an enemy to Allah, he disassociated himself from him. Indeed was Abraham compassionate and patient. (114) And Allah would not let a people stray after He has guided them until He makes clear to them what they should avoid. Indeed, Allah is Knowing of all things. (115)

Quran 60:3-7

لَن تَنفَعَكُمْ أَرْحَامُكُمْ وَلَآ أَوْلَٰدُكُمْ يَوْمَ ٱلْقِيَٰمَةِ يَفْصِلُ بَيْنَكُمْ وَٱللَّهُ بِمَا تَعْمَلُونَ بَصِيرٌ (٣) قَدْ كَانَتْ لَكُمْ أُسْوَةٌ حَسَنَةٌ فِىٓ إِبْرَٰهِيمَ وَٱلَّذِينَ مَعَهُ ٓ إِذْ قَالُوا۟ لِقَوْمِهِمْ إِنَّا بُرَءَٰٓؤُا۟ مِنكُمْ وَمِمَّا تَعْبُدُونَ مِن دُونِ ٱللَّهِ كَفَرْنَا بِكُمْ وَبَدَا بَيْنَنَا وَبَيْنَكُمُ ٱلْعَدَٰوَةُ وَٱلْبَغْضَآءُ أَبَدًا حَتَّىٰ تُؤْمِنُوا۟ بِٱللَّهِ وَحْدَهُ ٓ إِلَّا قَوْلَ إِبْرَٰهِيمَ لِأَبِيهِ لَأَسْتَغْفِرَنَّ لَكَ وَمَآ أَمْلِكُ لَكَ مِنَ ٱللَّهِ مِن شَىْءٍ رَّبَّنَا عَلَيْكَ تَوَكَّلْنَا وَإِلَيْكَ أَنَبْنَا وَإِلَيْكَ ٱلْمَصِيرُ (٤) رَبَّنَا لَا تَجْعَلْنَا فِتْنَةً لِّلَّذِينَ كَفَرُوا۟ وَٱغْفِرْ لَنَا رَبَّنَآ إِنَّكَ أَنتَ ٱلْعَزِيزُ ٱلْحَكِيمُ (٥) لَقَدْ كَانَ لَكُمْ فِيهِمْ أُسْوَةٌ حَسَنَةٌ لِّمَن كَانَ يَرْجُوا۟ ٱللَّهَ وَٱلْيَوْمَ ٱلْءَاخِرَ وَمَن يَتَوَلَّ فَإِنَّ ٱللَّهَ هُوَ ٱلْغَنِىُّ ٱلْحَمِيدُ (٦) ۞ عَسَى ٱللَّهُ أَن يَجْعَلَ بَيْنَكُمْ وَبَيْنَ ٱلَّذِينَ عَادَيْتُم مِّنْهُم مَّوَدَّةً وَٱللَّهُ قَدِيرٌ وَٱللَّهُ غَفُورٌ رَّحِيمٌ (٧)

Never will your relatives or your children benefit you; the Day of Resurrection He will judge between you. And

Allah, of what you do, is Seeing. (3) There has already been for you an excellent pattern in Abraham and those with him, when they said to their people, "Indeed, we are disassociated from you and from whatever you worship other than Allah. We have denied you, and there has appeared between us and you animosity and hatred forever until you believe in Allah alone" except for the saying of Abraham to his father, "I will surely ask forgiveness for you, but I have not [power to do] for you anything against Allah. Our Lord, upon You we have relied, and to You we have returned, and to You is the destination. (4) Our Lord, make us not [objects of] torment for the disbelievers and forgive us, our Lord. Indeed, it is You who is the Exalted in Might, the Wise." (5) There has certainly been for you in them an excellent pattern for anyone whose hope is in Allah and the Last Day. And whoever turns away - then indeed, Allah is the Free of need, the Praiseworthy. (6) Perhaps Allah will put, between you and those to whom you have been enemies among them, affection. And Allah is competent, and Allah is Forgiving and Merciful. (7)

Quran 37:83-113

۞ وَإِنَّ مِن شِيعَتِهِۦ لَإِبْرَٰهِيمَ (٨٣) إِذْ جَآءَ رَبَّهُۥ بِقَلْبٍ سَلِيمٍ (٨٤) إِذْ قَالَ لِأَبِيهِ وَقَوْمِهِۦ مَاذَا تَعْبُدُونَ (٨٥) أَئِفْكًا ءَالِهَةً دُونَ ٱللَّهِ تُرِيدُونَ (٨٦) فَمَا ظَنُّكُم بِرَبِّ ٱلْعَٰلَمِينَ (٨٧) فَنَظَرَ نَظْرَةً فِى ٱلنُّجُومِ (٨٨) فَقَالَ إِنِّى سَقِيمٌ (٨٩) فَتَوَلَّوْاْ عَنْهُ مُدْبِرِينَ (٩٠) فَرَاغَ إِلَىٰٓ ءَالِهَتِهِمْ فَقَالَ أَلَا تَأْكُلُونَ (٩١) مَا لَكُمْ لَا تَنطِقُونَ (٩٢) فَرَاغَ عَلَيْهِمْ ضَرْبًۢا بِٱلْيَمِينِ (٩٣) فَأَقْبَلُوٓاْ إِلَيْهِ يَزِفُّونَ

قَالَ أَتَعْبُدُونَ مَا تَنْحِتُونَ (٩٥) وَٱللَّهُ خَلَقَكُمْ وَمَا تَعْمَلُونَ (٩٦) قَالُواْ (٩٤)
ٱبْنُواْ لَهُ ۥ بُنْيَٰنًا فَأَلْقُوهُ فِى ٱلْجَحِيمِ (٩٧) فَأَرَادُواْ بِهِۦ كَيْدًا فَجَعَلْنَٰهُمُ ٱلْأَسْفَلِينَ
(٩٨) وَقَالَ إِنِّى ذَاهِبٌ إِلَىٰ رَبِّى سَيَهْدِينِ (٩٩) رَبِّ هَبْ لِى مِنَ ٱلصَّٰلِحِينَ
(١٠٠) فَبَشَّرْنَٰهُ بِغُلَٰمٍ حَلِيمٍ (١٠١) فَلَمَّا بَلَغَ مَعَهُ ٱلسَّعْىَ قَالَ يَٰبُنَىَّ إِنِّى أَرَىٰ
فِى ٱلْمَنَامِ أَنِّى أَذْبَحُكَ فَٱنظُرْ مَاذَا تَرَىٰ قَالَ يَٰٓأَبَتِ ٱفْعَلْ مَا تُؤْمَرُ سَتَجِدُنِى إِن
شَاءَ ٱللَّهُ مِنَ ٱلصَّٰبِرِينَ (١٠٢) فَلَمَّآ أَسْلَمَا وَتَلَّهُ ۥ لِلْجَبِينِ (١٠٣) وَنَٰدَيْنَٰهُ أَن
يَٰٓإِبْرَٰهِيمُ (١٠٤) قَدْ صَدَّقْتَ ٱلرُّءْيَآ إِنَّا كَذَٰلِكَ نَجْزِى ٱلْمُحْسِنِينَ (١٠٥) إِنَّ
هَٰذَا لَهُوَ ٱلْبَلَٰٓؤُاْ ٱلْمُبِينُ (١٠٦) وَفَدَيْنَٰهُ بِذِبْحٍ عَظِيمٍ (١٠٧) وَتَرَكْنَا عَلَيْهِ فِى
ٱلْءَاخِرِينَ (١٠٨) سَلَٰمٌ عَلَىٰٓ إِبْرَٰهِيمَ (١٠٩) كَذَٰلِكَ نَجْزِى ٱلْمُحْسِنِينَ (١١٠)
إِنَّهُ ۥ مِنْ عِبَادِنَا ٱلْمُؤْمِنِينَ (١١١) وَبَشَّرْنَٰهُ بِإِسْحَٰقَ نَبِيًّا مِّنَ ٱلصَّٰلِحِينَ
(١١٢) وَبَٰرَكْنَا عَلَيْهِ وَعَلَىٰٓ إِسْحَٰقَ وَمِن ذُرِّيَّتِهِمَا مُحْسِنٌ وَظَالِمٌ لِّنَفْسِهِۦ
مُبِينٌ (١١٣)

And indeed, among his kind was Abraham, (83) When he came to his Lord with a sound heart (84) [And] when he said to his father and his people, "What do you worship? (85) Is it falsehood [as] gods other than Allah you desire? (86) Then what is your thought about the Lord of the worlds?" (87) And he cast a look at the stars (88) And said, "Indeed, I am [about to be] ill." (89) So they turned away from him, departing. (90) Then he turned to their gods and said, "Do you not eat? (91) What is [wrong] with you that you do not speak?" (92) And he turned upon them a blow with [his] right hand. (93) Then the people came toward him, hastening. (94) He said, "Do you worship that which you [yourselves] carve, (95) While Allah created you and that which you do?" (96) They said, "Construct for him a furnace and throw him into the burning fire." (97) And they intended for him a plan, but We made them the most debased. (98) And [then] he said, "Indeed, I will go to [where I am ordered by] my Lord; He will guide me. (99) My Lord, grant me [a child] from among the righteous." (100) So We gave him good tidings of a forbearing boy. (101) And when he reached with him [the age of] exertion, he said, "O my son, indeed I have seen in a dream that I [must] sacrifice you, so see what you think." He said, "O my father, do as you are commanded. You will find me, if Allah wills, of the steadfast." (102) And when they had both submitted and he put him down upon his forehead, (103) We called to him, "O Abraham, (104) You have fulfilled the vision." Indeed, We thus reward the doers of good. (105) Indeed, this was the clear trial. (106) And We ransomed him with a great sacrifice, (107) And We left for him [favorable mention] among later generations: (108) "Peace upon Abraham." (109) Indeed, We thus reward the doers of good. (110) Indeed, he was of Our believing servants. (111) And We gave him good tidings of Isaac, a prophet from among the righteous. (112) And We blessed him and Isaac. But among their descendants is the doer of good and the clearly unjust to himself. (113)

Quran 4:54-55

أَمْ يَحْسُدُونَ ٱلنَّاسَ عَلَىٰ مَآ ءَاتَىٰهُمُ ٱللَّهُ مِن فَضْلِهِۦ فَقَدْ ءَاتَيْنَآ ءَالَ إِبْرَٰهِيمَ ٱلْكِتَٰبَ وَٱلْحِكْمَةَ وَءَاتَيْنَٰهُم مُّلْكًا عَظِيمًا (٥٤) فَمِنْهُم مَّنْ ءَامَنَ بِهِۦ وَمِنْهُم مَّن صَدَّ عَنْهُ وَكَفَىٰ بِجَهَنَّمَ سَعِيرًا (٥٥)

Or do they envy people for what Allah has given them of His bounty? But we had already given the family of Abraham the Scripture and wisdom and conferred upon them a great kingdom. (54) And some among them believed in it, and some among them were averse to it. And sufficient is Hell as a blaze. (55)

Quran 2:258-260

أَلَمْ تَرَ إِلَى ٱلَّذِى حَاجَّ إِبْرَٰهِۦمَ فِى رَبِّهِۦ أَنْ ءَاتَىٰهُ ٱللَّهُ ٱلْمُلْكَ إِذْ قَالَ إِبْرَٰهِۦمُ رَبِّىَ ٱلَّذِى يُحْىِۦ وَيُمِيتُ قَالَ أَنَا۠ أُحْىِۦ وَأُمِيتُ قَالَ إِبْرَٰهِۦمُ فَإِنَّ ٱللَّهَ يَأْتِى بِٱلشَّمْسِ مِنَ ٱلْمَشْرِقِ فَأْتِ بِهَا مِنَ ٱلْمَغْرِبِ فَبُهِتَ ٱلَّذِى كَفَرَ وَٱللَّهُ لَا يَهْدِى ٱلْقَوْمَ ٱلظَّٰلِمِينَ (٢٥٨) أَوْ كَٱلَّذِى مَرَّ عَلَىٰ قَرْيَةٍ وَهِىَ خَاوِيَةٌ عَلَىٰ عُرُوشِهَا قَالَ أَنَّىٰ يُحْىِۦ هَٰذِهِ ٱللَّهُ بَعْدَ مَوْتِهَا فَأَمَاتَهُ ٱللَّهُ مِائَةَ عَامٍ ثُمَّ بَعَثَهُ قَالَ كَمْ لَبِثْتَ قَالَ لَبِثْتُ يَوْمًا أَوْ بَعْضَ يَوْمٍ قَالَ بَل لَّبِثْتَ مِائَةَ عَامٍ فَٱنظُرْ إِلَىٰ طَعَامِكَ وَشَرَابِكَ لَمْ يَتَسَنَّهْ وَٱنظُرْ إِلَىٰ حِمَارِكَ وَلِنَجْعَلَكَ ءَايَةً لِّلنَّاسِ وَٱنظُرْ إِلَى ٱلْعِظَامِ كَيْفَ نُنشِزُهَا ثُمَّ نَكْسُوهَا لَحْمًا فَلَمَّا تَبَيَّنَ لَهُۥ قَالَ أَعْلَمُ أَنَّ ٱللَّهَ عَلَىٰ كُلِّ شَىْءٍ قَدِيرٌ (٢٥٩) وَإِذْ قَالَ إِبْرَٰهِۦمُ رَبِّ أَرِنِى كَيْفَ تُحْىِ ٱلْمَوْتَىٰ قَالَ أَوَلَمْ تُؤْمِن قَالَ بَلَىٰ وَلَٰكِن لِّيَطْمَئِنَّ قَلْبِى قَالَ فَخُذْ أَرْبَعَةً مِّنَ ٱلطَّيْرِ فَصُرْهُنَّ إِلَيْكَ ثُمَّ ٱجْعَلْ عَلَىٰ كُلِّ جَبَلٍ مِّنْهُنَّ جُزْءًا ثُمَّ ٱدْعُهُنَّ يَأْتِينَكَ سَعْيًا وَٱعْلَمْ أَنَّ ٱللَّهَ عَزِيزٌ حَكِيمٌ (٢٦٠)

Have you not considered the one who argued with Abraham about his Lord [merely] because Allah had given him kingship? When Abraham said, "My Lord is the one who gives life and causes death," he said, "I give life and cause death." Abraham said, "Indeed, Allah brings up the sun from the east, so bring it up from the west." So the disbeliever was overwhelmed [by astonishment], and Allah does not guide the wrongdoing people. (258) Or [consider such an example] as the one who passed by a township which had fallen into ruin. He said, "How will Allah bring this to life after its death?" So Allah caused him to die for a hundred years; then He revived him. He said, "How long have you remained?" The man said, "I have remained a day or part of a day." He said, "Rather, you have remained one hundred years. Look at your food and your drink; it has not changed with time. And look at your donkey; and We will make you a sign for the people. And look at the bones [of this donkey] - how We raise them and then We cover them with flesh." And when it became clear to him, he said, "I know that Allah is over all things competent." (259) And [mention] when Abraham said, "My Lord, show me how You give life to the dead." [Allah] said, "Have you not believed?" He said, "Yes, but [I ask] only that my heart may be satisfied." [Allah] said, "Take four birds and commit them to yourself. Then [after slaughtering them] put on each hill a portion of them; then call them - they will come [flying] to you in haste. And know that Allah is Exalted in Might and Wise." (260)

Quran 22:26-29

وَإِذْ بَوَّأْنَا لِإِبْرَٰهِيمَ مَكَانَ ٱلْبَيْتِ أَن لَّا تُشْرِكْ بِى شَيْـًٔا وَطَهِّرْ بَيْتِىَ لِلطَّآئِفِينَ
وَٱلْقَآئِمِينَ وَٱلرُّكَّعِ ٱلسُّجُودِ (٢٦) وَأَذِّن فِى ٱلنَّاسِ بِٱلْحَجِّ يَأْتُوكَ رِجَالًا
وَعَلَىٰ كُلِّ ضَامِرٍ يَأْتِينَ مِن كُلِّ فَجٍّ عَمِيقٍ (٢٧) لِّيَشْهَدُوا۟ مَنَٰفِعَ لَهُمْ
وَيَذْكُرُوا۟ ٱسْمَ ٱللَّهِ فِىٓ أَيَّامٍ مَّعْلُومَٰتٍ عَلَىٰ مَا رَزَقَهُم مِّنۢ بَهِيمَةِ ٱلْأَنْعَٰمِ ۖ فَكُلُوا۟

مِنْهَا وَأَطْعِمُواْ ٱلْبَآئِسَ ٱلْفَقِيرَ (٢٨) ثُمَّ لْيَقْضُواْ تَفَثَهُمْ وَلْيُوفُواْ نُذُورَهُمْ وَلْيَطَّوَّفُواْ بِٱلْبَيْتِ ٱلْعَتِيقِ (٢٩)

And [mention, O Muhammad], when We designated for Abraham the site of the House, [saying], "Do not associate anything with Me and purify My House for those who perform Tawaf and those who stand [in prayer] and those who bow and prostrate. (26) And proclaim to the people the Hajj [pilgrimage]; they will come to you on foot and on every lean camel; they will come from every distant pass - (27) That they may witness benefits for themselves and mention the name of Allah on known days over what He has provided for them of [sacrificial] animals. So eat of them and feed the miserable and poor. (28) Then let them end their untidiness and fulfill their vows and perform Tawaf around the ancient House." (29)

Quran 14:35-41

وَإِذْ قَالَ إِبْرَٰهِيمُ رَبِّ ٱجْعَلْ هَٰذَا ٱلْبَلَدَ ءَامِنًا وَٱجْنُبْنِى وَبَنِىَّ أَن نَّعْبُدَ ٱلْأَصْنَامَ (٣٥) رَبِّ إِنَّهُنَّ أَضْلَلْنَ كَثِيرًا مِّنَ ٱلنَّاسِ فَمَن تَبِعَنِى فَإِنَّهُ مِنِّى وَمَنْ عَصَانِى فَإِنَّكَ غَفُورٌ رَّحِيمٌ (٣٦) رَّبَّنَآ إِنِّىٓ أَسْكَنتُ مِن ذُرِّيَّتِى بِوَادٍ غَيْرِ ذِى زَرْعٍ عِندَ بَيْتِكَ ٱلْمُحَرَّمِ رَبَّنَا لِيُقِيمُواْ ٱلصَّلَوٰةَ فَٱجْعَلْ أَفْـِٔدَةً مِّنَ ٱلنَّاسِ تَهْوِىٓ إِلَيْهِمْ وَٱرْزُقْهُم مِّنَ ٱلثَّمَرَٰتِ لَعَلَّهُمْ يَشْكُرُونَ (٣٧) رَبَّنَآ إِنَّكَ تَعْلَمُ مَا نُخْفِى وَمَا نُعْلِنُ وَمَا يَخْفَىٰ عَلَى ٱللَّهِ مِن شَىْءٍ فِى ٱلْأَرْضِ وَلَا فِى ٱلسَّمَآءِ (٣٨) ٱلْحَمْدُ لِلَّهِ ٱلَّذِى وَهَبَ لِى عَلَى ٱلْكِبَرِ إِسْمَٰعِيلَ وَإِسْحَٰقَ إِنَّ رَبِّى لَسَمِيعُ ٱلدُّعَآءِ (٣٩) رَبِّ ٱجْعَلْنِى مُقِيمَ ٱلصَّلَوٰةِ وَمِن ذُرِّيَّتِى رَبَّنَا وَتَقَبَّلْ دُعَآءِ (٤٠) رَبَّنَا ٱغْفِرْ لِى وَلِوَٰلِدَىَّ وَلِلْمُؤْمِنِينَ يَوْمَ يَقُومُ ٱلْحِسَابُ (٤١)

And [mention, O Muhammad], when Abraham said, "My Lord, make this city [Makkah] secure and keep me and my sons away from worshipping idols. (35) My Lord, indeed they have led astray many among the people. So whoever follows me - then he is of me; and whoever disobeys me - indeed, You are [yet] Forgiving and Merciful. (36) Our Lord, I have settled some of my descendants in an uncultivated valley near Your sacred House, our Lord, that they may establish prayer. So make hearts among the people incline toward them and provide for them from the fruits that they might be grateful. (37) Our Lord, indeed You know what we conceal and what we declare, and nothing is hidden from Allah on the earth or in the heaven. (38) Praise to Allah, who has granted to me in old age Ishmael and Isaac. Indeed, my Lord is the Hearer of supplication. (39) My Lord, make me an establisher of prayer, and [many] from my descendants. Our Lord, and accept my supplication. (40) Our Lord, forgive me and my parents and the believers the Day the account is established." (41)

Quran 2:124-141

۞ وَإِذِ ٱبْتَلَىٰٓ إِبْرَٰهِـۧمَ رَبُّهُۥ بِكَلِمَٰتٍ فَأَتَمَّهُنَّ قَالَ إِنِّى جَاعِلُكَ لِلنَّاسِ إِمَامًا قَالَ وَمِن ذُرِّيَّتِى قَالَ لَا يَنَالُ عَهْدِى ٱلظَّٰلِمِينَ (١٢٤) وَإِذْ جَعَلْنَا ٱلْبَيْتَ مَثَابَةً لِّلنَّاسِ وَأَمْنًا وَٱتَّخِذُواْ مِن مَّقَامِ إِبْرَٰهِـۧمَ مُصَلًّى وَعَهِدْنَآ إِلَىٰٓ إِبْرَٰهِـۧمَ وَإِسْمَٰعِيلَ أَن طَهِّرَا بَيْتِىَ لِلطَّآئِفِينَ وَٱلْعَٰكِفِينَ وَٱلرُّكَّعِ ٱلسُّجُودِ (١٢٥) وَإِذْ قَالَ إِبْرَٰهِـۧمُ رَبِّ ٱجْعَلْ هَٰذَا بَلَدًا ءَامِنًا وَٱرْزُقْ أَهْلَهُۥ مِنَ ٱلثَّمَرَٰتِ مَنْ ءَامَنَ مِنْهُم بِٱللَّهِ وَٱلْيَوْمِ ٱلْءَاخِرِ قَالَ وَمَن كَفَرَ فَأُمَتِّعُهُۥ قَلِيلًا ثُمَّ أَضْطَرُّهُۥٓ إِلَىٰ عَذَابِ ٱلنَّارِ

وَبِئْسَ ٱلْمَصِيرُ (١٢٦) وَإِذْ يَرْفَعُ إِبْرَٰهِۦمُ ٱلْقَوَاعِدَ مِنَ ٱلْبَيْتِ وَإِسْمَٰعِيلُ رَبَّنَا تَقَبَّلْ مِنَّآ إِنَّكَ أَنتَ ٱلسَّمِيعُ ٱلْعَلِيمُ (١٢٧) رَبَّنَا وَٱجْعَلْنَا مُسْلِمَيْنِ لَكَ وَمِن ذُرِّيَّتِنَآ أُمَّةً مُّسْلِمَةً لَّكَ وَأَرِنَا مَنَاسِكَنَا وَتُبْ عَلَيْنَآ إِنَّكَ أَنتَ ٱلتَّوَّابُ ٱلرَّحِيمُ (١٢٨) رَبَّنَا وَٱبْعَثْ فِيهِمْ رَسُولًا مِّنْهُمْ يَتْلُواْ عَلَيْهِمْ ءَايَٰتِكَ وَيُعَلِّمُهُمُ ٱلْكِتَٰبَ وَٱلْحِكْمَةَ وَيُزَكِّيهِمْ إِنَّكَ أَنتَ ٱلْعَزِيزُ ٱلْحَكِيمُ (١٢٩) وَمَن يَرْغَبُ عَن مِّلَّةِ إِبْرَٰهِۦمَ إِلَّا مَن سَفِهَ نَفْسَهُۥ وَلَقَدِ ٱصْطَفَيْنَٰهُ فِى ٱلدُّنْيَا وَإِنَّهُۥ فِى ٱلْءَاخِرَةِ لَمِنَ ٱلصَّٰلِحِينَ (١٣٠) إِذْ قَالَ لَهُۥ رَبُّهُۥٓ أَسْلِمْ قَالَ أَسْلَمْتُ لِرَبِّ ٱلْعَٰلَمِينَ (١٣١) وَوَصَّىٰ بِهَآ إِبْرَٰهِۦمُ بَنِيهِ وَيَعْقُوبُ يَٰبَنِىَّ إِنَّ ٱللَّهَ ٱصْطَفَىٰ لَكُمُ ٱلدِّينَ فَلَا تَمُوتُنَّ إِلَّا وَأَنتُم مُّسْلِمُونَ (١٣٢) أَمْ كُنتُمْ شُهَدَآءَ إِذْ حَضَرَ يَعْقُوبَ ٱلْمَوْتُ إِذْ قَالَ لِبَنِيهِ مَا تَعْبُدُونَ مِنۢ بَعْدِى قَالُواْ نَعْبُدُ إِلَٰهَكَ وَإِلَٰهَ ءَابَآئِكَ إِبْرَٰهِۦمَ وَإِسْمَٰعِيلَ وَإِسْحَٰقَ إِلَٰهًا وَٰحِدًا وَنَحْنُ لَهُۥ مُسْلِمُونَ (١٣٣) تِلْكَ أُمَّةٌ قَدْ خَلَتْ لَهَا مَا كَسَبَتْ وَلَكُم مَّا كَسَبْتُمْ وَلَا تُسْـَٔلُونَ عَمَّا كَانُواْ يَعْمَلُونَ (١٣٤) وَقَالُواْ كُونُواْ هُودًا أَوْ نَصَٰرَىٰ تَهْتَدُواْ قُلْ بَلْ مِلَّةَ إِبْرَٰهِۦمَ حَنِيفًا وَمَا كَانَ مِنَ ٱلْمُشْرِكِينَ (١٣٥) قُولُوٓاْ ءَامَنَّا بِٱللَّهِ وَمَآ أُنزِلَ إِلَيْنَا وَمَآ أُنزِلَ إِلَىٰٓ إِبْرَٰهِۦمَ وَإِسْمَٰعِيلَ وَإِسْحَٰقَ وَيَعْقُوبَ وَٱلْأَسْبَاطِ وَمَآ أُوتِىَ مُوسَىٰ وَعِيسَىٰ وَمَآ أُوتِىَ ٱلنَّبِيُّونَ مِن رَّبِّهِمْ لَا نُفَرِّقُ بَيْنَ أَحَدٍ مِّنْهُمْ وَنَحْنُ لَهُۥ مُسْلِمُونَ (١٣٦) فَإِنْ ءَامَنُواْ بِمِثْلِ مَآ ءَامَنتُم بِهِۦ فَقَدِ ٱهْتَدَواْ وَّإِن تَوَلَّوْاْ فَإِنَّمَا هُمْ فِى شِقَاقٍ فَسَيَكْفِيكَهُمُ ٱللَّهُ وَهُوَ ٱلسَّمِيعُ ٱلْعَلِيمُ (١٣٧) صِبْغَةَ ٱللَّهِ وَمَنْ أَحْسَنُ مِنَ ٱللَّهِ صِبْغَةً وَنَحْنُ لَهُۥ عَٰبِدُونَ (١٣٨) قُلْ أَتُحَآجُّونَنَا فِى ٱللَّهِ وَهُوَ رَبُّنَا وَرَبُّكُمْ وَلَنَآ أَعْمَٰلُنَا وَلَكُمْ أَعْمَٰلُكُمْ وَنَحْنُ لَهُۥ مُخْلِصُونَ (١٣٩) أَمْ تَقُولُونَ إِنَّ إِبْرَٰهِۦمَ وَإِسْمَٰعِيلَ وَإِسْحَٰقَ وَيَعْقُوبَ وَٱلْأَسْبَاطَ كَانُواْ هُودًا أَوْ نَصَٰرَىٰ قُلْ ءَأَنتُمْ أَعْلَمُ أَمِ ٱللَّهُ وَمَنْ أَظْلَمُ مِمَّن كَتَمَ شَهَٰدَةً عِندَهُۥ مِنَ ٱللَّهِ وَمَا ٱللَّهُ بِغَٰفِلٍ عَمَّا تَعْمَلُونَ (١٤٠) تِلْكَ أُمَّةٌ قَدْ خَلَتْ لَهَا مَا كَسَبَتْ وَلَكُم مَّا كَسَبْتُمْ وَلَا تُسْـَٔلُونَ عَمَّا كَانُواْ يَعْمَلُونَ (١٤١)

And [mention, O Muhammad], when Abraham was tried by his Lord with commands and he fulfilled them. [Allah] said, "Indeed, I will make you a leader for the people." [Abraham] said, "And of my descendants?" [Allah] said,

"My covenant does not include the wrongdoers." (124) And [mention] when We made the House a place of return for the people and [a place of] security. And take, [O believers], from the standing place of Abraham a place of prayer. And We charged Abraham and Ishmael, [saying], "Purify My House for those who perform Tawaf and those who are staying [there] for worship and those who bow and prostrate [in prayer]." (125) And [mention] when Abraham said, "My Lord, make this a secure city and provide its people with fruits - whoever of them believes in Allah and the Last Day." [Allah] said. "And whoever disbelieves - I will grant him enjoyment for a little; then I will force him to the punishment of the Fire, and wretched is the destination." (126) And [mention] when Abraham was raising the foundations of the House and [with him] Ishmael, [saying], "Our Lord, accept [this] from us. Indeed You are the Hearing, the Knowing. (127) Our Lord, and make us Muslims [in submission] to You and from our descendants a Muslim nation [in submission] to You. And show us our rites and accept our repentance. Indeed, You are the Accepting of repentance, the Merciful. (128) Our Lord, and send among them a messenger from themselves who will recite to them Your verses and teach them the Book and wisdom and purify them. Indeed, You are the Exalted in Might, the Wise." (129) And who would be averse to the religion of Abraham except one who makes a fool of himself. And

*We had chosen him in this world, and indeed he, in the
Hereafter, will be among the righteous. (130) When his
Lord said to him, "Submit", he said "I have submitted
[in Islam] to the Lord of the worlds." (131) And
Abraham instructed his sons [to do the same] and [so
did] Jacob, [saying], "O my sons, indeed Allah has
chosen for you this religion, so do not die except while
you are Muslims." (132) Or were you witnesses when
death approached Jacob, when he said to his sons, "What
will you worship after me?" They said, "We will worship
your God and the God of your fathers, Abraham and
Ishmael and Isaac - one God. And we are Muslims [in
submission] to Him." (133) That was a nation which has
passed on. It will have [the consequence of] what it
earned, and you will have what you have earned. And
you will not be asked about what they used to do. (134)
They say, "Be Jews or Christians [so] you will be
guided." Say, "Rather, [we follow] the religion of
Abraham, inclining toward truth, and he was not of the
polytheists." (135) Say, [O believers], "We have believed
in Allah and what has been revealed to us and what has
been revealed to Abraham and Ishmael and Isaac and
Jacob and the Descendants and what was given to Moses
and Jesus and what was given to the prophets from their
Lord. We make no distinction between any of them, and
we are Muslims [in submission] to Him." (136) So if
they believe in the same as you believe in, then they have*

been [rightly] guided; but if they turn away, they are only in dissension, and Allah will be sufficient for you against them. And He is the Hearing, the Knowing. (137) [And say, "Ours is] the religion of Allah. And who is better than Allah in [ordaining] religion? And we are worshippers of Him." (138) Say, "Do you argue with us about Allah while He is our Lord and your Lord? For us are our deeds, and for you are your deeds. And we are sincere [in deed and intention] to Him." (139) Or do you say that Abraham and Ishmael and Isaac and Jacob and the Descendants were Jews or Christians? Say, "Are you more knowing or is Allah?" And who is more unjust than one who conceals a testimony he has from Allah? And Allah is not unaware of what you do. (140) That is a nation which has passed on. It will have [the consequence of] what it earned, and you will have what you have earned. And you will not be asked about what they used to do. (141)

Quran 16:120-125

إِنَّ إِبْرَاهِيمَ كَانَ أُمَّةً قَانِتًا لِّلَّهِ حَنِيفًا وَلَمْ يَكُ مِنَ ٱلْمُشْرِكِينَ (١٢٠) شَاكِرًا لِّأَنْعُمِهِ ٱجْتَبَاهُ وَهَدَاهُ إِلَىٰ صِرَاطٍ مُّسْتَقِيمٍ (١٢١) وَءَاتَيْنَاهُ فِى ٱلدُّنْيَا حَسَنَةً وَإِنَّهُ فِى ٱلْآخِرَةِ لَمِنَ ٱلصَّالِحِينَ (١٢٢) ثُمَّ أَوْحَيْنَآ إِلَيْكَ أَنِ ٱتَّبِعْ مِلَّةَ إِبْرَاهِيمَ حَنِيفًا وَمَا كَانَ مِنَ ٱلْمُشْرِكِينَ (١٢٣) إِنَّمَا جُعِلَ ٱلسَّبْتُ عَلَى ٱلَّذِينَ ٱخْتَلَفُواْ فِيهِ وَإِنَّ رَبَّكَ لَيَحْكُمُ بَيْنَهُمْ يَوْمَ ٱلْقِيَٰمَةِ فِيمَا كَانُواْ فِيهِ يَخْتَلِفُونَ (١٢٤) ٱدْعُ إِلَىٰ سَبِيلِ رَبِّكَ بِٱلْحِكْمَةِ وَٱلْمَوْعِظَةِ ٱلْحَسَنَةِ وَجَٰدِلْهُم بِٱلَّتِى هِىَ أَحْسَنُ إِنَّ رَبَّكَ هُوَ أَعْلَمُ بِمَن ضَلَّ عَن سَبِيلِهِ وَهُوَ أَعْلَمُ بِٱلْمُهْتَدِينَ (١٢٥)

Indeed, Abraham was a [comprehensive] leader, devoutly obedient to Allah, inclining toward truth, and he was not of those who associate others with Allah. (120) [He was] grateful for His favors. Allah chose him and guided him to a straight path. (121) And We gave him good in this world, and indeed, in the Hereafter he will be among the righteous. (122) Then We revealed to you, [O Muhammad], to follow the religion of Abraham, inclining toward truth; and he was not of those who associate with Allah. (123) The sabbath was only appointed for those who differed over it. And indeed, your Lord will judge between them on the Day of Resurrection concerning that over which they used to differ. (124) Invite to the way of your Lord with wisdom and good instruction, and argue with them in a way that is best. Indeed, your Lord is most knowing of who has strayed from His way, and He is most knowing of who is [rightly] guided. (125)

Quran 11:69-76

وَلَقَدْ جَاءَتْ رُسُلُنَا إِبْرَاهِيمَ بِالْبُشْرَىٰ قَالُواْ سَلَامًا قَالَ سَلَامٌ فَمَا لَبِثَ أَن جَاءَ بِعِجْلٍ حَنِيذٍ (٦٩) فَلَمَّا رَءَا أَيْدِيَهُمْ لَا تَصِلُ إِلَيْهِ نَكِرَهُمْ وَأَوْجَسَ مِنْهُمْ خِيفَةٌ قَالُواْ لَا تَخَفْ إِنَّا أُرْسِلْنَا إِلَىٰ قَوْمِ لُوطٍ (٧٠) وَامْرَأَتُهُ قَآئِمَةٌ فَضَحِكَتْ فَبَشَّرْنَاهَا بِإِسْحَاقَ وَمِن وَرَاءِ إِسْحَاقَ يَعْقُوبَ (٧١) قَالَتْ يَاوَيْلَتَىٰ ءَأَلِدُ وَأَنَا عَجُوزٌ وَهَاذَا بَعْلِى شَيْخًا إِنَّ هَاذَا لَشَىْءٌ عَجِيبٌ (٧٢) قَالُواْ أَتَعْجَبِينَ مِنْ أَمْرِ اللَّهِ رَحْمَتُ اللَّهِ وَبَرَكَاتُهُ عَلَيْكُمْ أَهْلَ الْبَيْتِ إِنَّهُ حَمِيدٌ مَجِيدٌ (٧٣) فَلَمَّا ذَهَبَ عَنْ إِبْرَاهِيمَ الرَّوْعُ وَجَاءَتْهُ الْبُشْرَىٰ يُجَادِلُنَا فِى قَوْمِ لُوطٍ (٧٤) إِنَّ إِبْرَاهِيمَ

لَحَلِيمٌ أَوَّاهٌ مُّنِيبٌ (٧٥) يَـٰٓإِبْرَٰهِيمُ أَعْرِضْ عَنْ هَـٰذَآ إِنَّهُ ۗ قَدْ جَآءَ أَمْرُ رَبِّكَ وَإِنَّهُمْ ءَاتِيهِمْ عَذَابٌ غَيْرُ مَرْدُودٍ (٧٦)

And certainly did Our messengers come to Abraham with good tidings; they said, "Peace." He said, "Peace," and did not delay in bringing [them] a roasted calf. (69) But when he saw their hands not reaching for it, he distrusted them and felt from them apprehension. They said, "Fear not. We have been sent to the people of Lot." (70) And his Wife was standing, and she smiled. Then We gave her good tidings of Isaac and after Isaac, Jacob. (71) She said, "Woe to me! Shall I give birth while I am an old woman and this, my husband, is an old man? Indeed, this is an amazing thing!" (72) They said, "Are you amazed at the decree of Allah? May the mercy of Allah and His blessings be upon you, people of the house. Indeed, He is Praiseworthy and Honorable." (73) And when the fright had left Abraham and the good tidings had reached him, he began to argue with Us concerning the people of Lot. (74) Indeed, Abraham was forbearing, grieving and [frequently] returning [to Allah]. (75) [The angels said], "O Abraham, give up this [plea]. Indeed, the command of your Lord has come, and indeed, there will reach them a punishment that cannot be repelled." (76)

Quran 15:51-60

وَنَبِّئْهُمْ عَن ضَيْفِ إِبْرَٰهِيمَ (٥١) إِذْ دَخَلُوا۟ عَلَيْهِ فَقَالُوا۟ سَلَٰمًا قَالَ إِنَّا مِنكُمْ وَجِلُونَ (٥٢) قَالُوا۟ لَا تَوْجَلْ إِنَّا نُبَشِّرُكَ بِغُلَٰمٍ عَلِيمٍ (٥٣) قَالَ أَبَشَّرْتُمُونِى عَلَىٰٓ أَن مَّسَّنِىَ ٱلْكِبَرُ فَبِمَ تُبَشِّرُونَ (٥٤) قَالُوا۟ بَشَّرْنَٰكَ بِٱلْحَقِّ فَلَا تَكُن مِّنَ ٱلْقَٰنِطِينَ (٥٥) قَالَ وَمَن يَقْنَطُ مِن رَّحْمَةِ رَبِّهِۦٓ إِلَّا ٱلضَّآلُّونَ (٥٦) قَالَ فَمَا خَطْبُكُمْ أَيُّهَا ٱلْمُرْسَلُونَ (٥٧) قَالُوٓا۟ إِنَّآ أُرْسِلْنَآ إِلَىٰ قَوْمٍ مُّجْرِمِينَ (٥٨) إِلَّآ ءَالَ لُوطٍ إِنَّا لَمُنَجُّوهُمْ أَجْمَعِينَ (٥٩) إِلَّا ٱمْرَأَتَهُۥ قَدَّرْنَآ إِنَّهَا لَمِنَ ٱلْغَٰبِرِينَ (٦٠)

And inform them about the guests of Abraham, (51) When they entered upon him and said, "Peace." [Abraham] said, "Indeed, we are fearful of you." (52) [The angels] said, "Fear not. Indeed, we give you good tidings of a learned boy." (53) He said, "Have you given me good tidings although old age has come upon me? Then of what [wonder] do you inform?" (54) They said, "We have given you good tidings in truth, so do not be of the despairing." (55) He said, "And who despairs of the mercy of his Lord except for those astray?" (56) [Abraham] said, "Then what is your business [here], O messengers?" (57) They said, "Indeed, we have been sent to a people of criminals, (58) Except the family of Lot; indeed, we will save them all (59) Except his wife." Allah decreed that she is of those who remain behind. (60)

Quran 29:31-32

وَلَمَّا جَآءَتْ رُسُلُنَآ إِبْرَٰهِيمَ بِٱلْبُشْرَىٰ قَالُوٓا۟ إِنَّا مُهْلِكُوٓا۟ أَهْلِ هَٰذِهِ ٱلْقَرْيَةِ إِنَّ أَهْلَهَا كَانُوا۟ ظَٰلِمِينَ (٣١) قَالَ إِنَّ فِيهَا لُوطًا قَالُوا۟ نَحْنُ أَعْلَمُ بِمَن فِيهَا لَنُنَجِّيَنَّهُۥ وَأَهْلَهُۥٓ إِلَّا ٱمْرَأَتَهُۥ كَانَتْ مِنَ ٱلْغَٰبِرِينَ (٣٢)

And when Our messengers came to Abraham with the good tidings, they said, "Indeed, we will destroy the people of that Lot's city. Indeed, its people have been wrongdoers." (31) [Abraham] said, "Indeed, within it is Lot." They said, "We are more knowing of who is within it. We will surely save him and his family, except his wife. She is to be of those who remain behind." (32)

Quran 51:24-37

هَلْ أَتَىٰكَ حَدِيثُ ضَيْفِ إِبْرَٰهِيمَ ٱلْمُكْرَمِينَ (٢٤) إِذْ دَخَلُواْ عَلَيْهِ فَقَالُواْ سَلَـٰمًا قَالَ سَلَـٰمٌ قَوْمٌ مُّنكَرُونَ (٢٥) فَرَاغَ إِلَىٰٓ أَهْلِهِۦ فَجَآءَ بِعِجْلٍ سَمِينٍ (٢٦) فَقَرَّبَهُۥ إِلَيْهِمْ قَالَ أَلَا تَأْكُلُونَ (٢٧) فَأَوْجَسَ مِنْهُمْ خِيفَةًۖ قَالُواْ لَا تَخَفْۖ وَبَشَّرُوهُ بِغُلَـٰمٍ عَلِيمٍ (٢٨) فَأَقْبَلَتِ ٱمْرَأَتُهُۥ فِى صَرَّةٍ فَصَكَّتْ وَجْهَهَا وَقَالَتْ عَجُوزٌ عَقِيمٌ (٢٩) قَالُواْ كَذَٰلِكِ قَالَ رَبُّكِۖ إِنَّهُۥ هُوَ ٱلْحَكِيمُ ٱلْعَلِيمُ (٣٠) ۞ قَالَ فَمَا خَطْبُكُمْ أَيُّهَا ٱلْمُرْسَلُونَ (٣١) قَالُوٓاْ إِنَّآ أُرْسِلْنَآ إِلَىٰ قَوْمٍ مُّجْرِمِينَ (٣٢) لِنُرْسِلَ عَلَيْهِمْ حِجَارَةً مِّن طِينٍ (٣٣) مُّسَوَّمَةً عِندَ رَبِّكَ لِلْمُسْرِفِينَ (٣٤) فَأَخْرَجْنَا مَن كَانَ فِيهَا مِنَ ٱلْمُؤْمِنِينَ (٣٥) فَمَا وَجَدْنَا فِيهَا غَيْرَ بَيْتٍ مِّنَ ٱلْمُسْلِمِينَ (٣٦) وَتَرَكْنَا فِيهَآ ءَايَةً لِّلَّذِينَ يَخَافُونَ ٱلْعَذَابَ ٱلْأَلِيمَ (٣٧)

Has there reached you the story of the honored guests of Abraham? - (24) When they entered upon him and said, "[We greet you with] peace." He answered, "[And upon you] peace, [you are] a people unknown. (25) Then he went to his family and came with a fat [roasted] calf (26) And placed it near them; he said, "Will you not eat?" (27) And he felt from them apprehension. They said, "Fear not," and gave him good tidings of a learned boy. (28) And his wife approached with a cry [of alarm] and

struck her face and said, "[I am] a barren old woman!"
(29) They said, "Thus has said your Lord; indeed, He is
the Wise, the Knowing." (30) [Abraham] said, "Then
what is your business [here], O messengers?" (31) They
said, "Indeed, we have been sent to a people of criminals
(32) To send down upon them stones of clay, (33)
Marked in the presence of your Lord for the
transgressors." (34) So We brought out whoever was in
the cities of the believers. (35) And We found not within
them other than a [single] house of Muslims. (36) And
We left therein a sign for those who fear the painful
punishment. (37)

Quran 42:13-16

۞ شَرَعَ لَكُم مِّنَ ٱلدِّينِ مَا وَصَّىٰ بِهِۦ نُوحًا وَٱلَّذِىٓ أَوْحَيْنَآ إِلَيْكَ وَمَا وَصَّيْنَا
بِهِۦٓ إِبْرَٰهِيمَ وَمُوسَىٰ وَعِيسَىٰٓ أَنْ أَقِيمُواْ ٱلدِّينَ وَلَا تَتَفَرَّقُواْ فِيهِۚ كَبُرَ عَلَى
ٱلْمُشْرِكِينَ مَا تَدْعُوهُمْ إِلَيْهِۚ ٱللَّهُ يَجْتَبِىٓ إِلَيْهِ مَن يَشَآءُ وَيَهْدِىٓ إِلَيْهِ مَن يُنِيبُ
(١٣) وَمَا تَفَرَّقُوٓاْ إِلَّا مِنۢ بَعْدِ مَا جَآءَهُمُ ٱلْعِلْمُ بَغْيًۢا بَيْنَهُمْۚ وَلَوْلَا كَلِمَةٌ سَبَقَتْ
مِن رَّبِّكَ إِلَىٰٓ أَجَلٍ مُّسَمًّى لَّقُضِىَ بَيْنَهُمْۚ وَإِنَّ ٱلَّذِينَ أُورِثُواْ ٱلْكِتَٰبَ مِنۢ بَعْدِهِمْ
لَفِى شَكٍّ مِّنْهُ مُرِيبٍ (١٤) فَلِذَٰلِكَ فَٱدْعُ وَٱسْتَقِمْ كَمَآ أُمِرْتَۖ وَلَا تَتَّبِعْ
أَهْوَآءَهُمْۖ وَقُلْ ءَامَنتُ بِمَآ أَنزَلَ ٱللَّهُ مِن كِتَٰبٍۖ وَأُمِرْتُ لِأَعْدِلَ بَيْنَكُمُۖ ٱللَّهُ رَبُّنَا
وَرَبُّكُمْۖ لَنَآ أَعْمَٰلُنَا وَلَكُمْ أَعْمَٰلُكُمْۖ لَا حُجَّةَ بَيْنَنَا وَبَيْنَكُمُۖ ٱللَّهُ يَجْمَعُ بَيْنَنَاۖ وَإِلَيْهِ
ٱلْمَصِيرُ (١٥) وَٱلَّذِينَ يُحَآجُّونَ فِى ٱللَّهِ مِنۢ بَعْدِ مَا ٱسْتُجِيبَ لَهُۥ حُجَّتُهُمْ
دَاحِضَةٌ عِندَ رَبِّهِمْ وَعَلَيْهِمْ غَضَبٌ وَلَهُمْ عَذَابٌ شَدِيدٌ (١٦)

He has ordained for you of religion what He enjoined
upon Noah and that which We have revealed to you, [O
Muhammad], and what We enjoined upon Abraham and

Moses and Jesus - to establish the religion and not be divided therein. Difficult for those who associate others with Allah is that to which you invite them. Allah chooses for Himself whom He wills and guides to Himself whoever turns back [to Him]. (13) And they did not become divided until after knowledge had come to them - out of jealous animosity between themselves. And if not for a word that preceded from your Lord [postponing the penalty] until a specified time, it would have been concluded between them. And indeed, those who were granted inheritance of the Scripture after them are, concerning it, in disquieting doubt. (14) So to that [religion of Allah] invite, [O Muhammad], and remain on a right course as you are commanded and do not follow their inclinations but say, "I have believed in what Allah has revealed of the Qur'an, and I have been commanded to do justice among you. Allah is our Lord and your Lord. For us are our deeds, and for you your deeds. There is no [need for] argument between us and you. Allah will bring us together, and to Him is the [final] destination." (15) And those who argue concerning Allah after He has been responded to - their argument is invalid with their Lord, and upon them is [His] wrath, and for them is a severe punishment. (16)

Quran 57:25-29

لَقَدْ أَرْسَلْنَا رُسُلَنَا بِالْبَيِّنَـٰتِ وَأَنزَلْنَا مَعَهُمُ الْكِتَـٰبَ وَالْمِيزَانَ لِيَقُومَ النَّاسُ بِالْقِسْطِ ۖ وَأَنزَلْنَا الْحَدِيدَ فِيهِ بَأْسٌ شَدِيدٌ وَمَنَـٰفِعُ لِلنَّاسِ وَلِيَعْلَمَ اللَّهُ مَن يَنصُرُهُ ۥ وَرُسُلَهُ ۥ بِالْغَيْبِ ۚ إِنَّ اللَّهَ قَوِىٌّ عَزِيزٌ (٢٥) وَلَقَدْ أَرْسَلْنَا نُوحًا وَإِبْرَٰهِيمَ وَجَعَلْنَا فِى ذُرِّيَّتِهِمَا النُّبُوَّةَ وَالْكِتَـٰبَ ۖ فَمِنْهُم مُّهْتَدٍ ۖ وَكَثِيرٌ مِّنْهُمْ فَـٰسِقُونَ (٢٦) ثُمَّ قَفَّيْنَا عَلَىٰٓ ءَاثَـٰرِهِم بِرُسُلِنَا وَقَفَّيْنَا بِعِيسَى ابْنِ مَرْيَمَ وَءَاتَيْنَـٰهُ الْإِنجِيلَ وَجَعَلْنَا فِى قُلُوبِ الَّذِينَ اتَّبَعُوهُ رَأْفَةً وَرَحْمَةً وَرَهْبَانِيَّةً ابْتَدَعُوهَا مَا كَتَبْنَـٰهَا عَلَيْهِمْ إِلَّا ابْتِغَآءَ رِضْوَٰنِ اللَّهِ فَمَا رَعَوْهَا حَقَّ رِعَايَتِهَا ۖ فَـَٔاتَيْنَا الَّذِينَ ءَامَنُوا مِنْهُمْ أَجْرَهُمْ ۖ وَكَثِيرٌ مِّنْهُمْ فَـٰسِقُونَ (٢٧) يَـٰٓأَيُّهَا الَّذِينَ ءَامَنُوا اتَّقُوا اللَّهَ وَءَامِنُوا بِرَسُولِهِ ۦ يُؤْتِكُمْ كِفْلَيْنِ مِن رَّحْمَتِهِ ۦ وَيَجْعَل لَّكُمْ نُورًا تَمْشُونَ بِهِ ۦ وَيَغْفِرْ لَكُمْ ۚ وَاللَّهُ غَفُورٌ رَّحِيمٌ (٢٨) لِّئَلَّا يَعْلَمَ أَهْلُ الْكِتَـٰبِ أَلَّا يَقْدِرُونَ عَلَىٰ شَىْءٍ مِّن فَضْلِ اللَّهِ ۙ وَأَنَّ الْفَضْلَ بِيَدِ اللَّهِ يُؤْتِيهِ مَن يَشَآءُ ۚ وَاللَّهُ ذُو الْفَضْلِ الْعَظِيمِ (٢٩)

We have already sent Our messengers with clear evidences and sent down with them the Scripture and the balance that the people may maintain [their affairs] in justice. And We sent down iron, wherein is great military might and benefits for the people, and so that Allah may make evident those who support Him and His messengers unseen. Indeed, Allah is Powerful and Exalted in Might. (25) And We have already sent Noah and Abraham and placed in their descendants prophethood and scripture; and among them is he who is guided, but many of them are defiantly disobedient. (26) Then We sent following their footsteps Our messengers and followed [them] with Jesus, the son of Mary, and gave him the Injeel. And We placed in the hearts of those who followed him compassion and mercy and monasticism, which they innovated; We did not prescribe

it for them except [that they did so] seeking the approval
of Allah. But they did not observe it with due observance.
So We gave the ones who believed among them their
reward, but many of them are defiantly disobedient. (27)
O you who have believed, fear Allah and believe in His
Messenger; He will [then] give you a double portion of
His mercy and make for you a light by which you will
walk and forgive you; and Allah is Forgiving and
Merciful. (28) [This is] so that the People of the Scripture
may know that they are not able [to obtain] anything
from the bounty of Allah and that [all] bounty is in the
hand of Allah; He gives it to whom He wills. And Allah
is the possessor of great bounty. (29)

Quran 3:60-71

ٱلْحَقُّ مِن رَّبِّكَ فَلَا تَكُن مِّنَ ٱلْمُمْتَرِينَ (٦٠) فَمَنْ حَاجَّكَ فِيهِ مِنْ بَعْدِ مَا
جَاءَكَ مِنَ ٱلْعِلْمِ فَقُلْ تَعَالَوْاْ نَدْعُ أَبْنَاءَنَا وَأَبْنَاءَكُمْ وَنِسَاءَنَا وَنِسَاءَكُمْ وَأَنفُسَنَا
وَأَنفُسَكُمْ ثُمَّ نَبْتَهِلْ فَنَجْعَل لَّعْنَتَ ٱللَّهِ عَلَى ٱلْكَٰذِبِينَ (٦١) إِنَّ هَٰذَا لَهُوَ
ٱلْقَصَصُ ٱلْحَقُّ وَمَا مِنْ إِلَٰهٍ إِلَّا ٱللَّهُ وَإِنَّ ٱللَّهَ لَهُوَ ٱلْعَزِيزُ ٱلْحَكِيمُ (٦٢) فَإِن
تَوَلَّوْاْ فَإِنَّ ٱللَّهَ عَلِيمٌ بِٱلْمُفْسِدِينَ (٦٣) قُلْ يَٰأَهْلَ ٱلْكِتَٰبِ تَعَالَوْاْ إِلَىٰ كَلِمَةٍ
سَوَاءٍ بَيْنَنَا وَبَيْنَكُمْ أَلَّا نَعْبُدَ إِلَّا ٱللَّهَ وَلَا نُشْرِكَ بِهِۦ شَيْئًا وَلَا يَتَّخِذَ بَعْضُنَا
بَعْضًا أَرْبَابًا مِّن دُونِ ٱللَّهِ فَإِن تَوَلَّوْاْ فَقُولُواْ ٱشْهَدُواْ بِأَنَّا مُسْلِمُونَ (٦٤) يَٰأَهْلَ
ٱلْكِتَٰبِ لِمَ تُحَاجُّونَ فِىٓ إِبْرَٰهِيمَ وَمَآ أُنزِلَتِ ٱلتَّوْرَىٰةُ وَٱلْإِنجِيلُ إِلَّا مِنۢ بَعْدِهِۦ
أَفَلَا تَعْقِلُونَ (٦٥) هَٰٓأَنتُمْ هَٰٓؤُلَاءِ حَاجَجْتُمْ فِيمَا لَكُم بِهِۦ عِلْمٌ فَلِمَ تُحَاجُّونَ فِيمَا
لَيْسَ لَكُم بِهِۦ عِلْمٌ وَٱللَّهُ يَعْلَمُ وَأَنتُمْ لَا تَعْلَمُونَ (٦٦) مَا كَانَ إِبْرَٰهِيمُ يَهُودِيًّا
وَلَا نَصْرَانِيًّا وَلَٰكِن كَانَ حَنِيفًا مُّسْلِمًا وَمَا كَانَ مِنَ ٱلْمُشْرِكِينَ (٦٧) إِنَّ أَوْلَى
ٱلنَّاسِ بِإِبْرَٰهِيمَ لَلَّذِينَ ٱتَّبَعُوهُ وَهَٰذَا ٱلنَّبِىُّ وَٱلَّذِينَ ءَامَنُواْ وَٱللَّهُ وَلِىُّ ٱلْمُؤْمِنِينَ
(٦٨) وَدَّت طَّآئِفَةٌ مِّنْ أَهْلِ ٱلْكِتَٰبِ لَوْ يُضِلُّونَكُمْ وَمَا يُضِلُّونَ إِلَّا أَنفُسَهُمْ وَمَا

يَشْعُرُونَ (٦٩) يَـٰٓأَهْلَ ٱلْكِتَـٰبِ لِمَ تَكْفُرُونَ بِـَٔايَـٰتِ ٱللَّهِ وَأَنتُمْ تَشْهَدُونَ (٧٠)
يَـٰٓأَهْلَ ٱلْكِتَـٰبِ لِمَ تَلْبِسُونَ ٱلْحَقَّ بِٱلْبَـٰطِلِ وَتَكْتُمُونَ ٱلْحَقَّ وَأَنتُمْ تَعْلَمُونَ (٧١)

*The truth is from your Lord, so do not be among the
doubters. (60) Then whoever argues with you about it
after [this] knowledge has come to you - say, "Come, let
us call our sons and your sons, our women and your
women, ourselves and yourselves, then supplicate
earnestly [together] and invoke the curse of Allah upon
the liars [among us]." (61) Indeed, this is the true
narration. And there is no deity except Allah. And
indeed, Allah is the Exalted in Might, the Wise. (62) But
if they turn away, then indeed - Allah is Knowing of the
corrupters. (63) Say, "O People of the Scripture, come to
a word that is equitable between us and you - that we
will not worship except Allah and not associate anything
with Him and not take one another as lords instead of
Allah." But if they turn away, then say, "Bear witness
that we are Muslims [submitting to Him]." (64) O
People of the Scripture, why do you argue about
Abraham while the Torah and the Injeel were not
revealed until after him? Then will you not reason? (65)
Here you are - those who have argued about that of which
you have [some] knowledge, but why do you argue about
that of which you have no knowledge? And Allah knows,
while you know not. (66) Abraham was neither a Jew nor
a Christian, but he was one inclining toward truth, a
Muslim [submitting to Allah]. And he was not of the*

polytheists. (67) Indeed, the most worthy of Abraham
among the people are those who followed him [in
submission to Allah] and this prophet, and those who
believe [in his message]. And Allah is the ally of the
believers. (68) A faction of the people of the Scripture
wish they could mislead you. But they do not mislead
except themselves, and they perceive [it] not. (69) O
People of the Scripture, why do you disbelieve in the
verses of Allah while you witness [to their truth]? (70) O
People of the Scripture, why do you confuse the truth
with falsehood and conceal the truth while you know [it]?
(71)

Quran 3:77-90

إِنَّ ٱلَّذِينَ يَشْتَرُونَ بِعَهْدِ ٱللَّهِ وَأَيْمَـٰنِهِمْ ثَمَنًا قَلِيلًا أُوْلَـٰئِكَ لَا خَلَـٰقَ لَهُمْ فِى
ٱلْأَخِرَةِ وَلَا يُكَلِّمُهُمُ ٱللَّهُ وَلَا يَنظُرُ إِلَيْهِمْ يَوْمَ ٱلْقِيَـٰمَةِ وَلَا يُزَكِّيهِمْ وَلَهُمْ
عَذَابٌ أَلِيمٌ (٧٧) وَإِنَّ مِنْهُمْ لَفَرِيقًا يَلْوُ ۥنَ أَلْسِنَتَهُم بِٱلْكِتَـٰبِ لِتَحْسَبُوهُ مِنَ
ٱلْكِتَـٰبِ وَمَا هُوَ مِنَ ٱلْكِتَـٰبِ وَيَقُولُونَ هُوَ مِنْ عِندِ ٱللَّهِ وَمَا هُوَ مِنْ عِندِ ٱللَّهِ
وَيَقُولُونَ عَلَى ٱللَّهِ ٱلْكَذِبَ وَهُمْ يَعْلَمُونَ (٧٨) مَا كَانَ لِبَشَرٍ أَن يُؤْتِيَهُ ٱللَّهُ
ٱلْكِتَـٰبَ وَٱلْحُكْمَ وَٱلنُّبُوَّةَ ثُمَّ يَقُولَ لِلنَّاسِ كُونُوا۟ عِبَادًا لِّى مِن دُونِ ٱللَّهِ وَلَـٰكِن
كُونُوا۟ رَبَّـٰنِيِّنَ بِمَا كُنتُمْ تُعَلِّمُونَ ٱلْكِتَـٰبَ وَبِمَا كُنتُمْ تَدْرُسُونَ (٧٩) وَلَا يَأْمُرَكُمْ
أَن تَتَّخِذُوا۟ ٱلْمَلَـٰئِكَةَ وَٱلنَّبِيِّنَ أَرْبَابًا أَيَأْمُرُكُم بِٱلْكُفْرِ بَعْدَ إِذْ أَنتُم مُّسْلِمُونَ (٨٠)
وَإِذْ أَخَذَ ٱللَّهُ مِيثَـٰقَ ٱلنَّبِيِّنَ لَمَا ءَاتَيْتُكُم مِّن كِتَـٰبٍ وَحِكْمَةٍ ثُمَّ جَاءَكُمْ
رَسُولٌ مُّصَدِّقٌ لِّمَا مَعَكُمْ لَتُؤْمِنُنَّ بِهِ وَلَتَنصُرُنَّهُ قَالَ ءَأَقْرَرْتُمْ وَأَخَذْتُمْ عَلَىٰ
ذَٰلِكُمْ إِصْرِى قَالُوا۟ أَقْرَرْنَا قَالَ فَٱشْهَدُوا۟ وَأَنَا۠ مَعَكُم مِّنَ ٱلشَّـٰهِدِينَ (٨١) فَمَن
تَوَلَّىٰ بَعْدَ ذَٰلِكَ فَأُوْلَـٰئِكَ هُمُ ٱلْفَـٰسِقُونَ (٨٢) أَفَغَيْرَ دِينِ ٱللَّهِ يَبْغُونَ وَلَهُ أَسْلَمَ
مَن فِى ٱلسَّمَـٰوَٰتِ وَٱلْأَرْضِ طَوْعًا وَكَرْهًا وَإِلَيْهِ يُرْجَعُونَ (٨٣) قُلْ ءَامَنَّا
بِٱللَّهِ وَمَا أُنزِلَ عَلَيْنَا وَمَا أُنزِلَ عَلَىٰ إِبْرَٰهِيمَ وَإِسْمَـٰعِيلَ وَإِسْحَـٰقَ وَيَعْقُوبَ

وَٱلْأَسْبَاطِ وَمَآ أُوتِىَ مُوسَىٰ وَعِيسَىٰ وَٱلنَّبِيُّونَ مِن رَّبِّهِمْ لَا نُفَرِّقُ بَيْنَ أَحَدٍ مِّنْهُمْ وَنَحْنُ لَهُۥ مُسْلِمُونَ (٨٤) وَمَن يَبْتَغِ غَيْرَ ٱلْإِسْلَٰمِ دِينًا فَلَن يُقْبَلَ مِنْهُ وَهُوَ فِى ٱلْأَخِرَةِ مِنَ ٱلْخَٰسِرِينَ (٨٥) كَيْفَ يَهْدِى ٱللَّهُ قَوْمًا كَفَرُواْ بَعْدَ إِيمَٰنِهِمْ وَشَهِدُوٓاْ أَنَّ ٱلرَّسُولَ حَقٌّ وَجَآءَهُمُ ٱلْبَيِّنَٰتُ وَٱللَّهُ لَا يَهْدِى ٱلْقَوْمَ ٱلظَّٰلِمِينَ (٨٦) أُوْلَٰٓئِكَ جَزَآؤُهُمْ أَنَّ عَلَيْهِمْ لَعْنَةَ ٱللَّهِ وَٱلْمَلَٰٓئِكَةِ وَٱلنَّاسِ أَجْمَعِينَ (٨٧) خَٰلِدِينَ فِيهَا لَا يُخَفَّفُ عَنْهُمُ ٱلْعَذَابُ وَلَا هُمْ يُنظَرُونَ (٨٨) إِلَّا ٱلَّذِينَ تَابُواْ مِنۢ بَعْدِ ذَٰلِكَ وَأَصْلَحُواْ فَإِنَّ ٱللَّهَ غَفُورٌ رَّحِيمٌ (٨٩) إِنَّ ٱلَّذِينَ كَفَرُواْ بَعْدَ إِيمَٰنِهِمْ ثُمَّ ٱزْدَادُواْ كُفْرًا لَّن تُقْبَلَ تَوْبَتُهُمْ وَأُوْلَٰٓئِكَ هُمُ ٱلضَّآلُّونَ (٩٠)

Indeed, those who exchange the covenant of Allah and their [own] oaths for a small price will have no share in the Hereafter, and Allah will not speak to them or look at them on the Day of Resurrection, nor will He purify them; and they will have a painful punishment. (77) And indeed, there is among them a party who alter the Scripture with their tongues so you may think it is from the Scripture, but it is not from the Scripture. And they say, "This is from Allah," but it is not from Allah. And they speak untruth about Allah while they know. (78) It is not for a human [prophet] that Allah should give him the Scripture and authority and prophethood and then he would say to the people, "Be servants to me rather than Allah," but [instead, he would say], "Be pious scholars of the Lord because of what you have taught of the Scripture and because of what you have studied." (79) Nor could he order you to take the angels and prophets as lords. Would he order you to disbelief after you had been Muslims? (80) And [recall, O People of the Scripture], when Allah took the covenant of the prophets, [saying], "Whatever I give you of the Scripture and wisdom and then there comes to you a messenger confirming what is with you, you [must] believe in him and support him." [Allah] said, "Have you acknowledged and taken upon that My commitment?" They said, "We have acknowledged it." He said, "Then bear witness, and I am with you among the witnesses." (81) And whoever turned away after that - they were the defiantly disobedient. (82) So is it other than the religion of Allah they desire, while to Him have submitted [all] those within the heavens and earth, willingly or by compulsion, and to Him they will be returned? (83) Say, "We have believed in Allah and in what was revealed to us and what was revealed to Abraham, Ishmael, Isaac, Jacob, and the Descendants, and in what was given to Moses and Jesus and to the prophets from their Lord. We make no distinction between any of them, and we are Muslims [submitting] to Him." (84) And whoever desires other than Islam as religion - never will it be accepted from him, and he, in the Hereafter, will be among the losers. (85) How shall Allah guide a people who disbelieved after their belief and had witnessed that the Messenger is true and clear signs had come to them? And Allah does not guide the wrongdoing people. (86) Those - their recompense will be that upon them is the curse of Allah and the angels and the people, all together, (87) Abiding eternally therein.

The punishment will not be lightened for them, nor will they be reprieved. (88) Except for those who repent after that and correct themselves. For indeed, Allah is Forgiving and Merciful. (89) Indeed, those who reject the message after their belief and then increase in disbelief - never will their [claimed] repentance be accepted, and they are the ones astray. (90)

Quran 3:95-102

قُلْ صَدَقَ ٱللَّهُ فَٱتَّبِعُواْ مِلَّةَ إِبْرَٰهِيمَ حَنِيفًا وَمَا كَانَ مِنَ ٱلْمُشْرِكِينَ (٩٥) إِنَّ أَوَّلَ بَيْتٍ وُضِعَ لِلنَّاسِ لَلَّذِى بِبَكَّةَ مُبَارَكًا وَهُدًى لِّلْعَٰلَمِينَ (٩٦) فِيهِ ءَايَٰتٌ بَيِّنَٰتٌ مَّقَامُ إِبْرَٰهِيمَ ۖ وَمَن دَخَلَهُ ۥ كَانَ ءَامِنًا ۗ وَلِلَّهِ عَلَى ٱلنَّاسِ حِجُّ ٱلْبَيْتِ مَنِ ٱسْتَطَاعَ إِلَيْهِ سَبِيلًا ۚ وَمَن كَفَرَ فَإِنَّ ٱللَّهَ غَنِىٌّ عَنِ ٱلْعَٰلَمِينَ (٩٧) قُلْ يَٰأَهْلَ ٱلْكِتَٰبِ لِمَ تَكْفُرُونَ بِـَٔايَٰتِ ٱللَّهِ وَٱللَّهُ شَهِيدٌ عَلَىٰ مَا تَعْمَلُونَ (٩٨) قُلْ يَٰأَهْلَ ٱلْكِتَٰبِ لِمَ تَصُدُّونَ عَن سَبِيلِ ٱللَّهِ مَنْ ءَامَنَ تَبْغُونَهَا عِوَجًا وَأَنتُمْ شُهَدَآءُ ۗ وَمَا ٱللَّهُ بِغَٰفِلٍ عَمَّا تَعْمَلُونَ (٩٩) يَٰأَيُّهَا ٱلَّذِينَ ءَامَنُوٓاْ إِن تُطِيعُواْ فَرِيقًا مِّنَ ٱلَّذِينَ أُوتُواْ ٱلْكِتَٰبَ يَرُدُّوكُم بَعْدَ إِيمَٰنِكُمْ كَٰفِرِينَ (١٠٠) وَكَيْفَ تَكْفُرُونَ وَأَنتُمْ تُتْلَىٰ عَلَيْكُمْ ءَايَٰتُ ٱللَّهِ وَفِيكُمْ رَسُولُهُ ۥ ۗ وَمَن يَعْتَصِم بِٱللَّهِ فَقَدْ هُدِىَ إِلَىٰ صِرَٰطٍ مُّسْتَقِيمٍ (١٠١) يَٰأَيُّهَا ٱلَّذِينَ ءَامَنُواْ ٱتَّقُواْ ٱللَّهَ حَقَّ تُقَاتِهِ ۦ وَلَا تَمُوتُنَّ إِلَّا وَأَنتُم مُّسْلِمُونَ (١٠٢)

Say, "Allah has told the truth. So follow the religion of Abraham, inclining toward truth; and he was not of the polytheists." (95) Indeed, the first House [of worship] established for mankind was that at Makkah - blessed and a guidance for the worlds. (96) In it are clear signs [such as] the standing place of Abraham. And whoever enters it shall be safe. And [due] to Allah from the people is a

pilgrimage to the House - for whoever is able to find
thereto a way. But whoever disbelieves - then indeed,
Allah is free from need of the worlds. (97) Say, "O People
of the Scripture, why do you disbelieve in the verses of
Allah while Allah is Witness over what you do?" (98)
Say, "O People of the Scripture, why do you avert from
the way of Allah those who believe, seeking to make it
[seem] deviant, while you are witnesses [to the truth]?
And Allah is not unaware of what you do." (99) O you
who have believed, if you obey a party of those who were
given the Scripture, they would turn you back, after your
belief, [to being] unbelievers. (100) And how could you
disbelieve while to you are being recited the verses of
Allah and among you is His Messenger? And whoever
holds firmly to Allah has [indeed] been guided to a
straight path. (101) O you who have believed, fear Allah
as He should be feared and do not die except as Muslims
[in submission to Him]. (102)

Quran 4:123-125

لَّيْسَ بِأَمَانِيِّكُمْ وَلَا أَمَانِيِّ أَهْلِ ٱلْكِتَـٰبِ مَن يَعْمَلْ سُوٓءًا يُجْزَ بِهِۦ وَلَا يَجِدْ لَهُۥ
مِن دُونِ ٱللَّهِ وَلِيًّا وَلَا نَصِيرًا (١٢٣) وَمَن يَعْمَلْ مِنَ ٱلصَّـٰلِحَـٰتِ مِن ذَكَرٍ
أَوْ أُنثَىٰ وَهُوَ مُؤْمِنٌ فَأُوْلَـٰئِكَ يَدْخُلُونَ ٱلْجَنَّةَ وَلَا يُظْلَمُونَ نَقِيرًا (١٢٤) وَمَنْ
أَحْسَنُ دِينًا مِّمَّنْ أَسْلَمَ وَجْهَهُۥ لِلَّهِ وَهُوَ مُحْسِنٌ وَٱتَّبَعَ مِلَّةَ إِبْرَٰهِيمَ حَنِيفًا وَٱتَّخَذَ
ٱللَّهُ إِبْرَٰهِيمَ خَلِيلًا (١٢٥)

Paradise is not [obtained] by your wishful thinking nor
by that of the People of the Scripture. Whoever does a

wrong will be recompensed for it, and he will not find besides Allah a protector or a helper. (123) And whoever does righteous deeds, whether male or female, while being a believer - those will enter Paradise and will not be wronged, [even as much as] the speck on a date seed. (124) And who is better in religion than one who submits himself to Allah while being a doer of good and follows the religion of Abraham, inclining toward truth? And Allah took Abraham as an intimate friend. (125)

Quran 4:150-166

إِنَّ ٱلَّذِينَ يَكْفُرُونَ بِٱللَّهِ وَرُسُلِهِۦ وَيُرِيدُونَ أَن يُفَرِّقُواْ بَيْنَ ٱللَّهِ وَرُسُلِهِۦ وَيَقُولُونَ نُؤْمِنُ بِبَعْضٍ وَنَكْفُرُ بِبَعْضٍ وَيُرِيدُونَ أَن يَتَّخِذُواْ بَيْنَ ذَٰلِكَ سَبِيلاً (١٥٠) أُوْلَـٰئِكَ هُمُ ٱلْكَـٰفِرُونَ حَقًّا وَأَعْتَدْنَا لِلْكَـٰفِرِينَ عَذَابًا مُّهِينًا (١٥١) وَٱلَّذِينَ ءَامَنُواْ بِٱللَّهِ وَرُسُلِهِۦ وَلَمْ يُفَرِّقُواْ بَيْنَ أَحَدٍ مِّنْهُمْ أُوْلَـٰئِكَ سَوْفَ يُؤْتِيهِمْ أُجُورَهُمْ وَكَانَ ٱللَّهُ غَفُورًا رَّحِيمًا (١٥٢) يَسْئَلُكَ أَهْلُ ٱلْكِتَـٰبِ أَن تُنَزِّلَ عَلَيْهِمْ كِتَـٰبًا مِّنَ ٱلسَّمَاءِ فَقَدْ سَأَلُواْ مُوسَىٰ أَكْبَرَ مِن ذَٰلِكَ فَقَالُواْ أَرِنَا ٱللَّهَ جَهْرَةً فَأَخَذَتْهُمُ ٱلصَّـٰعِقَةُ بِظُلْمِهِمْ ثُمَّ ٱتَّخَذُواْ ٱلْعِجْلَ مِنْ بَعْدِ مَا جَاءَتْهُمُ ٱلْبَيِّنَـٰتُ فَعَفَوْنَا عَن ذَٰلِكَ وَءَاتَيْنَا مُوسَىٰ سُلْطَـٰنًا مُّبِينًا (١٥٣) وَرَفَعْنَا فَوْقَهُمُ ٱلطُّورَ بِمِيثَـٰقِهِمْ وَقُلْنَا لَهُمُ ٱدْخُلُواْ ٱلْبَابَ سُجَّدًا وَقُلْنَا لَهُمْ لَا تَعْدُواْ فِى ٱلسَّبْتِ وَأَخَذْنَا مِنْهُم مِّيثَـٰقًا غَلِيظًا (١٥٤) فَبِمَا نَقْضِهِم مِّيثَـٰقَهُمْ وَكُفْرِهِم بِـَٔايَـٰتِ ٱللَّهِ وَقَتْلِهِمُ ٱلْأَنۢبِيَاءَ بِغَيْرِ حَقٍّ وَقَوْلِهِمْ قُلُوبُنَا غُلْفٌ بَلْ طَبَعَ ٱللَّهُ عَلَيْهَا بِكُفْرِهِمْ فَلَا يُؤْمِنُونَ إِلَّا قَلِيلاً (١٥٥) وَبِكُفْرِهِمْ وَقَوْلِهِمْ عَلَىٰ مَرْيَمَ بُهْتَـٰنًا عَظِيمًا (١٥٦) وَقَوْلِهِمْ إِنَّا قَتَلْنَا ٱلْمَسِيحَ عِيسَى ٱبْنَ مَرْيَمَ رَسُولَ ٱللَّهِ وَمَا قَتَلُوهُ وَمَا صَلَبُوهُ وَلَـٰكِن شُبِّهَ لَهُمْ وَإِنَّ ٱلَّذِينَ ٱخْتَلَفُواْ فِيهِ لَفِى شَكٍّ مِّنْهُ مَا لَهُم بِهِۦ مِنْ عِلْمٍ إِلَّا ٱتِّبَاعَ ٱلظَّنِّ وَمَا قَتَلُوهُ يَقِينًا (١٥٧) بَل رَّفَعَهُ ٱللَّهُ إِلَيْهِ وَكَانَ ٱللَّهُ عَزِيزًا حَكِيمًا (١٥٨) وَإِن مِّنْ أَهْلِ ٱلْكِتَـٰبِ إِلَّا لَيُؤْمِنَنَّ بِهِۦ قَبْلَ مَوْتِهِۦ وَيَوْمَ ٱلْقِيَـٰمَةِ يَكُونُ عَلَيْهِمْ شَهِيدًا (١٥٩) فَبِظُلْمٍ مِّنَ ٱلَّذِينَ هَادُواْ حَرَّمْنَا عَلَيْهِمْ طَيِّبَـٰتٍ أُحِلَّتْ لَهُمْ وَبِصَدِّهِمْ عَن

سَبِيلِ ٱللَّهِ كَثِيرًا (١٦٠) وَأَخْذِهِمُ ٱلرِّبَوٰا۟ وَقَدْ نُهُوا۟ عَنْهُ وَأَكْلِهِمْ أَمْوَٰلَ ٱلنَّاسِ بِٱلْبَٰطِلِ ۚ وَأَعْتَدْنَا لِلْكَٰفِرِينَ مِنْهُمْ عَذَابًا أَلِيمًا (١٦١) لَّٰكِنِ ٱلرَّٰسِخُونَ فِى ٱلْعِلْمِ مِنْهُمْ وَٱلْمُؤْمِنُونَ يُؤْمِنُونَ بِمَآ أُنزِلَ إِلَيْكَ وَمَآ أُنزِلَ مِن قَبْلِكَ ۚ وَٱلْمُقِيمِينَ ٱلصَّلَوٰةَ ۚ وَٱلْمُؤْتُونَ ٱلزَّكَوٰةَ وَٱلْمُؤْمِنُونَ بِٱللَّهِ وَٱلْيَوْمِ ٱلْءَاخِرِ أُو۟لَٰٓئِكَ سَنُؤْتِيهِمْ أَجْرًا عَظِيمًا (١٦٢) ۞ إِنَّآ أَوْحَيْنَآ إِلَيْكَ كَمَآ أَوْحَيْنَآ إِلَىٰ نُوحٍ وَٱلنَّبِيِّۦنَ مِنۢ بَعْدِهِۦ ۚ وَأَوْحَيْنَآ إِلَىٰٓ إِبْرَٰهِيمَ وَإِسْمَٰعِيلَ وَإِسْحَٰقَ وَيَعْقُوبَ وَٱلْأَسْبَاطِ وَعِيسَىٰ وَأَيُّوبَ وَيُونُسَ وَهَٰرُونَ وَسُلَيْمَٰنَ ۚ وَءَاتَيْنَا دَاوُۥدَ زَبُورًا (١٦٣) وَرُسُلًا قَدْ قَصَصْنَٰهُمْ عَلَيْكَ مِن قَبْلُ وَرُسُلًا لَّمْ نَقْصُصْهُمْ عَلَيْكَ ۚ وَكَلَّمَ ٱللَّهُ مُوسَىٰ تَكْلِيمًا (١٦٤) رُّسُلًا مُّبَشِّرِينَ وَمُنذِرِينَ لِئَلَّا يَكُونَ لِلنَّاسِ عَلَى ٱللَّهِ حُجَّةٌۢ بَعْدَ ٱلرُّسُلِ ۚ وَكَانَ ٱللَّهُ عَزِيزًا حَكِيمًا (١٦٥) لَّٰكِنِ ٱللَّهُ يَشْهَدُ بِمَآ أَنزَلَ إِلَيْكَ ۖ أَنزَلَهُۥ بِعِلْمِهِۦ ۖ وَٱلْمَلَٰٓئِكَةُ يَشْهَدُونَ ۚ وَكَفَىٰ بِٱللَّهِ شَهِيدًا (١٦٦)

Indeed, those who disbelieve in Allah and His messengers and wish to discriminate between Allah and His messengers and say, "We believe in some and disbelieve in others," and wish to adopt a way in between - (150) Those are the disbelievers, truly. And We have prepared for the disbelievers a humiliating punishment. (151) But they who believe in Allah and His messengers and do not discriminate between any of them - to those He is going to give their rewards. And ever is Allah Forgiving and Merciful. (152) The People of the Scripture ask you to bring down to them a book from the heaven. But they had asked of Moses [even] greater than that and said, "Show us Allah outright," so the thunderbolt struck them for their wrongdoing. Then they took the calf [for worship] after clear evidences had come to them, and We pardoned that. And We gave Moses a clear authority. (153) And

We raised over them the mount for [refusal of] their covenant; and We said to them, "Enter the gate bowing humbly", and We said to them, "Do not transgress on the sabbath", and We took from them a solemn covenant. (154) And [We cursed them] for their breaking of the covenant and their disbelief in the signs of Allah and their killing of the prophets without right and their saying, "Our hearts are wrapped". Rather, Allah has sealed them because of their disbelief, so they believe not, except for a few. (155) And [We cursed them] for their disbelief and their saying against Mary a great slander, (156) And [for] their saying, "Indeed, we have killed the Messiah, Jesus, the son of Mary, the messenger of Allah." And they did not kill him, nor did they crucify him; but [another] was made to resemble him to them. And indeed, those who differ over it are in doubt about it. They have no knowledge of it except the following of assumption. And they did not kill him, for certain. (157) Rather, Allah raised him to Himself. And ever is Allah Exalted in Might and Wise. (158) And there is none from the People of the Scripture but that he will surely believe in Jesus before his death. And on the Day of Resurrection he will be against them a witness. (159) For wrongdoing on the part of the Jews, We made unlawful for them [certain] good foods which had been lawful to them, and for their averting from the way of Allah many [people], (160) And [for] their taking of usury while they had been forbidden from it, and their consuming of the people's wealth unjustly. And we have prepared for the disbelievers among them a painful punishment. (161) But those firm in knowledge among them and the believers believe in what has been revealed to you, [O Muhammad], and what was revealed before you. And the establishers of prayer [especially] and the givers of zakah and the believers in Allah and the Last Day - those We will give a great reward. (162) Indeed, We have revealed to you, [O Muhammad], as We revealed to Noah and the prophets after him. And we revealed to Abraham, Ishmael, Isaac, Jacob, the Descendants, Jesus, Job, Jonah, Aaron, and Solomon, and to David We gave the book [of Psalms]. (163) And [We sent] messengers about whom We have related [their stories] to you before and messengers about whom We have not related to you. And Allah spoke to Moses with [direct] speech. (164) [We sent] messengers as bringers of good tidings and warners so that mankind will have no argument against Allah after the messengers. And ever is Allah Exalted in Might and Wise. (165) But Allah bears witness to that which He has revealed to you. He has sent it down with His knowledge, and the angels bear witness [as well]. And sufficient is Allah as Witness. (166)

Quran 22:72-78

وَإِذَا تُتْلَىٰ عَلَيْهِمْ ءَايَٰتُنَا بَيِّنَٰتٍ تَعْرِفُ فِى وُجُوهِ ٱلَّذِينَ كَفَرُواْ ٱلْمُنكَرَ يَكَادُونَ يَسْطُونَ بِٱلَّذِينَ يَتْلُونَ عَلَيْهِمْ ءَايَٰتِنَا قُلْ أَفَأُنَبِّئُكُم بِشَرٍّ مِّن ذَٰلِكُمُ ٱلنَّارُ وَعَدَهَا ٱللَّهُ ٱلَّذِينَ كَفَرُواْ وَبِئْسَ ٱلْمَصِيرُ (٧٢) يَٰٓأَيُّهَا ٱلنَّاسُ ضُرِبَ مَثَلٌ فَٱسْتَمِعُواْ لَهُۥ إِنَّ ٱلَّذِينَ تَدْعُونَ مِن دُونِ ٱللَّهِ لَن يَخْلُقُواْ ذُبَابًا وَلَوِ ٱجْتَمَعُواْ لَهُۥ وَإِن يَسْلُبْهُمُ ٱلذُّبَابُ شَيْـًٔا لَّا يَسْتَنقِذُوهُ مِنْهُ ضَعُفَ ٱلطَّالِبُ وَٱلْمَطْلُوبُ (٧٣) مَا قَدَرُواْ ٱللَّهَ حَقَّ قَدْرِهِۦٓ إِنَّ ٱللَّهَ لَقَوِىٌّ عَزِيزٌ (٧٤) ٱللَّهُ يَصْطَفِى مِنَ ٱلْمَلَٰٓئِكَةِ رُسُلًا وَمِنَ ٱلنَّاسِ إِنَّ ٱللَّهَ سَمِيعٌۢ بَصِيرٌ (٧٥) يَعْلَمُ مَا بَيْنَ أَيْدِيهِمْ وَمَا خَلْفَهُمْ وَإِلَى ٱللَّهِ تُرْجَعُ ٱلْأُمُورُ (٧٦) يَٰٓأَيُّهَا ٱلَّذِينَ ءَامَنُواْ ٱرْكَعُواْ وَٱسْجُدُواْ وَٱعْبُدُواْ رَبَّكُمْ وَٱفْعَلُواْ ٱلْخَيْرَ لَعَلَّكُمْ تُفْلِحُونَ ۩ (٧٧) وَجَٰهِدُواْ فِى ٱللَّهِ حَقَّ جِهَادِهِۦ هُوَ ٱجْتَبَٰكُمْ وَمَا جَعَلَ عَلَيْكُمْ فِى ٱلدِّينِ مِنْ حَرَجٍ مِّلَّةَ أَبِيكُمْ إِبْرَٰهِيمَ هُوَ سَمَّىٰكُمُ ٱلْمُسْلِمِينَ مِن قَبْلُ وَفِى هَٰذَا لِيَكُونَ ٱلرَّسُولُ شَهِيدًا عَلَيْكُمْ وَتَكُونُواْ شُهَدَآءَ عَلَى ٱلنَّاسِ فَأَقِيمُواْ ٱلصَّلَوٰةَ وَءَاتُواْ ٱلزَّكَوٰةَ وَٱعْتَصِمُواْ بِٱللَّهِ هُوَ مَوْلَىٰكُمْ فَنِعْمَ ٱلْمَوْلَىٰ وَنِعْمَ ٱلنَّصِيرُ (٧٨)

And when Our verses are recited to them as clear evidences, you recognize in the faces of those who disbelieve disapproval. They are almost on the verge of assaulting those who recite to them Our verses. Say, "Then shall I inform you of [what is] worse than that? [It is] the Fire which Allah has promised those who disbelieve, and wretched is the destination." (72) O people, an example is presented, so listen to it. Indeed, those you invoke besides Allah will never create [as much as] a fly, even if they gathered together for that purpose. And if the fly should steal away from them a [tiny] thing, they could not recover it from him. Weak are the pursuer and pursued. (73) They have not appraised Allah with true appraisal. Indeed, Allah is Powerful and Exalted in

Might. (74) Allah chooses from the angels messengers and from the people. Indeed, Allah is Hearing and Seeing. (75) He knows what is [presently] before them and what will be after them. And to Allah will be returned [all] matters. (76) O you who have believed, bow and prostrate and worship your Lord and do good - that you may succeed. (77) And strive for Allah with the striving due to Him. He has chosen you and has not placed upon you in the religion any difficulty. [It is] the religion of your father, Abraham. Allah named you "Muslims" before [in former scriptures] and in this [revelation] that the Messenger may be a witness over you and you may be witnesses over the people. So establish prayer and give zakah(charity) and hold fast to Allah. He is your protector; and excellent is the protector, and excellent is the helper. (78)

It was narrated from Abul-Khaleel that 'Ali said:

I heard a man asking for forgiveness for his parents and they were mushrikeen. I said: Are you asking for forgiveness for your parents when they are mushrikeen? He said: Didn`t Ibraheem ask for forgiveness for his father when he was a mushrik? I mentioned that to the Prophet (ﷺ) and these verses were revealed: "It is not (proper) for the Prophet (ﷺ) and those who believe to ask Allah`s forgiveness for the Mushrikeen" [At-Tawbah 9:113-114]. 'Abdur-Rahman said: And Allah revealed [the words]. *"And Ibraheem`s (Abraham) invoking (of Allah) for his father`s forgiveness was only because of a promise he [Ibraheem (Abraham)] had made to him (his father)`.*

Source: Musnad Ahmad 1085 Grade: Hasan

It was narrated that 'Ali said:

I heard a man praying for forgiveness for his parents, who were mushrikeen. I said: Would a man pray for forgiveness for his parents when they are mushrikeen? He said: Didn`t Abraham pray for forgiveness for his father? I mentioned that to the Prophet (ﷺ) and the words `It is not proper for the Prophet and those who believe to ask Allah`s forgiveness for the Mushrikoon, even though they be of kin, after it has become clear to them that they are the dwellers of the Fire (because they died in a state of disbelief). And Ibrahim`s (Abraham) invoking (of Allah) for his father`s forgiveness was only because of a promise he [Ibrahim (Abraham]] had made to him (his father). But when it became clear to him that he (his father) is an enemy of Allah, he dissociated himself from him" At- Tawbah [9:113-114] were revealed. He [the Prophet (ﷺ) ] said: `[That was] when he died.`

Source: Musnad Ahmad 771 Grade: Hasan

Narrated Abu Huraira:

The Prophet (ﷺ) said, "On the Day of Resurrection Abraham will meet his father Azar whose face will be dark and covered with dust.(The Prophet (ﷺ) Abraham will say to him): 'Didn't I tell you not to disobey me?' His father will reply: 'Today I will not disobey you.' 'Abraham will say: 'O Lord! You promised me not to disgrace me on the Day of Resurrection; and what will be more disgraceful to me than cursing and dishonoring my father?' Then Allah will say (to him):' 'I have forbidden Paradise for the disbelievers." Then he will be addressed, 'O Abraham! Look! What is underneath your feet?' He will look and there he will see a Dhabh (an animal,) blood-stained, which will be caught by the legs and thrown in the (Hell) Fire."

Source: Sahih al-Bukhari 3350

Ibn 'Abbas narrated that the Prophet said:

"The people will be gathered on the Day of Resurrection naked and uncircumcised. The first one to be clothed will be Abraham." Then he recited: As We began the first creation, We shall repeat it"

Source: Sunan an-Nasa'i 2082 Grade: Sahih

Anas said:

A man said to the Messenger of Allah: O best of all creatures! The Messenger of Allah said : That was Abraham (peace be upon him).

Source: Sunan Abi Dawud 4672 Grade: Sahih

Narrated Ibn `Abbas:

'Allah is Sufficient for us and He Is the Best Disposer of affairs," was said by Abraham when he was thrown into the fire; and it was said by Muhammad when they (i.e. hypocrites) said, "A great army is gathering against you, therefore, fear them," but it only increased their faith and they said: "Allah is Sufficient for us, and He is the Best Disposer (of affairs, for us)." (3:173)

Source: Sahih al-Bukhari 4563

Narrated Um Sharik:

Allah's Messenger (ﷺ) ordered that the salamander should be killed and said, "It (i.e. the salamander) blew (the fire) on Abraham."

Source: Sahih al-Bukhari 3359

Sa'ibah, the freed slave woman of Fakih bin Mughirah, narrated that she entered upon 'Aishah and saw a spear in her house. She said:

"O Mother of the Believers, what do you do with this?" She said: "We kill these house lizards with it, for the Prophet of Allah (ﷺ) told us that when Abraham was thrown into the fire, there was no beast on earth that did not try to put it out, apart from the house lizard that

blew on it. So the Messenger of Allah (ﷺ) commanded that they should be killed."

Source: Sunan Ibn Majah 3231 Grade: Hasan

Narrated Abu Huraira:

The Prophet (ﷺ) said, "The Prophet (ﷺ) Abraham emigrated with Sarah and entered a village where there was a king or a tyrant. (The king) was told that Abraham had entered (the village) accompanied by a woman who was one of the most charming women. So, the king sent for Abraham and asked, 'O Abraham! Who is this lady accompanying you?' Abraham replied, 'She is my sister (i.e. in religion).' Then Abraham returned to her and said, 'Do not contradict my statement, for I have informed them that you are my sister. By Allah, there are no true believers on this land except you and I.' Then Abraham sent her to the king. When the king got to her, she got up and performed ablution, prayed and said, 'O Allah! If I have believed in You and Your Apostle, and have saved my private parts from everybody except my husband, then please do not let this pagan overpower me.' On that the king fell in a mood of agitation and started moving his legs. Seeing the condition of the king, Sarah said, 'O Allah! If he should die, the people will say that I have killed him.' The king regained his power, and proceeded towards her but she got up again and performed ablution, prayed and said, 'O Allah! If I have believed in You and Your Apostle and have kept my private parts safe from all except my husband, then please do not let this pagan overpower me.' The king again fell in a mood of agitation and started moving his legs. On seeing that state of the king, Sarah said, 'O Allah! If he should die, the people will say that I have killed him.' The king got either two or three attacks, and after recovering from the last attack he said, 'By Allah! You have sent a satan to me. Take her to Abraham and give her Hajar.' So she came back to Abraham and said, 'Allah humiliated the pagan and gave us a slave-girl for service."

Source: Sahih al-Bukhari 2217

Narrated Abu Huraira:

Abraham did not tell a lie except on three occasion. Twice for the Sake of Allah when he said, "I am sick," and he said, "(I have not done this but) the big idol has done it." The (third was) that while Abraham and Sarah (his wife) were going (on a journey) they passed by (the territory of) a tyrant. Someone said to the tyrant, "This man (i.e. Abraham) is accompanied by a very charming lady." So, he sent for Abraham and asked him about Sarah saying, "Who is this lady?" Abraham said, "She is my sister." Abraham went to Sarah and said, "O Sarah! There are no believers on the surface of the earth except you and I. This man asked me about you and I have told him that

*you are my sister, so don't contradict my statement."
The tyrant then called Sarah and when she went to him,
he tried to take hold of her with his hand, but (his hand
got stiff and) he was confounded. He asked Sarah. "Pray
to Allah for me, and I shall not harm you." So Sarah
asked Allah to cure him and he got cured. He tried to take
hold of her for the second time, but (his hand got as stiff
as or stiffer than before and) was more confounded. He
again requested Sarah, "Pray to Allah for me, and I will
not harm you." Sarah asked Allah again and he became
alright. He then called one of his guards (who had
brought her) and said, "You have not brought me a
human being but have brought me a devil." The tyrant
then gave Hajar as a girl-servant to Sarah. Sarah came
back (to Abraham) while he was praying. Abraham,
gesturing with his hand, asked, "What has happened?"
She replied, "Allah has spoiled the evil plot of the infidel
(or immoral person) and gave me Hajar for service."
(Abu Huraira then addressed his listeners saying, "That
(Hajar) was your mother, O Bani Ma-is-Sama (i.e. the
Arabs, the descendants of Ishmael, Hajar's son).*

Source: Sahih al-Bukhari 3358

Narrated Ibn `Abbas:

*The first lady to use a girdle was the mother of Ishmael.
She used a girdle so that she might hide her tracks from
Sarah. Abraham brought her and her son Ishmael while*

she was suckling him, to a place near the Ka`ba under a tree on the spot of Zamzam, at the highest place in the mosque. During those days there was nobody in Mecca, nor was there any water So he made them sit over there and placed near them a leather bag containing some dates, and a small water-skin containing some water, and set out homeward. Ishmael's mother followed him saying, "O Abraham! Where are you going, leaving us in this valley where there is no person whose company we may enjoy, nor is there anything (to enjoy)?" She repeated that to him many times, but he did not look back at her Then she asked him, "Has Allah ordered you to do so?" He said, "Yes." She said, "Then He will not neglect us," and returned while Abraham proceeded onwards, and on reaching the Thaniya where they could not see him, he faced the Ka`ba, and raising both hands, invoked Allah saying the following prayers: 'O our Lord! I have made some of my offspring dwell in a valley without cultivation, by Your Sacred House (Ka`ba at Mecca) in order, O our Lord, that they may offer prayer perfectly. So fill some hearts among men with love towards them, and (O Allah) provide them with fruits, so that they may give thanks.' (14:37) Ishmael's mother went on suckling Ishmael and drinking from the water (she had). When the water in the water-skin had all been used up, she became thirsty and her child also became thirsty. She started looking at him (i.e. Ishmael) tossing in agony. She left *him, for she could not endure looking at him, and found that the mountain of Safa was the nearest mountain to her on that land. She stood on it and started looking at the valley keenly so that she might see somebody, but she could not see anybody. Then she descended from Safa and when she reached the valley, she tucked up her robe and ran in the valley like a person in distress and trouble, till she crossed the valley and reached the Marwa mountain where she stood and started looking, expecting to see somebody, but she could not see anybody. She repeated that (running between Safa and Marwa) seven times." The Prophet (ﷺ) said, "This is the source of the tradition of the walking of people between them (i.e. Safa and Marwa). When she reached the Marwa (for the last time) she heard a voice and she asked herself to be quiet and listened attentively. She heard the voice again and said, 'O, (whoever you may be)! You have made me hear your voice; have you got something to help me?" And behold! She saw an angel at the place of Zamzam, digging the earth with his heel (or his wing), till water flowed from that place. She started to make something like a basin around it, using her hand in this way, and started filling her water-skin with water with her hands, and the water was flowing out after she had scooped some of it." The Prophet (ﷺ) added, "May Allah bestow Mercy on Ishmael's mother! Had she let the Zamzam (flow without trying to control it) (or had she not scooped from that*

*water) (to fill her water-skin), Zamzam would have been
a stream flowing on the surface of the earth." The
Prophet (ﷺ) further added, "Then she drank (water) and
suckled her child. The angel said to her, 'Don't be afraid
of being neglected, for this is the House of Allah which
will be built by this boy and his father, and Allah never
neglects His people.' The House (i.e. Ka`ba) at that time
was on a high place resembling a hillock, and when
torrents came, they flowed to its right and left. She lived
in that way till some people from the tribe of Jurhum or a
family from Jurhum passed by her and her child, as they
(i.e. the Jurhum people) were coming through the way of
Kada'. They landed in the lower part of Mecca where
they saw a bird that had the habit of flying around water
and not leaving it. They said, 'This bird must be flying
around water, though we know that there is no water in
this valley.' They sent one or two messengers who
discovered the source of water, and returned to inform
them of the water. So, they all came (towards the water)."
The Prophet (ﷺ) added, "Ishmael's mother was sitting
near the water. They asked her, 'Do you allow us to stay
with you?" She replied, 'Yes, but you will have no right
to possess the water.' They agreed to that." The Prophet
(ﷺ) further said, "Ishmael's mother was pleased with the
whole situation as she used to love to enjoy the company
of the people. So, they settled there, and later on they sent
for their families who came and settled with them so that*

some families became permanent residents there. The child (i.e. Ishmael) grew up and learnt Arabic from them and (his virtues) caused them to love and admire him as he grew up, and when he reached the age of puberty they made him marry a woman from amongst them. After Ishmael's mother had died, Abraham came after Ishmael's marriage in order to see his family that he had left before, but he did not find Ishmael there. When he asked Ishmael's wife about him, she replied, 'He has gone in search of our livelihood.' Then he asked her about their way of living and their condition, and she replied, 'We are living in misery; we are living in hardship and destitution,' complaining to him. He said, 'When your husband returns, convey my salutation to him and tell him to change the threshold of the gate (of his house).' When Ishmael came, he seemed to have felt something unusual, so he asked his wife, 'Has anyone visited you?' She replied, 'Yes, an old man of so-and-so description came and asked me about you and I informed him, and he asked about our state of living, and I told him that we were living in a hardship and poverty.' On that Ishmael said, 'Did he advise you anything?' She replied, 'Yes, he told me to convey his salutation to you and to tell you to change the threshold of your gate.' Ishmael said, 'It was my father, and he has ordered me to divorce you. Go back to your family.' So, Ishmael divorced her and married another woman from amongst them (i.e. Jurhum). Then

Abraham stayed away from them for a period as long as Allah wished and called on them again but did not find Ishmael. So he came to Ishmael's wife and asked her about Ishmael. She said, 'He has gone in search of our livelihood.' Abraham asked her, 'How are you getting on?' asking her about their sustenance and living. She replied, 'We are prosperous and well-off (i.e. we have everything in abundance).' Then she thanked Allah' Abraham said, 'What kind of food do you eat?' She said. 'Meat.' He said, 'What do you drink?' She said, 'Water." He said, "O Allah! Bless their meat and water." The Prophet added, "At that time they did not have grain, and if they had grain, he would have also invoked Allah to bless it." The Prophet (ﷺ) added, "If somebody has only these two things as his sustenance, his health and disposition will be badly affected, unless he lives in Mecca." The Prophet (ﷺ) added," Then Abraham said to Ishmael's wife, "When your husband comes, give my regards to him and tell him that he should keep firm the threshold of his gate.' When Ishmael came back, he asked his wife, 'Did anyone call on you?' She replied, 'Yes, a good-looking old man came to me,' so she praised him and added. 'He asked about you, and I informed him, and he asked about our livelihood and I told him that we were in a good condition.' Ishmael asked her, 'Did he give you any piece of advice?' She said, 'Yes, he told me to give his regards to you and ordered that you should keep firm the *threshold of your gate.' On that Ishmael said, 'It was my father, and you are the threshold (of the gate). He has ordered me to keep you with me.' Then Abraham stayed away from them for a period as long as Allah wished, and called on them afterwards. He saw Ishmael under a tree near Zamzam, sharpening his arrows. When he saw Abraham, he rose up to welcome him (and they greeted each other as a father does with his son or a son does with his father). Abraham said, 'O Ishmael! Allah has given me an order.' Ishmael said, 'Do what your Lord has ordered you to do.' Abraham asked, 'Will you help me?' Ishmael said, 'I will help you.' Abraham said, Allah has ordered me to build a house here,' pointing to a hillock higher than the land surrounding it." The Prophet (ﷺ) added, "Then they raised the foundations of the House (i.e. the Ka`ba). Ishmael brought the stones and Abraham was building, and when the walls became high, Ishmael brought this stone and put it for Abraham who stood over it and carried on building, while Ishmael was handing him the stones, and both of them were saying, 'O our Lord! Accept (this service) from us, Verily, You are the All-Hearing, the All-Knowing.' The Prophet (ﷺ) added, "Then both of them went on building and going round the Ka`ba saying: O our Lord ! Accept (this service) from us, Verily, You are the All-Hearing, the All-Knowing." (2:127)*

Source: Sahih al-Bukhari 3364

Narrated Abu Huraira:

Allah's Messenger (ﷺ) said "The Prophet) Abraham circumcised himself after he had passed the age of eighty years and he circumcised himself with an adze."

Source: Sahih al-Bukhari 6298

Yahya related to me from Malik from Yahya ibn Said that Said ibn al-Musayyub said,

"Abraham, may Allah bless him and grant him peace, was the first to give hospitality to the guest and the first person to be circumcised and the first person to trim the moustache and the first person to see grey hair. He said, 'O Lord! What is this?' Allah the Blessed, the Exalted, said, 'It is dignity, Abraham.' He said, 'Lord, increase me in dignity!' "

Yahya said that he had heard Malik say, "One takes from the moustache until the edge of the lip appears, that is the rim. One does not cut if off completely so that one mutilates oneself."

Source: Muwatta by Imam Malik Chapter 49 section 3 hadith 4

Amr bin Dinar narrated from Amr bin Abdulah bin Safwan, that Yazid bin Shaiban said:

"Ibn Mirba Al-Ansari came to us while we were standing at our places" (Amr bin Sinar said:) a place that

Amr (bin Abdullah) indicated was far - "and he said: 'I am a messenger whom the Messenger of Allah sent to you to say: 'Stay with your (Hajj) rites, for indeed you are following a legacy left by Abraham.'"

Source: Jami` at-Tirmidhi 883 Grade: Sahih

It was narrated that Ibn 'Umar said:

"The Messenger of Allah performed ablution washing each part once. He said: 'This is the ablution of the person from whom Allah will not accept his prayer without it.' Then he performed ablution washing each part twice, and he said: 'This is the ablution that Allah appreciates.' Then he performed ablution washing each part three times, and said: 'This is how ablution is performed properly, and this is my ablution and the ablution of the Close Friend of Allah, Abraham. Whoever performs ablution like this, then on completing it says: 'Ashhadu an la ilaha illallah, wa ashhadu anna Muhammadan 'abduhu wa rasuluhu' (I bear witness that none has the right to be worshipped but Allah, and I bear witness that Muhammed is His servant and His Messenger), eight gates of Paradise will be opened to him and he may enter through whichever one he wants.'"

Source: Sunan Ibn Majah 419 Grade: Daif

It was narrated from Abu Hurairah that the Prophet (ﷺ) said:

"O Allah! Abraham was Your Friend and Prophet, and You declared Makkah to be sacred through Abraham. O Allah! I am Your slave and Prophet, and I declare what is between its two lava fields to be sacred."

Source: Sunan Ibn Majah 3113 Grade: Sahih

Jabir reported Allah's Apostle (ﷺ) as saying:

Abraham declared Mecca as sacred; I declare Medina, that between the two mountains, as inviolable. No tree should be lopped and no game is to be molested.

Source: Sahih Muslim 1362

Narrated `Abdullah bin Zaid:

The Prophet (ﷺ) said, "The Prophet (ﷺ) Abraham made Mecca a sanctuary, and asked for Allah's blessing in it. I made Medina a sanctuary as Abraham made Mecca a sanctuary and I asked for Allah's Blessing in its measures the Mudd and the Sa as Abraham did for Mecca.

Source: Sahih al-Bukhari 2129

It was narrated that Jabir said:

"When Allah's Messenger (ﷺ) finished circumambulating the House, he came to Maqam Abraham. 'Umar said: 'O Messenger of Allah, this is the Maqam of our father Abraham, about which Allah says,

"And take you (people) the Maqam (place) of Abraham as a place of prayer.'" [Quran 2:125]

Source: Sunan Ibn Majah 2960 Grade: Sahih

Narrated `Amr bin Maimuin:

"The Prophet (ﷺ) sent Mu`adh to Yemen and he (led the people) in the Fajr prayer and recited: 'Allah took Abraham as a Khalil(close friend). A man behind him said, "(How) glad the mother of Abraham is!"

Source: Sahih al-Bukhari 4348

Narrated Ibn `Abbas:

The Prophet used to seek Refuge with Allah for Al-Hasan and Al-Husain and say: "Your forefather (i.e. Abraham) used to seek Refuge with Allah for Ishmael and Isaac by reciting the following: 'O Allah! I seek Refuge with Your Perfect Words from every devil and from poisonous pests and from every evil, harmful, envious eye.' "

Source: Sahih al-Bukhari 3371

Narrated `Aisha:

(the wife of the Prophet) that Allah's Messenger (ﷺ) said to her, "Do you know that when your people (Quraish) rebuilt the Ka`ba, they decreased it from its original foundation laid by Abraham?" I said, "O Allah's Messenger (ﷺ)! Why don't you rebuild it on its original

foundation laid by Abraham?" He replied, "Were it not for the fact that your people are close to the Pre-Islamic Period of ignorance (i.e. they have recently become Muslims) I would have done so." The sub-narrator, `Abdullah (bin `Umar) stated: `Aisha 'must have heard this from Allah's Messenger (ﷺ) for in my opinion Allah's Messenger (ﷺ) had not placed his hand over the two corners of the Ka`ba opposite Al-Hijr only because the Ka`ba was not rebuilt on its original foundations laid by Abraham.

Source: Sahih al-Bukhari 1583

Narrated Yazid bin Ruman from `Urwa:

`Aisha said that the Prophet (ﷺ) said to her, "O Aisha! Were your nation not close to the Pre-Islamic Period of Ignorance, I would have had the Ka`ba demolished and would have included in it the portion which had been left, and would have made it at a level with the ground and would have made two doors for it, one towards the east and the other towards the west, and then by doing this it would have been built on the foundations laid by Abraham." That was what urged Ibn-Az-Zubair to demolish the Ka`ba. Jazz said, "I saw Ibn-Az-Zubair when he demolished and rebuilt the Ka`ba and included in it a portion of Al-Hijr (the unroofed portion of Ka`ba which is at present in the form of a compound towards the northwest of the Ka`ba). I saw the original

foundations of Abraham which were of stones resembling the humps of camels." So Jarir asked Yazid, "Where was the place of those stones?" Jazz said, "I will just now show it to you." So Jarir accompanied Yazid and entered Al-Hijr, and Jazz pointed to a place and said, "Here it is." Jarir said, "It appeared to me about six cubits from Al-Hijr or so."

Source: Sahih al-Bukhari 1586

Jundub reported:

I heard from the Messenger of Allah (ﷺ) five days before his death and he said: I stand acquitted before Allah that I took any one of you as friend, for Allah has taken me as His friend, as he took Abraham as His friend. Had I taken any one of my Ummah as a friend, I would have taken Abu Bakr as a friend. Beware of those who preceded you and used to take the graves of their prophets and righteous men as places of worship, but you must not take graves as mosques; I forbid you to do that.

Source: Sahih Muslim 532

Narrated Ibn 'Umar:

Zaid bin 'Amr bin Nufail went to Sham, inquiring about a true religion to follow. He met a Jewish religious scholar and asked him about their religion. He said, "I intend to embrace your religion, so tell me something about it." The Jew said, "You will not embrace our religion unless you receive your share of Allah's Anger." Zaid said, "'I do not run except from Allah's Anger, and I will never bear a bit of it if I have the power to avoid it. Can you tell me of some other religion?" He said, "I do not know any other religion except the Hanif." Zaid enquired, "What is Hanif?" He said, "Hanif is the religion of (the prophet) Abraham who was neither a Jew nor a Christian, and he used to worship None but Allah (Alone)" Then Zaid went out and met a Christian religious scholar and told him the same as before. The Christian said, "You will not embrace our religion unless you get a share of Allah's Curse." Zaid replied, "I do not run except from Allah's Curse, and I will never bear any of Allah's Curse and His Anger if I have the power to avoid them. Will you tell me of some other religion?" He replied, "I do not know any other religion except Hanif." Zaid enquired, "What is Hanif?" He replied, Hanif is the religion of (the prophet) Abraham who was neither a Jew nor a Christian and he used to worship None but Allah (Alone)" When Zaid heard their Statement about (the religion of) Abraham, he left that place, and when he came out, he raised both his hands and said, "O Allah! I make You my Witness that I am on the religion of Abraham."

Source: Sahih al-Bukhari 3827

Narrated Ibn `Abbas:

The Prophet (ﷺ) entered the Ka`ba and found in it the pictures of (Prophet) Abraham and Mary. On that he said' "What is the matter with them (i.e. Quraish)? They have already heard that angels do not enter a house in which there are pictures; yet this is the picture of Abraham. And why is he depicted as practicing divination by arrows?"

Source: Sahih al-Bukhari 3351

Narrated Ibn `Abbas:

When the Prophet (ﷺ) saw pictures in the Ka`ba, he did not enter it till he ordered them to be erased. When he saw (the pictures of Abraham and Ishmael carrying the arrows of divination, he said, "May Allah curse them (i.e. the Quraish)! By Allah, neither Abraham nor Ishmael practiced divination by arrows."

Source: Sahih al-Bukhari 3352

Narrated Abu Huraira:

The people said, "O Allah's Messenger (ﷺ)! Who is the most honorable amongst the people (in Allah's Sight)?" He said, "The most righteous amongst them." They said, "We do not ask you, about this. " He said, "Then Joseph, Allah's Prophet, the son of Allah's Prophet, The son of Allah's Prophet the son of Allah's Khalil (i.e. Abraham)." They said, "We do not want to ask about this," He said' "Then you want to ask about the descent of the Arabs.

Those who were the best in the pre-lslamic period of ignorance will be the best in Islam provided they comprehend the religious knowledge."

Source: Sahih al-Bukhari 3353

It was narrated that abu Sa'eed Al-Khudri said:

"We said: 'O Messenger of Allah (ﷺ), we know how to send salams upon you, but how should we send salah upon you?' He said: 'Say: "Allahumma salli 'ala Muhammadin 'abdika wa rasulika kama salaita 'ala Ibrahim wa barik 'ala Muhammadin wa 'ala ali Muhammadin kama barakta 'ala Ibrahim (O Allah, send salah upon Muhammad, Your slave and Messenger , as You sent Salah upon Abraham, and send blessings upon Muhammad and upon the family of Muhammad as You sent blessings upon Abraham)."

Source: Sunan an-Nasa'i 1293 Grade: Sahih

Abu Hurairah reported that the Prophet said,

"If anyone says, 'O Allah, bless Muhammad and the family of Muhammad as You blessed Abraham and the family of Abraham. Shower blessings on Muhammad and the family of Muhammad as You showered blessings on Abraham and the family of Abraham. Show mercy to Muhammad and the family of Muhammad as You showed mercy to Abraham and the family of Abraham,' I

will testify for him on the Day of Rising and I will intercede for him."

Source: Al-Adab Al-Mufrad 641 Grade: Daif

Interestingly these last two hadith coincide with the previously mentioned verse of the Hebrew Bible Genesis 12:3 which says God said he will bless those who bless Abraham. This is interesting because everytime a Muslim prays, whether its one of the obligatory 5 daily prayers or an optional prayer, they specifically ask Allah to bless Abraham in the Durood of Abraham and his family. Therefore according to the text of Genesis in the bible, everytime Muslims pray God is simultaneously blessing them. Likewise in each unit of those prayers, at least 17 times a day minimum while reciting the last verse of Surah Fatihah the Muslim begs Allah to guide them to the path of those who are blessed and not the path of those who earned God's anger or the path of those who went astray. While Adi bin Hatim reported in a hadith graded to be Hasan that the Prophet Muhammad said: *"The Jews are those who Allah is wrath with, and the Christians have strayed."* So contextually many times a day Muslims are upon firm conviction that Allah blessed Abraham, his family and followers and that the blessed path of Abraham and all the prophets is different than the path of Jews and Christians. The preceding Quran verses couldn't be more clear as they say as such explicitly announcing in many different plain terms that Jews and Christians are not following the Abrahamic faith despite their rival claims of exclusivity. Islam also teaches us much about Abraham's doctrine of monotheism by including quotations of his debates with people of other faiths and his immense intolerance for their religions and the people upon falsehood. Abraham destroyed idols that his father, nicknamed Azar, created and was persecuted as a result of such opposition. Abraham and his followers announced that until the people believe in the same deity as Abraham does and worship exactly as Abraham did then there is nothing but enmity between them until they choose to repent from their crimes. Islam presents a clear portrayal of Abraham, there is more historical Abrahamic data but I refrained from mentioning anything not directly attributed to Allah or Muhammad. The picture of Abraham is so vividly anti-interfaith and exclusivist that I almost decided its not even worth composing this book because nobody who reads the Quran could be confused unless they had a disease in their soul. Literally one or two statements from Allah succinctly refutes the entire interfaith platform irreparably. It is also a proof of the miraculous nature of the Quran that Allah refuted the pluralist Abrahamic faith notions long before they ever became a trend.

This Abrahamic faiths doctrine was first traced to Yoakim Moubarac in the 1950s CE. Yoakim Moubarac was a Lebanese Maronite priest who had been ordained June 29, 1947 CE, about 1 month after the state of Israel was created. His mentor was a French Catholic orientalist named Louis Massignon who was influential during the Second Vatican Council changing certain Church doctrines and a friend of the famous British T.E. Lawrence. A graduate of "Jesus College" in Oxford, England, during WWI T.E. Lawrence was the guy who tricked the Arab Muslims to fight against the Ottomon Empire in support of the British. This then led to the British conquering Palestine and the allied powers taking much of the middle eastern Muslim lands. T.E. Lawrence's friend Louis Massignon made it his life mission to enforce French control and influence over Muslim lands and ensure Palestinians and Arabs accepted the Israeli occupation. Louis Massignon said that Catholicism and Islam were both Abrahamic faiths in order to make the Muslims in French colonies stop waging Jihad. Massignon's student Yoakim Moubarac continued the Israeli platform of his mentor's mission adding Judaism and broadened the club to include Judaism, Christianity and Islam as Abrahamic faiths. Why? This was because Israel was waging a religious war against Islam and Christianity in the name of Judaism. Whereas Israel could not win such a war unless the Muslims and Christians didn't fight back. Thus the Abrahamic faith mythology of Judaism, Christianity and Islam all stemming from Abraham was formulated and has been preached ever since in the name of tolerance and peace. So this Abrahamic faiths notion is partially Zionist propaganda so the state of Israel can fight a religious war in the holy land without having the other religious groups fight back. If any claims otherwise then ask for proof of this Abrahamic faiths doctrine being preached by Jews, Christians or Muslims prior to the state of Israel being created in 1947. The Anti-Semitic Europeans never heard this doctrine before WWII. This Abrahamic faiths doctrine is false and constitutes disbelief in Judaism, and in Christianity and in Islam. Yet this is the premise of "inter-faith". Abraham did not teach, preach or practice 3 different religions. To show the stupidity of this "inter-faith" corruption you can just say, "*Well most every religion agrees that mankind all comes from one original pair of humans. Therefore all the religions go back to Adam because we are all his descendants. Thus all religions are Adamic faiths which stem from his teachings. Since God made us all and we have religions then they must all count and all must lead to heaven. So that means everyone's religion is correct. Hooray! Let's all love each other while we wait to go to paradise, every human goes to heaven. It's impossible to be wrong! If you are a human then your religion is automatically correct. Now we could say only aliens go to hell, but then might have to change that belief if we meet aliens. We could say hell isn't real and God loves everybody but few will fall for that because we know it's not true. Thus our doctrine shall be God loves everybody except for those who say God hates people for what they believe. So only those intolerant extremists who hate people for believing something different than they believe will go to hell. Of course this doesn't mean we think we will go to hell, because we don't hate the haters we love them, even though they are crazy intolerant extremists. God loves everyone who loves everyone and God hates anyone who hates anyone.*" Obviously such a doctrine is sheer satanic stupidity, similar to the Santa Claus methodology of X being true only if you believe it is and X being false if you don't believe X is true, but it's exactly the same as the "Abrahamic faiths" movement. This disease is based on promoting tolerance and love in order to achieve peace. Not one prophet in the world taught this. So were all the prophets extremists who killed everyone who disagreed with them? No. Were they intolerant of every other religion? Yes. Were they peaceful? Yes. Did they love everyone? No. Did they hate other people because of what they believed? Yes. The fundamental issue with "inter-faith" is that it's not prophetic and is an entirely different religion that's based on a hatred for intolerance. Which is ironic because such people claim to be all about tolerance and combating extremism but in reality they are extremists who are intolerant towards the very intolerance the prophets preached and practiced. Intolerance doesn't mean violence! What if Abraham walked into one of "Abrahamic faiths" events? Would Abraham say, "*All your religions are true, you Jews keep on being Jews, you Christians keep on being Christians, you Muslims keep on being Muslims. Nobody should change, but if anyone does it doesn't matter because all of you are going to heaven despite having 3 different faiths and I only taught 1.*" Likewise do you think Jesus would attend such a meeting and tell Jews to remain as Jews, Christians to stay Christians and Muslims to remain Muslims? No, Jesus would tell at least 2 groups to change their faith, as would all the prophets. In fact as we included in this book in John 8:37-46 biblical Jesus himself says explicitly that Jews are not related to the faith of Abraham but are related to the devil and are nothing but liars. Why don't Christians quote that bible verse during Interfaith seminars? In context the biblical Jews were pulling the same ruse people preach today saying Jews, Christians and Muslims are all "children of Abraham". The bible itself says Jesus said NO and he even told Jews he knows their lineages to link to Abraham but he still said their father was the devil and their religion was the devil's. If you say Jews, Christians and Muslims are all "children of Abraham" then you might as well say everyone is because Abraham was reportedly the first human to start wearing underwear under their pants, so technically anyone who wears underwear is following the religion of Abraham. But who would dare say because you wear underwear that makes you a follower of Abraham on the road to heaven and God loves you? A heaven-bound global Abrahamic underwear club makes more sense than the Abrahamic faiths doctrine. By wearing underwear you have more in common with Abraham than those preaching there are 3 or 8 Abrahamic faiths depending on how you count them. The funny part is those who preach the "Abrahamic faiths" mythology don't even know Abraham is reportedly the first to wear underwear. That's how little they know about Abraham. The names they use show how ridiculous and illegitimate the concept is. They'll use the term inter-faith and Abrahamic faiths together. Which label is it? They'll claim to be both types but in reality are neither. So how is it people today fall for this "inter-faith Abrahamic faiths" stuff? They are simply idiots who don't know at least 3 religions. All those who know religion know this and all who promote inter-faith are extremists upon different faiths than the very faiths they are trying to bring together. The real word for "Abrahamic faiths" is pluralism. Pluralism is the religion that says more than one religion is true and that people can believe in different religions and still all end up in paradise. Abraham was not a pluralist, those preaching Abrahamic faiths in his name as well as most types of "Inter-faith" types are. Those who promote the Abrahamic faiths coexistence movement have the least to do with the religion of Abraham out of all 3 or 8 groups claiming to be connected to Abraham.

The thing is we can all be tolerant of persons with different religious opinions but we cannot be tolerant of different religions. There is a difference between peaceful intolerance and violent intolerance and extremist intolerance and violent extremist intolerance. The first 2 are prophetic, the second 2 are satanic. There is no such thing in the prophetic religion as peaceful tolerance. Moses, Jesus and Muhammad taught both peaceful intolerance as well as violent intolerance when certain situations arose. Yet I personally know some people who don't understand what prophetic peaceful intolerance is. It is more accurate to say Publicly Peaceful Aggressive Intolerance which is sometimes polite depending on the specific person or people one is communicating with. One thing many fail to understand is that while prophets were frequently peaceful, during those peaceful moments they were not always polite. The majority of the time prophets interacted with disbelievers they were confrontational. Sometimes the prophets were rudely confrontational but they were politely confrontational more. Rarely were prophets peacefully politely non-confrontational with disbelievers when it came to discussing religion. They would act like that only with people who were genuinely deeply interested in learning about what they believed and preached. Usually the prophets were boldly confrontational because confrontation causes motivation for the one confronted to quickly and comprehensively resolve the confrontation. Unfortunately many people, particularly in the West, are not confrontational when discussing religion with disbelievers when they should be. While those who are, might sometimes be only confrontational, too confrontational, or not as polite as they should be because they lack knowledge and manners. Yet overall the world in general, due to secularism, freedom, equality, tolerance, etc, has forgotten that confrontationalism is central to religion. This causes most today to incorrectly mistake confrontational people as extreme just because they are confrontational. The true prophetic religion as taught by Prophet Abraham is only spread by theological confrontation.

Diluting the differences between religions due to fear of frightening disagreement is a plan of the devil to distort the prophetic faith of Abraham. Monotheism itself implies there is only one way of truth and one way to paradise. There is no such thing as multi-monotheisms. You cannot unite people who believe in different prophets and who practice different laws/lifestyles just because they all agree that one human was a prophet which they all claim to respect. All 8 of the alleged Abrahamic faiths agree that nobody on earth is permitted to follow just Prophet Abraham and ignore the prophets who came after him. They all agree that following Abraham exclusively ignoring the revelations revealed afterwards and the prophets who came afterwards is disbelief in the prophetic faith of Abraham no matter what is claimed.

Abraham made little distinction between idolatry and idolaters, in fact when you actually think about it the idolaters are worse than the idols themselves because most idols aren't capable of doing idolatry or any other sin. So to ever hate an idol you have to hate the idolater even more. Most idols are innocent. Abraham is known for intolerance and the prophets who claim to be upon orders from the God of Abraham such as Jesus and Muhammad further stressed intolerance towards disbelievers in their prophethood and extra intolerance towards those who rejected their religions in the name of following Abraham. I could go on pages and pages ranting about the ramifications of interfaith dilution violating Abrahamic principles but I grow weary and disgusted of the subject. Every book I've ever written has technically been dealing with the subject of this prophetic Abrahamic faith. What more can be said? Those who accept the evidence presented herein will accept and those who don't won't no matter how many books are written or how many explanations and admonishments they receive. The Quranic evidence was clear, in need of no explanation so what else is there to say after the words of Allah on the matter? The testimony of Allah that Abraham was neither a Jew nor a Christian and that he and his descendants were true Muslims upon Islam closes the case for discussion. We are left to submit similarly or await the consequences of disputing with God and lying. My personal belief is Islam is the true religion of Abraham and that Muhammad is the final link in the chain of prophets after the virgin born Jesus son of Mary. The correct Islam is not the interfaith peaceful extremism increasingly preached under the guise of anti-terrorist dawah by hypocrites who Allah exposes as such to those blessed with insight. Nor is the correct Islam the overboard extremism of the sword-mongers whether they be Madhhab fanatics in imitation of the original Madhhab fanatics of sinful Shiism or the Khawarij revolutionary protesters who promote chaos and instability that leads to the very compromises they denounce as betrayal of the faith. The true Islam is that as taught by the prophets and understood by the contemporary original Companions of the prophets and the first three generations of Muhammadean Muslims. We lost access to the religion of Abraham and his Scripture and it is no longer valid to even follow the Abrahamic Shariah or laws in this modern era. Jews claim to follow Moses' laws, Christians Jesus' laws and Muslims Muhammad's laws all originating from God. All agree that the Abrahamic faith is no longer accepted by someone alive today. Please kindly tell all who claim to be following the Abrahamic faith today that they have to stop that and follow the prophet of their era(Muhammad) or be doomed to eternal hellfire. There is absolutely no way two religions can ever be true, much less three or more.

This book is not about proving the prophethood of other prophets. It is about disproving the claims of the interfaith Abrahamic faiths crowd showing how the primary religious texts are irreconcilable and what they do agree on is that Abraham didn't tolerate other religious understandings accompanying his own. It was always you either follow Abraham or go to hell. Then Abraham died and other prophets came and it was/is you either follow them as they come or go to hell. That is what Abraham was upon, pure prophetic partisanship which doomed all those fools who disagreed.

Abraham was not wrong to express prejudicial hatred and exclusivity, or as it's called a monopoly on salvation. It all depends on how and why you do it, but people getting upset with it doesn't mean it's wrong or sinful rather sometimes it's good and obligatory to preach in such a manner. To express hatred for disbelief AND disbelievers is part of the prophetic way of preaching, if you don't do it at all then one would not be preaching the prophetic way. Yet it's important to stress this must be done with wisdom. "With wisdom" doesn't mean that it's not to be done as some may claim under the excuse of wisdom, but that it's best to do it smartly. You can publicly express hatred, opposition and intolerance for disbelief and disbelievers without doing it in an overtly offensive or reckless manner. Thus my hatred comes with lots of context and reasons, and it's polite. You don't have to use the word hatred to express your hatred, if you have a large vocabulary you can say very hateful things in public and have people smile at you even when they know you are expressing hatred because you use clean words when doing it. It's not that hatred is offensive in itself, most of the times its vulgarity that's offensive. You don't have to be vulgar or crude and the prophets weren't. With most people in person I don't even explicitly state I hate them, but imply how, "*There is only 1 true religion and God would hate all who aren't following it, so if Me and You are upon different religions then God must hate at least one of us. While if we believe in God we must hate who God hates, thus one of us or both of us should change our religion for the true one so that God can love us both and we are both on the road to paradise.*" Then I can have a genuine religious conversation with the person who knows I hate them because I think they are disbelievers, but I still care about them and want us to be on the same team to go to paradise with them, whereupon I believe Islam is God's only team and that their team is that of the devil. It also lets them know that I know they hate me for being upon a different religion, Islam, and it's expected/normal for them to hate me for that reason and they need not hide it or pretend that they don't. That's what I call hate preaching and most people have no issues with this at all and appreciate the honesty, unless they don't believe in the fundamental concept that only 1 religion is true. In that case then we can discuss/debate/prove that on the spot. So this is what I consider to be the prophetic hate preaching. The faith of equality and freedom forbid and oppose this type of hate preaching because those are false faiths which get refuted by it. So if people don't like this type of preaching it's due to their religion, and any such religion is an evil religion that will lead them to hell. Abraham never compromised the truth in the name of tolerance. I propose the groups promoting tolerance in the name of Abraham cease and desist from such sinful slander and heresy. Hypocrites will persist however regardless of the warnings and will find excuses to continue their combat of God disguised as cooperation upon goodness. Yet Abraham taught us to fight such falsehood as part of our faith, for false faiths will always fail their followers and fight the truth-tellers for influence in competition for creating a united like-minded society. Certainly, truth and falsehood never unite.

Please research the prophetic religion every day to save yourself from ruinous deviation or bigoted arrogance or ignorance. I conclude this discourse with a comprehensive prayer to the God of prophet Abraham which I challenge the reader and interfaith folk to witness and pray sincerely as individuals, and then strive accordingly until death.

May the God of Abraham curse all those who falsely lay claim to be following his religion, particularly those in the devilish interfaith movements, until they sincerely contritely repent from creed based crimes and lesser sins.

May the God of Abraham give speedy destruction to the liars and falsifiers who claim to be sincere upon Abraham's faith who are nothing but sinful though they are too stupid or satanic to admit to it.

May the God of Abraham forgive those who err in their quest for guidance and repent but for those who err and continue in error then please increase them in error making them joyfully heedless and harmless before you punish them severely in their lifetime and for eternity as an everlasting example of perfect justice.

May the God of Abraham bless those who make this prayer and quickly curse those who invoke other than the God of Abraham as we expect you to, and please guide all of the devils and allies of devils among humans and jinn to your prophetic faith of Abraham making us all true believers following the prophet of our era with sincerity, knowledge and consistent good deeds until we die.

May the God of Abraham guide us to the single prophetic way of those who are blessed and not the many ways of those who have earned your anger nor the many ways of those who have gone astray.